INCAPACITY AND ACCESS TO FAMILY JUSTICE

This edited collection explores the question of how those with limited capacity are enabled to take their part as members of society within the context of both a legal framework and the expectations of their family and community.

The book is divided into three parts, firstly looking at the current legal position on incapacity in a number of jurisdictions. It discusses the recent European project FLEUR, and the associated debates developing around whether legislation dealing with incapacity should aim to support or control the vulnerable person.

Secondly, the book looks at the experience of families with vulnerable members. Chapters examine developments in Australia, Spain, Bulgaria and Argentina, while part three looks at France, Turkey, Canada, the Netherlands, Poland and Ukraine. It asks questions such as: What are the contemporary demands for full financial protection by the state in the Netherlands? What can happen in an emergency? How did the Polish system provide for the needs of refugees in wartime, in the case of the recent flight from Ukraine into Poland?

An important dimension is added to the debate, asking how we can provide support and control within a social network or group whose members have different aims and needs in a family or a community.

Oñati International Series in Law and Society

A SERIES PUBLISHED FOR THE OÑATI INSTITUTE
FOR THE SOCIOLOGY OF LAW

Recent titles in this series

The Right to the Continuous Improvement of Living Conditions: Responding to Complex Global Challenges
Edited by Jessie Hohmann and Beth Goldblatt

Supporting Legal Capacity in Socio-Legal Context
Edited by Mary Donnelly, Rosie Harding and Ezgi Tascioglu

What Is a Family Justice System For?
Edited by Mavis Maclean, Rachel Treloar and Bregje Dijksterhuis

Combining the Legal and the Social in Sociology of Law: An Homage to Reza Banakar
Edited by Håkan Hydén, Roger Cotterrell, David Nelken and Ulrike Schultz

Criminal Justice and The Ideal Defendant in the Making of Remorse and Responsibility
Edited by Stewart Field and Cyrus Tata

Socio-Legal Trajectories Across Europe: Comparative Perspectives
Edited by Christian Boulanger, Naomi Creutzfeldt and Jennifer Hendry

Parole Futures: Rationalities, Institutions and Practices
Edited by Harry Annison, Nicola Carr and Thomas Guiney

The Socio-Politics of Legal Design and its Epistemic Consequences
Edited by Siddharth Peter de Souza and Joaquín Santuber

Digital Intermediaries in Domestic and Care Work
Edited by Lorena Poblete and Eva Kocher

Incapacity and Access to Family Justice
Edited by Mavis Maclean

For the complete list of titles in this series see www.bloomsbury.com/uk/series/oñati-international-series-in-law-and-society

Incapacity and Access to Family Justice

Edited by
Mavis Maclean

Oñati International Series in Law and Society

A SERIES PUBLISHED FOR THE OÑATI INSTITUTE FOR THE SOCIOLOGY OF LAW

•HART•
OXFORD • LONDON • NEW YORK • NEW DELHI • SYDNEY

HART PUBLISHING
Bloomsbury Publishing Plc
Kemp House, Chawley Park, Cumnor Hill, Oxford, OX2 9PH, UK
1385 Broadway, New York, NY 10018, USA
Bloomsbury Publishing Ireland Limited, 29 Earlsfort Terrace, Dublin 2, D02 AY28, Ireland

First published in Great Britain 2026

1

A catalogue record for this book is available from the British Library.

A catalogue record for this book is available from the Library of Congress.

ISBN: HB: 978-1-50998-342-1
ePDF: 978-1-50998-344-5
ePub: 978-1-50998-343-8

Typeset by Amnet

For product safety related questions contact productsafety@bloomsbury.com

To find out more about our authors and books visit www.hartpublishing.co.uk. Here you will find extracts, author information, details of forthcoming events and the option to sign up for our newsletters.

Acknowledgments

We wish to thank the Onati Institute for enabling us to hold our last online Workshop and then to enjoy the return to a meeting in person. Both were productive and successful, but the opportunity to exchange ideas and information is always further stimulated by face-to-face contact whether in the Residencia, the Institute, or sharing walks in the surrounding countryside. We are most grateful to Sarah Castle, the Official Solicitor for England and Wales, for suggesting that sociologists of family law could contribute to the development of legal work where lack of capacity is an issue.

Contents

PART III
UNDERLYING POLICIES

List of Contributors

Mavis Maclean, CBE, is a Senior Research Fellow of St Hilda's College, University of Oxford

Masha Antokolskaia is Full Professor Family Law Vrije Universiteit, Amsterdam, and the chair of FL-EUR.

Benoit Bastard is Directeur of Research Émérite at CNRS, École Supérieure de Paris Sacle, France

Sarah Castle is the Official Solicitor and Public Trustee, London

Bregje Dijksterhuis is Assistant Professor of Family Law, University of Amsterdam, Netherlands, working with research team Jelle Landman and Anja Hoekstra

Belinda Fehlberg is Professor of Law, University of Melbourne, Australia

Małgorzata Fuszara is Professor in the Institute for Applied Social Science, University of Warsaw, Poland

Verda İrtiş is Scientific Collaborator, Université libre de Bruxelles, CRPSD, Faculty of Law and Criminology

Richard Ingleby Victorian Bar and University of Western Australia

Jacek Kurczewski is Professor of Sociology and Anthropology of Custom and Law, University of Warsaw, Poland

Jelle Landman is a Partner at Forza Adviesgroep (Oud-Beijerland, the Netherlands).

Laura Lora is Research Professor Faculty of Law, University of Buenos Aires

Julieta Marotta is Assistant Professor of Law and Policy, Maastricht University, Netherlands

Thomas Meysen is Director of SOCLES University of Heidelberg, Germany

Cheryl Morris is a lawyer in the Office of the Official Solicitor and Public Trustee, London

Teresa Picontó Novales is Professor of Law, University of Zaragoza, Spain

Jens Scherpe is Director of NORDFAM and Professor of Law, University of Aalborg, Denmark

Rieneke Stelma-Roorda is Assistant Professor Family Law at Vrije Universiteit, Amsterdam, and secretary of FL-EUR.

Velina Todorova is Professor of Law, University of Plovdiv, Bulgaria

Anja Vaandering-Hoekstra is a Lawyer at Klaver & Janssen Lawyers in Alkmaar.

Part I

Introduction and Existing Legal Frameworks

1

Introduction

MAVIS MACLEAN

THE CONTRIBUTORS TO this volume have benefitted from working together for many years as members of the International Sociological Association Research Committee on the Sociology of Law, supported by the IISL Onati, with the aim of increasing understanding of the role of law in the relationship between the individual, the family and the state. We have carried out empirical research in a number of jurisdictions. We have looked at the social context and functioning of a range of family justice systems, and most recently at the changing role of the state in family matters. For example, Polish governments have recently been encouraging access to courts in order to avoid undue private pressure on the individual from family and church in family matters. In Australia and the UK, governments with concerns about the rising cost of their family justice systems have sought to discourage and control access to family courts in the period of austerity following the financial crash of 2008, and instead have been placing increasing emphasis on promoting private individual problem solving using alternative forms of dispute resolution. We have also studied the increasingly prevalent question of how to ensure that a justice system can function fairly and efficiently in societies with diverse cultures and values. For example, in communities where both state law and Sharia law are important to citizens this may give rise to a range of conflicting expectations about the resolution of family issues. But we have only recently begun to think, at the suggestion of Sarah Castle, the Official Solicitor for England and Wales, in London, about the relationship between family matters and individual vulnerability, which may perhaps be giving rise to concerns about individual legal capacity. The problems often relate either to age or disability, but may also arise from issues associated with conditions for residence, or adherence to a different belief system. But as the Official Solicitor pointed out to us in our online workshop in Onati, in 2022, incapacity can often give rise to family problems related to allocation of resources, choice of residence, or participation in a household. These may be followed by further problems arising from the choices made about ways of coping with the outcomes of these kinds of decisions, which can so easily lead to disputes between family members,[1] and may require access to the family justice system. These issues are becoming increasingly prevalent as societies age, and also as we develop more complex forms of family grouping and organisation. The increase in different forms of partnering to include not only marriage but also cohabitation, and the experience of multiple partner and parenting relationships over time have led to complex disputes. For example, a recent Australian case concerned whether the longstanding and devoted de facto partner of a widow had any claim on his partner's original family property since the latter had lost capacity with the onset of dementia. She had needed to be moved out of the family home and into residential care, but he had nowhere else to go if the house were to be sold and the equity passed to the widow's adult children.[2] Matters can also become complex when there are post-separation parenting arrangements to be made, and where there are children from different parents sharing a single household. Furthermore, there are different culture-based approaches to property ownership in different societies which contribute to potential conflict in the context of complex legal and social norms and limited general understanding. For example, is a wealthy elderly man who lacks legal capacity still able to spend as he wishes? Or is there a responsibility to consider the needs and expectations of the wider family and even the community, which may then require the support of state intervention in the form of a court-appointed financial guardian? This latter form of guardianship is accepted in the Netherlands, but would be considered a gross violation of individual privacy in other jurisdictions, for example Australia. Moreover, the role of the guardian is very demanding, as guardians are required to provide expert financial advice as well as helping with family negotiations, and questions are now arising about whether it is still feasible to seek performance of this double role. This issue is discussed further in chapter twelve, which presents empirical data on the work of guardians from a research team in Amsterdam, which included a former practising guardian. There is also discussion and debate about the developing tendency to define incapacity not as a set of medical phenomena but as an interactive state, where the capacity of a vulnerable person is dependent to some extent on the attitudes and behaviour of other family members. Here the UN thinking on human rights may be the most useful starting point.[3]

The Official Solicitor (OS) and her staff first raised some of these questions at our earlier meeting entitled 'What is a Family Justice System For?', in 2021, asking why family lawyers, and particularly sociologists of family law, have not been interested in legal capacity when the associated issues are so often connected with family needs? The question resonated with this group, particularly a case described to us by the OS where a local authority had applied to take into care

[1] See ch 5 below.
[2] See ch 5.
[3] See, for example, C Kong and A Ruck Keene 'Overcoming challenges in the Mental Capacity Act 2005' (2019 Kingsley, London).

a vulnerable baby born in the UK to a young mother who had been trafficked from Eastern Europe. But at the same time the local authority was asking the OS to represent the mother in seeking an order for foster care rather than adoption, so that it might be possible for her to continue to have contact with the child. The OS 'stands in the shoes' of a vulnerable person in a family case. She also described a case at the other end of the age range: a 91-year-old man, Mr P and his cat, Fluffy. A relative had reported concerns to the local authority regarding Mr P who had dementia and other health issues and was living alone. The local authority visited and immediately took him into care and placed him in a secure residential home. Over a year later, the OS was asked to help when other relatives asked for help in showing that he did have sufficient support to stay in his flat. He was then returned to his home and reunited with his cat and awarded compensation by the court for wrongful deprivation of liberty. These cases stimulated both discussion and empirical work, following the second online meeting of the group at IISL in 2022, and were discussed in person in Onati in 2023. We suggest that the focus of family law on reconciling conflicting and changing needs while protecting the rights of individuals within a family group over time, in order to develop their full potential within that group, could be helpful to those having difficulty in working for the rights of a disabled or vulnerable person to develop their full potential and meet their needs within their family and over a period of time. The discussion continued to develop further at the IISL meeting entitled 'Family Justice and Mental Incapacity', which was held in July 2023, and the findings are presented in this volume.

The volume has three parts: Part 1, Introduction and Existing Legal Frameworks , describes questions arising in the context of current legal frameworks beginning in chapter two with the UK, and presenting the position of the Official Solicitor in England and Wales, and in chapter three drawing on the work of the FL-EUR Project in over 30 European jurisdictions whose report was first published in 2019.[4] This part then goes on to introduce the need to see situations from various perspectives, for example in chapter four looking at the needs of a child with parents who lack the capacity to parent. Part 2, Legislative Change, describes the impact of recent attempts to introduce new forms of legislation, in chapter five in Australia and in chapters six and seven in Spain and Bulgaria, including emerging aims which are less concerned with controlling those with capacity limited by age or disability than with attempting to increase their support and extend their range of activities. Chapter eight turns to the specific question of response to capacity as it increases with age as children grow up, and how the judiciary are developing the ability to match capacity to activity in Argentina rather than using fixed cut-off points. Part 3, Underlying Policies, considers the range of policies and ideologies underpinning the design and delivery of these interventions, eg in France and Turkey, asking

[4] FLEUR report link https://fl-eur.eu/.

who is in control and who is aiming to do what. We are then able, in chapter eleven, to give a detailed research-based account of how financial guardianship is currently working steadily in the Netherlands. This is followed by a report from Poland in chapter twelve on what can happen in a period of crisis when a new need arises to be able to work around current legal requirements for showing capacity to enter society. The chapter describes the recent emergency response to the sudden increase in cases of legal incapacity when refugees from the conflict in Ukraine began arriving at the Polish border without papers, but were nevertheless accepted and provided with ways of joining meaningfully in Polish society. The volume closes in chapter thirteen with some conclusions, which may be helpful, but perhaps most importantly with a number of new questions for further consideration about when and how legal intervention needs to be able to respond to a changing range of needs and circumstances in the interests of all members of a society.

In chapter one the editor sets out the origins and development of the project as discussed in the Onati Workshops and its relation to the ongoing stream of work from this group on the relationship between law, the individual, the family and the state. This is followed in chapter two which presents the questions raised by the Official Solicitor and Public Trustee for England and Wales, Sarah Castle. These questions concern the role of the OSPT, which is essentially to act as a litigation friend in civil (often family court) proceedings, for a person who lacks mental capacity, to ensure protection of their rights as a vulnerable person, whether this is a child or someone who lacks capacity according to the provisions of the Mental Capacity Act 2005. This legislation states that such a person is unable to make a decision if they cannot understand the information relevant to that decision, and cannot retain that information, or use or weigh up the information as a part of the process of making the required decision. It is thought necessary in England and Wales to call on the Official Solicitor, even where there are family members or friends willing to act, as the latter may have a fixed view before any court hearing, or be involved in the case in other ways. Currently, however, some leading practitioners are advocating a more interactionist view of disability which stresses the variety of roles played in mental capacity by relationships. Kong and Keene (see fn 2, p 9) stress 'the fact that people are situated within complex relationships that can support and disable as well as obstruct their ability to act and to secure their own interests . . . or even be in a fundamentally abusive relationship with the impaired person'. They go on to argue that the view of capacity as interactive, depending on a family situation, need not be regarded as incompatible with a human rights approach, supporting this claim by quoting Eleanor Roosevelt's eloquent question as the first Chairperson of the United Nations Commission on Human Rights (quoted p 10) saying 'Where after all do universal human rights begin? In small places, close to home, the world of the individual person . . . the school, the farm, the office . . . such are the places where every man woman and child seeks equal justice, equal opportunity, equal dignity without discrimination.'

The role of the Official Solicitor in England and Wales can be traced back to the Office of the Six Clerks in the eighteenth century. They have assisted destitute litigants, lunatics and infants in Chancery suits ever since. At the 2022 Onati IISL Workshop, Sarah Castle described her role as representation of the vulnerable, and is pleased to be seeing the development of protection, and welcomes no longer being required to delay proceedings by having to present an unarguable case (see *ECtHR RP and Others v The United Kingdom* 382/45/08). She is also able, as at the 2023 Workshop, to comment more broadly on issues facing the courts, for example the recent discussions of the concept of substituted parenting, whereby local authorities have been limiting the amount of help given to disabled parents on the grounds that this kind of substituted rather than supportive parenting would leave a child confused as to who their real parents are. Recent research has, however, indicated that the term is being used in judgments but lacks definition, and the courts seem to have responded rapidly to the advice to use support for parents rather than substitute care (see Court of Appeal *Re H (Parents with Learning Difficulties: Risk of Harm* [2003] EWCA Civ 59 (2 February 2023)). She is also able to intervene where the relevant rules do not make provision and the common law has had to step in. For example, where adult parties in care proceedings lack mental capacity and are deemed to be protected persons, the Official Solicitor can 'step into their shoes' and make applications on their behalf, requiring procedural fairness but without authority beyond the proceedings. Chapter three goes on to look at the present state of legal regulation concerning capacity. Professor Jens Scherpe, University of Aalborg, comments on the report from the 30 European states who participated in the FLEUR PROJECT, whose work was published in 2019. This project on Empowerment and Protection of Vulnerable Adults concluded by supporting autonomous decision making by adults with impairments for as long as possible, with supported decision making when needed, and supported representation as a last resort, together with the assurance that the application of such measures does not automatically lead to limitation of legal capacity. Finally the report recommends that assistance should be demand orientated, using the principle of best interests to refer to the vulnerable person's own will and preferences while seeking protection from abuse by third parties. These recommendations are designed to support the vulnerable person and their representative, and to offer protection from neglect but also from the effects of their own ill-considered decisions.

However, it is clear from the FLEUR survey that developing legislation to deal with incapacity is not an easy task, in particular, how might we aim to support or control the vulnerable person? Is it feasible or desirable to use a medically based definition of incapacity, or should human rights discourse be the preferred starting point?[5] Attempts to legislate have had varying outcomes

[5] Mary Donnelly, Rosie Harding and Ezgi Tascioglu (eds) 'Supporting Legal Capacity in Socio Legal Context' (Onati Series 2022).

in the jurisdictions scanned by FLEUR, who report that major reform was noted in Finland, Germany and Norway prior to ratification of the United Nations Convention on the Rights of Persons with Disabilities (UN CRPD) 2020, and after ratification of UN CRPD by Austria, Belgium, Czechia and Portugal, Slovenia and Switzerland. But reform has been patchy in Croatia, Denmark, Hungary, Russia, the Netherlands, Lithuania, Scotland and Sweden. Bills had been published in Bulgaria, England and Wales, and Ireland, but no reform had been achieved at the time of publication in Estonia, Greece, Poland or Serbia. There has also been a proposal from the European Commission for rules to protect people who have lost mental capacity in cross-border cases (STEP). The choice of actions to be taken arose from the context and history, as well as the character of the specific proposals, and we therefore go on in Part 2 to examine in more detail examples of attempts to improve the legislative position in three very different settings, Australia, Spain and Bulgaria, where the background, the aims and the capacity for change vary greatly. But first we can pause to enjoy and respond to the challenge from Thomas Meysen of SOCLES, University of Heidelberg, in chapter four to be careful about what underlying assumptions we wish to accept! He asks us to think about a situation where the process of managing incapacity by supporting the vulnerable may follow an unexpected pathway. He presents the case of children, usually thought of as vulnerable but progressing towards capacity, and adults, usually thought of as competent, but possibly likely to lose capacity in old age. He asks the reader to exchange the location of these characteristics and consider the situation of children with normal development and capacity who have parents who are vulnerable and lack legal capacity, and asks for consideration of a helpful policy response. (This follows in chapter eight.)

In Part 2 we consider three examples of recent attempts to reform the law relating to mental incapacity and access to family justice. The first case in chapter five comes from Australia, where Richard Ingleby and Belinda Fehlberg explore the operation of the recent Guardianship and Administration Act 2019 for the State of Victoria. In Australia, State governments have the power to make laws to support people with disabilities that reduce or remove their capacity to make their own decisions. The authors analyse the decisions made under the current 2019 Victorian guardianship legislation, and its predecessor the Guardianship and Administration Act 1986 (Victoria) by the Victorian and Civil Administrative Appeals Tribunal (VCAT), to see whether the 2019 legislative changes resulted in any changes in outcomes or approach. They then look more broadly at the issues arising most commonly in the reported cases. In Australia, orders to support adults with disabilities who lack legal capacity to make their own decisions are called guardianship and administrative orders, typically covering where the represented person lives, their health care, and their access to services and to people. A guardian must be a suitable person, whose interests do not conflict with those of the vulnerable person, a friend or relative, or an Officer of the Public Advocate representative (OPA). The OPA has independent powers to protect the vulnerable person, and assist with applications for guardianship, administration or powers of attorney for those who wish to plan ahead. The attorney cannot, however, make medical treatment decisions for the person. The VCAT provides a low cost, accessible service for dispute resolution, but it is not a court. An application must therefore be made to the Supreme Court of Victoria to enforce VCAT orders. The Act aimed to support those in need of help with decision making, taking into account the UN Convention on Rights of Persons with Disabilities. The study looked at all decisions made in 2022 under the 2019 Act, and in 2019 under the 1986 Act. But no discernible change was found in the approach or outcomes between the two data sets, and there were no appeals to the Supreme Court of Victoria. The identification of a medical decision maker is dealt with separately under the Medical Treatment Planning and Decision Act 2016 and the Power of Attorney Act 2014 (Vic). After dividing the cases into those where orders had been made and power of attorney or medical treatment had been decided, or no provision made, in the cases where something had changed this was usually in response to a question about the identity of a guardian. Overall, existing practice appeared already to have developed to a point compatible with the requirements of the recent legislation, which therefore appears to have been able to confirm existing practice. But where changes to guardianship had been sought and achieved, the great majority of cases had arisen from family disputes about management or control of the resources or the care of the vulnerable person. The authors of chapter five refer to the frequency of longstanding and extreme animosity between family members.

In chapter six we hear of a very different response to new legislation from Teresa Picontó about a transitional legal situation where radical reform of legal protection for persons with disabilities has recently been introduced by State Law 8/2021 for Spain, based on the principle of equality with other people in Aragon to exercise their rights and preferences. This law follows the New York Convention of 2006 in having a single definition for capacity, but adds support for the exercise of existing rights. In Aragon however the existing local law 5/2019 was based mainly on the older legal model of protection, and not all the legal operators in the region will comply with the innovation required in state law 8/2021 whereby autonomy is to displace best interests. The Catalan code is also being revised – see Draft Law 19/2021. However, because it derives from regulations to protect elderly people, it is based more firmly on the concept of assistance as being requested by the vulnerable person.

The third case study, which appears in chapter seven, is even less optimistic about change according to the account provided by Velina Todorova from Bulgaria. The Bulgarian constitution does not regulate legal capacity, but includes a special protection clause in Art 51 which places old persons who cannot support themselves, as well as persons with disabilities, under the special protection of the state. Until 2020, guardianship had been an easy way to place incapacitated adults in institutions where they remained forgotten. But more recently, following two cases at the European Court of Human Rights (in 2007 and 2012), violations of several human rights in incapacitated persons were found under the ECHR. The new Social Services Act 2020 stipulated that any placement in an institution should be based on a court order. There is now a draft law on Natural Persons and Supported Decisions, similar to Spanish law, with pilot experiments and work on the training of judges with advice from medical experts. There has been a large and sustained advocacy movement for change headed by parents and NCOs. But there is still little public interest, and no national system for care for vulnerable adults in Bulgaria.

The final chapter in Part 2, chapter eight, turns to the position of children and adolescents who are often 'invisible' in family legal processes. But in Argentina the law gives capacity gradually to adolescents in a way that is linked to their 'evolving capacities' and 'progressive autonomy'. Julieta Marotta and Laura Lora report exciting empirical research into the work of the interdisciplinary teams who assess the capacity of adolescents in order to advise the court. Information was collected from young people through participatory research, which included the opportunity to create something to reflect their experience with the family justice system, such as videos, songs, and even plays. In addition, the family courts have developed protocols on how to introduce themselves to young people. A judge stressed to the researchers the importance of 'making a child visible' and free to express himself, so enabling the court to understand directly how children see their situation, not simply through the views of their parents. Children's concepts of access to justice are highly valued.

In Part 3, however, we turn from the development of assessment of individual capacity in the justice system to the 'top down' issues of the development and implementation of policy with respect to vulnerable people (ie the character and role of the family justice system).

In chapter nine, Benoit Bastard comments on the tendency of European institutions to move towards favouring the autonomy of vulnerable people, while in France his empirical work for this project indicates a different perspective rooted in 'protection', with the use of various measures that frame and restrict the freedom of individuals despite the legislative changes that have been taking place over the last 50 years. In France, the juge de la protection remains the figure who decides in all cases whether a person is supposed to need a measure of protection. The definition of various categories of vulnerability has developed with subgroups and differing legal structures, and a greater emphasis on family support (habilitation familiale), where the family carer has full control, perhaps for economic reasons, with the aim of controlling public expenditure. But at the same time the question of assets has become more closely controlled by the state, with annual accounting procedures being required. He presents a detailed account of the involvement of three different actors: the judge, the guardian (mandataire de justice) and the family, finding diversity in practice but overall with a strong element of state protection.

We then turn, in chapter ten, to the description by Verda İrtiş of the current legal position in Turkey, and recent developments in practice for the vulnerable. By considering both international developments and local change, her analysis highlights the increasing effort to develop new ways of dealing with disability, and also the need to carry out further research in this area of legal incapacity.

We draw towards a close with two chapters which provide detailed accounts of two very different current systems and situations. In chapter eleven Bregje Dijksterhuis, and her colleagues Jelle Landman and Anja Hoekstra provide a detailed account of their research with state-appointed financial guardians in the Netherlands, where the state provides and even requires proactive protection, but where those performing this role are finding it increasingly difficult to balance the multiplicity of demands they face. The guardian is described as a person who helps the client to understand the consequences of freely made decisions and can also protect a client where he cannot cope with some of the consequences. Autonomy and freedom are seen as intertwined. As a member of the research team, Jelle Landman is able to give a particularly detailed and nuanced description of the work based on his own recent experience in the role. The authors quote the definition of Oliver Wendell Holmes who described freedom as how 'your right to swing your arms ends just where the others man's nose begins'. But the situation is more complex for the person who does not know where his arm ends or the other's nose begins. You may be free, but you do not know the effect it will have on your own autonomy. Dijksterhuis, Landman and Hoekstra say 'In the end you can be free, but not so free as to evade the consequences of the freely made decision'. In practice, the authors tell us that when a client makes a decision without the help of the guardian that has a negative effect on the client's assets, the guardian can reverse that decision.

A complex balance has been developed in the Netherlands between individual autonomy and group needs. But we end with another view of the question of balance between individual need and legal code, asking what should happen in an emergency situation where people lack legal capacity based on language and the requisite documentation but urgently need to escape from danger and access the benefits of a stable society? In chapter twelve, Professors Kurczewski and Fuszara from Warsaw and Professor Tashkinova, visiting from Ukraine, describe what happened in 2022 when Ukrainian refugees, mainly women and children, arrived without documents or language skills at the Polish border in flight from the invasion of their country. They were welcomed, and enabled to play a part in Polish society without question; a strange variation on the situation of those who are controlled by the state for their own benefit. These people in flight were released from control by the state for their benefit to the possible detriment of the hosts.

This final case study provides an unusually clear example of how a piece of legislation is not simply a rule with a single clear purpose, but rather a mechanism for balancing needs and safeguards in a society, where flexibility can be a life-saving device.

The balance between support and restraint, and between individual, family and community or state responsibilities gives rise to a number of questions which are considered in our concluding chapter thirteen. For example, should this balance be determined by lawyers or by welfare experts? Should family members give evidence in a public decision-making process or should this be done by welfare professionals? Or by lawyers? Should there be different systems for managing finance and personal life? How will we cope with an ageing population? and with more complex and changing family structures? What is the role of medicine in decision making? What is the role or responsibility of the state in encouraging individuals to make provision for future incapacity through arranging powers of attorney? Or does the responsibility lie with the state?

Can the UNDHR provide guidelines? Or even answers?

The debate is just beginning . . .

2

Access to Family Justice and Mental Incapacity in England and Wales: The Role of the Official Solicitor

SARAH CASTLE

INTRODUCTION

THIS CHAPTER SEEKS to explain the definition of mental capacity in England and Wales, and the role of the Official Solicitor as litigation friend, with particular reference to family law matters.

It then describes some recent changes to the understanding of family law issues and how these have affected the position of some parties within the family law system.[1]

Finally, it sets out the nature and extent of the development of the law relating to those who lack litigation capacity.

THE DEFINITION OF MENTAL CAPACITY IN ENGLAND AND WALES

The legal test for lack of capacity is contained in the Mental Capacity Act 2005 (MCA 2005). A person lacks mental capacity in relation to a matter if at the material time they suffer from an impairment of, or a disturbance in, the functioning of the mind or brain, which causes them to be unable to make a decision (MCA 2005, s 2(1)). The test is issue specific.

The MCA 2005 defines a person who lacks capacity as a person who is unable to understand the information relevant to a decision, to retain that information for sufficient time to decide, to make a decision, even if that decision is unwise,

[1] This chapter was drafted in 2022 and 2023, and represents the law as it then stood. It has not been updated to refer to any subsequent developments.

and to communicate that decision (MCA 2005, s 3). All possible efforts must be made to assist a party to attain this level of ability (MCA 2005, s 2).

In the context of litigation, the application of the test is also informed by common law. It has been held that capacity for this purpose means capacity to conduct the proceedings. The leading case regarding litigation capacity in fact pre-dates the MCA 2005.[2] In a post-MCA 2005 case decided by the Supreme Court, Lady Hale, who gave the leading judgment, held that the Court of Appeal had reached the correct conclusion in *Masterman-Lister*.

This is a functional test, so the fact that a parent is for example detained under the Mental Health Act 1983 for assessment or treatment for a mental illness, will not of itself mean that the parent lacks mental capacity to conduct family proceedings such as care proceedings. As previously stated, capacity is issue specific. The fact that a person is unable to deal with their finances does not mean that they are automatically considered to lack litigation capacity.

In family proceedings, a person who lacks mental capacity to conduct a case is called a protected party, and the court rules require that a protected party and children (subject to specified exemptions in the case of children) must act through a litigation friend (to bring or defend proceedings). There are similar court rules which apply in the civil courts and in the Court of Protection.

If a party is found to lack litigation capacity, no substantive steps may be taken in the proceedings to which they are a party until a litigation friend is appointed.

THE ROLE OF A LITIGATION FRIEND

The function of the litigation friend is to enable people who are vulnerable because of their lack of mental capacity, or because they are under 18 years of age, to access the civil justice system in order to bring or defend proceedings.

The purpose of appointing a litigation friend for a party who lacks mental capacity is both:

(a) to ensure that the legal rights of the mentally incapacitated and children are recognised and enforced; and
(b) to ensure other parties to the proceedings are not denied a remedy because essential parties to the proceedings are legally incompetent (because of lack of mental capacity or age).

While in many cases a family member or friend is prepared to act as a litigation friend of a protected party, in some cases, and particularly family cases, no-one is able and prepared to act. In those cases the Official Solicitor is asked by the court to act as litigation friend of last resort.

[2] *Masterman-Lister v Brutton & Co (Nos 1 and 2)* [2002] EWCA Civ 1889, [2003] 1 WLR 1511.

THE HISTORY AND ROLE OF THE OFFICIAL SOLICITOR

The history of the office of the Official Solicitor and its predecessors is a long and complicated one since it became established as a statutory office in the late nineteenth century. The first Official Solicitor, Henry Leigh Pemberton, was appointed in 1871, so the office recently celebrated its 150th anniversary. Sarah Castle, the current holder of the office is the twelfth Official Solicitor and the first woman to hold the office. She was appointed as Official Solicitor and Public Trustee, by the then Lord Chancellor under the Senior Courts Act 1981 on 4 July 2019. Prior to her appointment she had worked for local authorities, dealing with cases relating to child protection, adult social care and education.

The position of the Official Solicitor is unique within the system of the administration of justice in England and Wales.

Although the court's own solicitor, the Official Solicitor also acts for private individuals. Powers, duties and responsibilities may be conferred or imposed on her (or removed from her) from time to time in the following ways:

(a) by, or under, the Senior Courts Act 1981 or any other Act of Parliament;
(b) by, or in accordance with, a direction given by the Lord Chancellor;
(c) by, or under, rules of court;
(d) by common law; or
(e) in accordance with established practice.

In addition to the statutory provisions relating to the Official Solicitor, the Official Solicitor's functions, powers and duties have been extended by judicial decision making in specific cases. For example, the Official Solicitor may be asked by a judge to carry out investigations,[3] or to act as Advocate to the Court.

For those who may be unfamiliar with the latter concept, a court may seek the assistance of an Advocate to the Court when there is a danger of an important and difficult point of law being decided without the court hearing relevant argument. Unlike the situation in most of the Official Solicitor's work, when she acts as Advocate to the Court, she represents no-one. The function of the Official Solicitor is to give the court such assistance as she can on the relevant law and its application to the facts of the case. Ordinarily the Attorney-General acts as advocate to the court but the Official Solicitor can be asked to do so when the issue is one relating to the representation of adults under legal disability.

The primary function and purpose of the office is, however, to act as a litigation friend in civil proceedings, including family proceedings, when there is no other suitable person who is willing and able to act (ie as a last resort).

The Office of the Official Solicitor comprises 138 staff, 30 of whom are lawyers. Eighty-nine members of staff are involved in litigation casework. In addition to the family litigation team, the office has dedicated teams for civil

[3] See, for example, the case of *Harbin v Masterman* [1896] 1 Ch 351.

litigation and for Court of Protection work. There are parallels and overlaps between family proceedings and Court of Protection proceedings, and many family judges in England and Wales also sit as judges of the Court of Protection. This is because the Court of Protection has jurisdiction under the Mental Capacity Act 2005 to make decisions on financial or health or welfare matters for people who lack mental capacity to make those decisions, and the Official Solicitor may act for the same person in a Court of Protection case and in a concurrent family case.

The central core of the work of the Official Solicitor is the role of litigation friend (formerly called Next Friend or Guardian ad Litem) of last resort. There remain, however, areas of civil proceedings where the relevant rules do not make provision and the common law has to step in.

The Official Solicitor's position in relation to her appointment as litigation friend in tribunal proceedings is that the Lord Chancellor has not made any Direction, pursuant to the Senior Courts Act 1981, section 90(3), for the Official Solicitor to act as litigation friend in such cases. However, where the Rules allow for the appointment of a litigation friend she will consider acting as a litigation friend to assist parties who lack capacity to instruct solicitors in exceptional circumstances and subject always to her acceptance criteria.[4]

Since 2016, a litigation friend can be appointed, as a matter of common law for a party to a tribunal case who lacks mental capacity. This is because it was held in a number of cases that the common law concept of procedural fairness demanded that a litigation friend should be appointed to act on behalf of a party who lacked capacity, notwithstanding that a tribunal is not a formal court as such.[5]

Similarly, following a judicial review of the Parole Board[6] in which the Official Solicitor acted as litigation friend of a prisoner who lacked mental capacity to apply for parole, a litigation friend can now also be appointed for the purpose of a parole review but must consent to their appointment. This last is a new area of work and formal guidance about this was only issued in October 2021. Although doubtless beneficial to those affected, it has resource implications for the office.

In family proceedings, the majority of those for whom the Official Solicitor acts as litigation friend are protected parties, that is, adult parties who lack the mental capacity to conduct the proceedings, rather than children. The only children she acts for as litigation friend in family proceedings are parents who are themselves children and intervenors who are under 18.

An intervening child will generally be joined to a care case where the court is enquiring into the cause of injury to the child who is the subject of the care proceedings, and the other, intervening child is one of the possible perpetrators of the injury. As the intervening child's welfare is not the subject of the care

[4] See *AM (Afghanistan) v Secretary for State for the Home Department* [2017]EWCA Civ 1123, Sir Ernest Ryder, Senior President para 44.

[5] See *Bradbury & Ors v Paterson & Ors* [2014]EWHC 3992 (QB).

[6] See *R (EG) v Parole Board* [2020] EWHC 1457 (Admin).

proceedings, it falls to the Official Solicitor to represent that child. Children who are the subject of care proceedings have their interests protected by representation from the legal arm of the Children and Family Court Advisory Service.

As litigation friend, the Official Solicitor 'steps into the footsteps/shoes' of the protected party and gives instructions to the protected party's solicitors on their behalf.

Although the office is funded by the Ministry of Justice, independence in decision making is crucial to the Official Solicitor's work as litigation friend, as she acts for private individuals and the State may be a party to the proceedings. For example, all care proceedings in the Family Court are brought by the State in the form of the relevant local authority.

In family proceedings the Official Solicitor usually becomes involved as litigation friend when a judge asks her to accept the appointment. But she can and does also bring proceedings on behalf of a protected party, where some responsible person or body brings the facts to her attention and it appears that the protected party, on whose behalf she is invited to act, has a good cause of action. This is more common in private law – for example, when a protected party parent wants to have contact with their child and she accepts appointment in order to make the application.

THE OFFICIAL SOLICITOR'S CRITERIA FOR ACCEPTING AN INVITATION TO ACT FOR A PARTY

When there is a request for the Official Solicitor to act, she will always enquire as to whether there is satisfactory undisputed evidence regarding lack of capacity. This evidence must be produced and the question must be asked regardless of whether the party concerned accepts the opinion of the expert. If the party does not and asserts their own capacity, then it is for the judge, not for the Official Solicitor, to apply the law to the facts and make a decision as to whether the parent is in fact a protected party.

In addition she must ensure that funding is in place to permit her to instruct solicitors. This can be problematic in divorce cases, although less so in care proceedings.

THE ROLE OF LITIGATION FRIEND

Although the office of Official Solicitor is unique in the legal framework of England and Wales, the role of litigation friend is not unique to the Official Solicitor.

The Official Solicitor acts as litigation friend, not because she alone is able to act, but because there no one else suitable and willing to act in a given case. When she acts, she plays the same role as any other person appointed to act as litigation friend. Her position in litigation is no better and no worse than that of any other appointee. Except as regards costs, she is not in a privileged position simply because she is the Official Solicitor.

Any other person may act as a litigation friend, provided they can fairly and competently conduct the proceedings for the person for whom they are acting and have no adverse interest.

Family members often act as litigation friends in civil 'money' claims such as personal injury and clinical negligence claims, but do so less often in cases which have a bearing on family life.

This is not because a family member cannot do so. Perhaps the reasons why the Official Solicitor is more often asked to act in family proceedings (and similar reasons apply to Court of Protection proceedings) include the following:

- Where there is a family dispute, members of a family may find it difficult to take a balanced and even-handed approach to the relevant issues. They themselves may also be emotionally involved in the matters in dispute.
- Family members may be reluctant to take on the responsibility of acting as litigation friend because they are worried about the impact on their family relationships if they do so.
- Family members may have fixed views of their own either about the issues in dispute, about what can or should be achieved for the relative who has been found to lack mental capacity, or about the role of other parties (eg the local authority) in bringing or progressing the proceedings.
- Family members may have direct or ancillary involvement in the proceedings – as another party, as a witness or (in care proceedings) as a potential kinship carer.

Although it is healthy for the justice system to experience differing approaches to the discharge of a litigation friend's duties and responsibilities, it is only rarely that a family member is appointed as litigation friend for a parent in care proceedings. This is partly because family members do not put themselves forward, but also owing to concern on the part of the court or others regarding family members' abilities to discharge the duty of a litigation friend and because of the legal requirement that the litigation friend should have no adverse interest.

When acting as litigation friend, the Official Solicitor is discharging a 'private' role, as she is not doing anything that could not be done by someone else. This is different from the situation where she acts in any of her 'official' roles, for example, when acting as advocate to the court, as that is a role shared only with the Attorney-General and with the Children and Family Court Advisory Service (Cafcass).

CONDITIONS THAT CAUSE A LITIGATION FRIEND TO BE APPOINTED

A wide range of conditions can cause a lack of capacity, but the conditions the office of the Official Solicitor's staff see most often in family proceedings are mental illness, learning disability, brain injury, progressive neurological conditions and (increasingly) dementia. Often there is co-morbidity, or the party's condition is exacerbated by abuse of drugs or alcohol.

Although the majority of family referrals made to the office are in proceedings relating to children, the Official Solicitor may act as litigation friend in all forms of family proceedings; so she may act as litigation friend in family cases ranging from a care case arising out of serious injury to a child, to a 'big money' financial remedy case involving trusts.

CAPACITY OF A PROTECTED PARTY REVIEWED

The appointment of a litigation friend is not necessarily a once-and-for-all decision, as a protected party may lose or regain capacity at any point during proceedings. This means that the Official Solicitor may be appointed or discharged as litigation friend at any point. There have been cases when she has been appointed for only a short time before a trial, and similarly cases where she has been discharged on the eve of trial. Her office will always keep capacity under review if there is any possibility of the protected party recovering capacity during the proceedings, and will ask for further assessment if recovery appears likely.

The Official Solicitor's duty as litigation friend to the conduct of proceedings is to fairly and competently conduct the proceedings on behalf of the person for whom they are appointed to act – the duty does not depend on the nature of the proceedings. This remains the same across the board. The litigation friend may do anything which is required or authorised by the court rules to be done by a party to the proceedings, but the litigation friend's authority does not extend beyond the proceedings. This is not always understood by other parties.

The Official Solicitor cannot, for example, exercise parental responsibility in place of a parent simply because that parent is a protected party in the proceedings – so she cannot consent (or refuse consent) to medical treatment for their child, but as the parent's litigation friend she could support or oppose a court order authorising such treatment.

When acting as litigation friend in a family case, the office instructs external solicitors to conduct proceedings for the protected party or child. She relies on the solicitor (and barrister where appropriate) for legal advice about the steps the Official Solicitor should take on behalf of the protected party.

The Official Solicitor must ensure procedural fairness for the protected party and the steps and decisions she takes in the proceedings must be for the benefit of the protected party. However, when making decisions about the conduct of the proceedings, although she must take into account what the protected party wants, she cannot ignore what the evidence says or the legal framework and simply put forward whatever argument the protected party desires, although she will always ensure that the party's wishes and feelings are before the court.

However in children proceedings, for example, she cannot ignore the fact that the law requires the court to view the child's welfare as the paramount consideration and to apply the welfare checklist contained in the Children Act 1989.

Similarly, while she will put forward any realistic arguments and relevant evidence that may be available on behalf of the protected party in relation to the issues before the court, if she is advised by the parent's solicitor that there are no realistic arguments to be made, having regard to the evidence, she will not take a case to trial solely because that is what the parent wants. Generally, however in such circumstances she will not oppose rather than support or agree with the other party's case. She will, however, take a case to trial if advised that there are arguments which can reasonably be put, even if the legal advice is that it is unlikely that those arguments will actually succeed at trial.

This approach is informed by advice that the previous Official Solicitor obtained from Peter Jackson QC (now an Appeal Court judge) in 2007. He was instructed to review and advise about the approach the Official Solicitor should take, in the light of the Official Solicitor's obligations under the Human Rights Act 1998 and in particular having regard to the gravity of the issues for parents and children involved in cases where the local authority was proposing a plan for adoption. A number of potential approaches were identified by the Official Solicitor, including whether, as litigation friend, he should on principle oppose such an application on behalf of the parent. The advice (in line with the Official Solicitor's then existing practice) was that the correct course is for the Official Solicitor as litigation friend to present any realistic arguments and relevant evidence available on behalf of (ie in support of) the parent in relation to the issues, if the point is reasonably arguable but not that the case should be opposed regardless.

This approach has been tested.

In late 2006 Alastair Pitblado, the previous Official Solicitor, was appointed as litigation friend of a mother in care proceedings. Ultimately, a case was brought against the UK in the European Court of Human Rights (ECtHR) arising out of that appointment.[7] In that case the court held that in determining whether a case was arguable or not, it was necessary for the Official Solicitor to consider what was in the child's best interests, and that acting in the mother's best interests did not require the Official Solicitor to advance any argument the mother wished. The ECtHR held that on the contrary, it would not have been in the mother's – or in any party's – best interests for the Official Solicitor to have delayed proceedings by advancing an unarguable case.

In recent years, changes both in approach and to the court rules mean that vulnerable parties (not only protected parties) are now much better supported to participate in proceedings, as parties and as witnesses. There have been a number of very positive developments including:

[7] The judgment of the ECtHR is reported as *RP & Others v The United Kingdom* 38245/08.

- the introduction of Part 3A (Vulnerable Persons: Participation in Proceedings and Giving Evidence) into the Family Procedure Rules 2010 – Part 3A requires the court to consider whether 'participation directions' are required – that is, whether any adjustments to the usual methods of giving evidence should be made to assist a vulnerable person to give their evidence. This includes the use of screens around the witness box, or the witness giving evidence by video link, for example;
- the use of witness intermediaries (first introduced into criminal proceedings) to help parties with communication difficulties to understand the case as it progresses in court. This is now commonplace in family proceedings;
- the establishment of the online Advocates' Gateway which provides free access to practical guidance for barristers and solicitors about how to communicate with vulnerable witnesses and parties.

THE IMPACT OF THE PANDEMIC

On 23 March 2020, the then Prime Minister announced the first COVID-19 lockdown in the UK ordering people to 'stay at home'. Legal restrictions ended in England on 24 February 2022; in Wales the last restrictions ended on 30 May 2022.

The impact of the restrictions on an already struggling family justice system was profound – the lack of hearings in the early stage of the restrictions and then the move to remote hearings caused backlogs in the system to increase. Before the introduction of restrictions, care cases were allocated to a case manager within two working days of acceptance criteria being met, honouring a commitment made by my predecessor to the Family Justice Board. However, the pandemic had an impact on the office's ability to allocate cases. Happily the position has now returned to normal.

Anecdotally. my case managers have noticed that the care cases, in particular, received since the pandemic are more complex, and the problems families are facing are more profound. The difficulties clients had to contend with meant that many were highly vulnerable to further harm in the context of lockdown, which restricted access to services. Mental illnesses went undiagnosed or untreated, and drugs and alcohol became coping mechanisms. There were incidents of violence against children and others. The office has seen cases of parental deaths at the hands of their partners arising out of undiagnosed and therefore untreated mental illness.

TAKING OPPORTUNITIES TO RAISE ISSUES RELATING TO THE REPRESENTATION OF THE VULNERABLE

It is an important part of the work of the office to raise the issue of representation of the vulnerable when the opportunity presents itself – not to make political points but to highlight where there are gaps (as there often are)[8] in procedural fairness; how those who lack mental capacity can be enabled to participate; and to make suggestions about how things might be improved.

The Official Solicitor also responds to relevant government consultations and from time to time has agreed to participate in research. Office staff have also been involved for some years with the Working Together with Parents Network (WTPN) which works to improve support for parents with a learning disability and is convened by the Norah Fry Institute at Bristol University.

The Official Solicitor has recently been approached by the Civil Justice Council to take part in a working group to look at issues relating to the assessment of mental capacity in civil proceedings. This follows on from similar work the office undertook some years ago with the Family Justice Council, which led to the publication of guidance on the issue.

NEW INITIATIVES BEING PILOTED IN THE FAMILY JUSTICE SYSTEM

First, there is the introduction of the Pathfinder courts pilot announced on 8 March 2022 to deal with private law children cases. This pilot has now been launched in the family courts in North Wales[9] and Dorset[10] and is aimed at better supporting victims of domestic abuse.

It follows from a review of family courts which found that an adversarial process often exacerbated conflict between parents and had a damaging impact on victims and their children. The pilot scheme will encourage proceedings to be less adversarial, with more emphasis on investigating and addressing allegations of domestic abuse and other harmful behaviours. The steps include:

1. agencies gathering information and assessing whether there are any concerns for a child or person involved in a case from substance misuse, domestic abuse or other welfare issues;
2. a hearing to decide what interventions or decisions are required (including whether the case is suitable for mediation out of court).

The second is the introduction, on 4 July 2022, of a pilot of a dedicated court based at the Royal Courts of Justice to hear applications made to authorise the deprivation of liberty of a child.

A recent report from the Nuffield Family Justice Observatory,[11] which drew on national administrative data and research for the last 10 years, noted first

[8] Capacity to Litigate in Proceedings involving Children, Family Justice Council, 2018.

[9] Caernarfon, Mold, Prestatyn and Wrexham.

[10] Bournemouth and Weymouth.

[11] 'What do we know about children and young people deprived of their liberty in England and Wales? An evidence review' (Nuffield Family Justice Observatory (nuffieldfjo.org.uk) 2022).

that many more children are referred for a place in a secure children's home on welfare grounds than can be placed, and secondly that there is some evidence that there is a cohort of children with particularly complex needs who are seen as too 'challenging' to be suitable for a secure children's home. This has led to a significant increase in applications by local authorities for the exercise of the inherent jurisdiction of the High Court (a power of the court which is not spelt out in legislation) to authorise children being deprived of their liberty in alternative placements. In 2020/2021, there were 579 applications, a 462 per cent increase from 2017/2018. The author of the report notes that very little is known about where these children are placed, what restrictions are placed on their liberty, or what their outcomes are. There is some information in published judgments, but of course it is limited to preserve the confidentiality of the children concerned.

It is clear that much work still needs to be done. Whilst the Official Solicitor welcomes all initiatives which may help the struggling family justice system, it is noticeable that parties who lack capacity are seldom participants in pilots and therefore such pilots are not necessarily tested against this very vulnerable class of litigants. It is a source of regret that parties who lack mental capacity are not necessarily at the forefront of policymakers' minds when policy or new legislation is being developed and therefore 'gaps' persist, or new gaps emerge.

Enabling, to the fullest extent possible, the participation of those who lack mental capacity in decision making about either themselves or their children is of fundamental importance for a just legal system.

'SUBSTITUTED PARENTING'

This relates particularly to proceedings involving parents with learning disabilities.

In England and Wales, the local authority may remove a child from their parents if the child is likely to be suffering abuse or neglect and these flaws in parenting cannot be rectified by the parents.

There has been a trend for local authorities to state that they cannot give a substantial amount of support to learning-disabled parents because this would become 'substituted parenting'. According to some local authorities, children would become confused as to who were their parents, and would suffer attachment disorder as a result. They added that the disorder would be worsened, because carers might be changed frequently.

This seemed to the Official Solicitor to be an invalid argument, because children who have nannies, and might see them come and go during their childhoods, or be looked after by au pairs who could leave after a year do not appear to suffer from such a disorder. However, the office could not substantiate this, and care orders were regularly made on this basis.

Recently the Nuffield Foundation, a charity which funds research that informs social policy, primarily in education, welfare and justice, gave a grant to Bristol University to fund research into the subject of substituted parenting. One of the family lawyers working at the office was asked to chair the Advisory Group of this project.

The researchers spoke to lawyers, judges, social workers, children's guardians, and learning-disabled parents themselves. Their findings are now on the Bristol University website.[12]

The findings of the researchers were that although the term 'substituted parenting' is often used in judgments,[13] there appears to be no agreed definition of what this means. It became apparent that this was a term used by local authorities that had been accepted by all parties in care proceedings without any research to prove its veracity, and sometimes without any clear definition of its meaning.

Judgments which refer to substituted parenting do not seem to define it, or to analyse either what risk is perceived, or what might be done to minimise the risk.

The researchers found that duration, costs, resources, sustainability, and the impact on a child's emotional welfare are the main reasons adduced as to why substituted parenting is not considered to be desirable, feasible, or acceptable. 'Parenting by others' in a family context (and to a degree parenting by paid professionals) is distinguished from 'substituted parenting'.

If a court is being asked to weigh costs in the balance, researchers considered that specific information should be made available by the local authority, detailing those costs and setting out at what point (and why) such costs stop being 'sustainable' or 'feasible'.

The principal perceived risk of substituted parenting is that it would be inimical to a child's welfare, in terms of the child's emotional well-being, rather than physical safety (although in some cases this can also be of concern).

The researchers concluded that identifying and raising such a concern is important. However they concluded that it was essential that concerns are not just raised, but also carefully analysed to ensure that they are based on fact and not speculation, and that options should be explored to address, manage, mitigate, or even eliminate those concerns where possible.

This, they concluded, is particularly the case where the concerns are based on theoretical support packages, rather than actual evidence, and the potential consequences are so significant for the family.

Families are entitled to a fair process, whatever the eventual outcome.

[12] The report may be found at http://bristol.ac.uk/media-library/sites/sps/documents/wtpn/SP%20Report.pdf, the executive summary at http://www.bristol.ac.uk/medialibrary/sites/sps/documents/wtpn/SP520Summary.pdf and the policy summary at http://www.bristol.ac.uk/media-library/sites/sps/documents/wtpn/SP20%Policy%20Brief.pdf. An easy read version for parents is at http://www.bristol.ac.uk/media-library/sites/sps/dpcuments/wtpn/SP%20Easy%20Read.pdf.

[13] See, for example, *A Local Authority v G (Parent with Learning Disability) (Rev 1)* [2017] EWFC B94 (18 December 2017) (bailii.org).

Research is helpful to explore an area, but what makes this research particularly important is that it appears to have had an immediate effect. In the case of *Re H*[14] the Court of Appeal stated that:

> Judges need to be wary of arguments based on the concept of 'substituted parenting'. They should carefully scrutinise the evidence adduced by the local authority that the level of support required by the parents would be on a scale that would be adverse to the child's welfare and should look for options for ameliorating the risk of harm that might result from a high level of support. It is all encapsulated in the simple sentence in paragraph 1.4.4 of the Guidance quoted above – 'every effort should be made to support not supplant the parents'.

It would appear therefore that this research is already affecting the outcomes of cases.

THE TRANSPARENCY PROJECT

Unlike criminal courts, which are open to public access and frequently reported on, going through the family court is a private and confidential process. Because of this, many members of the public know very little about family law proceedings. Often their only exposure to the family court system is television programmes like Judge Rinder, and US-style televised litigation (eg Amber Heard vs Jonny Depp or the OJ Simpson trial). As a result, there is much misinformation and prejudice about family court judgments.

Until now, journalists, bloggers and reporters have not been allowed to sit in court during family proceedings (with some exceptions, and only with the judge's permission) and much of the information shared within family court cases is held to be private.

Any opening of the courts has had to navigate the tension between two major factors: the need to boost public trust in the family court and the need to maintain confidentiality and privacy for those who use the family court to resolve family disputes.

On Monday 30 January 2023, the Transparency Implementation Group Reporting Pilot launched in Cardiff, Leeds and Carlisle. The aim of the pilot is to introduce a presumption that accredited media and legal bloggers may report on what they see and hear during family court cases, subject to strict rules of anonymity. The ability to report is being piloted to make sure that it can be done safely and with minimum disruption to those involved in cases, and the courts. This will be done through judges in these courts making a Transparency Order, which sets out the rules of what can and cannot be reported.

[14] *H, Re (Parents with Learning Difficulties: Risk of Harm)* [2023] EWCA Civ 59 (2 February 2023).

The content of the transparency order is vitally important, particularly to the sort of cases involving the Official Solicitor. Although the President of the Family Division made it clear that he considered families' privacy to be vital, if pieces of information are available – the name of a small town, a school catchment area, a number of siblings – it is possible to piece together that information and guess at the identity of a particular party.

In a recent case in which the Official Solicitor was acting, a child and one parent suffered from a very rare illness. As a result of that and certain other factors disclosed during proceedings, anyone who knew the family would be able to identify them through this information. When the Official Solicitor made an application to the judge, he specifically recorded in the transparency order that no information about the illness should be disclosed by any reporter or blogger.

The aim of the pilot was to 'improve the accounting and transparency and to promote the public's confidence in the family justice system'. At the time of writing (July 2023), it has only been in operation for a few months, so it is too early draw conclusions. However, perhaps the biggest problem faced by this aim is the public's desire to read about sensational cases, which have little bearing on their own lives or any judgment that might affect them.

Meanwhile, the Official Solicitor must be careful to ensure that any transparency order that she makes limits information that is likely to identify her clients.

FORCED MARRIAGE PROTECTION ORDERS

Forced marriages are usually categorised as those in which one party is coerced into marrying another. However there is another type of forced marriage, which is one where a party is 'married' despite not having capacity to consent to a marriage.

This is not as odd as it sounds. A parent who is growing older may consider that the best way for their learning-disabled child to receive adequate care and attention after the parent is unable to provide that care is to find them a spouse who will care for them. This can have disastrous consequences for both parties. Sometimes, the able spouse will leave their partner after realising the extent of their disability. If the disabled partner does not have the ability to consent to sex, and the able partner does not appreciate that, the able partner might even be charged with rape. The area is fraught with difficulty.

Recently schools specialising in teaching learning-disabled pupils and children's social workers have been advising local authorities if a child mentions that they are going to be married.

This is a time when the Court of Protection work of the Official Solicitor becomes intertwined with family law. Under the Mental Capacity Act 2005, 'a person is not to be treated as unable to make a decision unless all practicable steps to help him to do so have been taken without success' (MCA 2005, s 1(3)).

But it is the Court of Protection that makes the decision about whether or not a person has capacity in the interim, and it is that court which will order an educational programme, as suggested by both parties, to see whether the disabled party can gain capacity to consent to marriage. Some local authorities, particularly those which are not used to dealing with forced marriage cases, may become over protective. In a recent case a 16-year-old decided she wanted to marry in accordance with her family's customs. The council applied for a Forced Marriage Protection Order. After numerous tests, it was decided that although her decision appeared unwise on the face of it, it was not made because she lacked capacity or because she was being coerced into marriage. In that case, therefore, the Official Solicitor had the rare opportunity to facilitate a marriage rather than stopping one.

3

The FL-EUR Comparative Research Project on Empowerment and Protection of Vulnerable Adults

RIENEKE STELMA-ROORDA, MASHA ANTOKOLSKAIA, AND JENS M SCHERPE[1]

INTRODUCTION

FAMILY LAW IN Europe: An Academic Network (FL-EUR) was founded in Amsterdam in 2019. The objective of FL-EUR is to promote spontaneous bottom-up harmonisation of the law of persons and family law in Europe by collecting, systematising, analysing and making available knowledge about relevant national laws in Europe to academics, practitioners, national and supranational governments and international organisations. The FL-EUR project focuses on substantive law only, but this of course includes what is commonly referred to as 'law in the books' as well as 'law in action', and thus puts the relevant laws in their context. FL-EUR also aspires to promote comparative and multidisciplinary research and education to facilitate learning from each other's experiences.

Importantly, FL-EUR is a purely academic initiative, not linked to any governments or international organisations. All participants take part in the network in their own personal capacity and enjoy full academic independence. Currently, the network brings together 34 leading experts: academics, judges and government employees, from 31 European jurisdictions, both from within

[1] Rieneke Stelma-Roorda is assistant professor of family law and the law of persons at the Vrije Universiteit Amsterdam, the Netherlands and secretary of FL-EUR. Masha Antokolskaia is professor of family law at the Vrije Universiteit Amsterdam, the Netherlands and the chair of FL-EUR. Jens M Scherpe is professor of comparative law at Aalborg Universitet, Denmark, Director of the Nordic Centre for Comparative and International Family Law (NorFam) and member of FL-EUR.

and outside the European Union,[2] with additional members expected to join in the future. The network is organised democratically: all members have a voice and a vote, and important decisions are taken jointly. FL-EUR has a smaller Coordinating Group, and this group is mainly in charge of preparatory and organisational work.

Currently FL-EUR is working on its first project: on the Empowerment and Protection of Vulnerable Adults. Experts from 29 jurisdictions were asked to write a country report based on a carefully designed questionnaire. With their subsequent analysis of these country reports, FL-EUR aims to uncover the common core, best practices and pitfalls in the field of empowerment and protection of vulnerable adults, putting together a range of possible solutions that could be used by national governments, European and international organisations, professionals and their associations. The national reports on this first topic were published in 2023.[3] Several teams of researchers from different countries are currently working on analysing the reports each looking at a different theme, including:

- statutory adult protection measures;
- voluntary measures, such as the continuing power of attorney; and
- *ex lege* measures.[4]

In this chapter we present the rationale for and importance of this work, looking at the theoretical and practical challenges around the theme of Empowerment and Protection of Vulnerable Adults (see the following section). We will then briefly address the methods used by FL-EUR to explore these challenges (see 'Methods Used by the FL-EUR' below) before ending with some short concluding thoughts (see 'Concluding Thoughts' below).

EMPOWERMENT AND PROTECTION OF VULNERABLE ADULTS – FIRST FINDINGS AND ISSUES ARISING

At their very first general meeting, FL-EUR members chose 'Empowerment and Protection of Vulnerable Adults' as the first topic for their work. This subject was chosen from a shortlist that also included issues in high-conflict divorces and new forms of parenthood including parenthood through surrogacy. That

[2] Austria, Belgium, Bulgaria, Croatia, Czech Republic, Denmark, England & Wales, Estonia, Finland, France, Germany, Greece, Hungary, Ireland, Italy, Latvia, Lithuania, North Macedonia, Norway, Poland, Portugal, Romania, Russia, Scotland, Serbia, Slovakia, Slovenia, Spain, Sweden, Switzerland, The Netherlands and Ukraine.

[3] The country reports are available open access on the FL-EUR website (www.fl-eur.eu) and on the website of the multidisciplinary open-access journal Family & Law (https://www.familyandlaw.eu/pagina/country_reports) (last accessed 6.2.2025).

[4] *Ex lege* measures can be defined as adult protection measures providing legal authority to other persons to act *ex lege* (by operation of law) on behalf of the adult, requiring neither a decision by a competent authority nor a voluntary measure by the adult.

the legal measures of empowerment and protection of vulnerable adults were chosen is illustrative of the rapidly growing interest in and importance of this area, triggered by the rapidly ageing population in developed countries and the coming into force of the United Nations Convention on the Rights of Persons with Disabilities (UNCRPD). Both developments have transformed the legal protection of vulnerable adults from a somewhat underappreciated and niche subject into a 'hot topic'.

The decision to choose this topic as the first area of work was timely, given the societal challenge developed countries will face in coming decades. According to figures provided by the World Health Organization, the proportion of the world's population over 60 years will increase from 12 per cent to 22 per cent between 2015 and 2050.[5] With age, certain age-related illnesses can and will occur. These include frailty, falls and delirium and heightened risks of diseases such as dementia. In 2020, there were over 50 million people worldwide living with dementia. This number is expected to increase to 82 million in 2030 and 152 million in 2050,[6] meaning that there will be an increasing number of people requiring support and care in the future. This support and care will probably have to be provided by a decreasing number of people, as many countries experience a so-called 'grey pressure phenomenon', where the ratio between the number people aged between 20 and 65 able to provide care and support for people aged 65 is decreasing significantly.[7]

This societal trend is also likely to have an impact on the care and support available for vulnerable adults more broadly. FL-EUR deliberately chose to focus not just on *older* adults with impaired capacity, but rather on vulnerable adults of *all* ages. Using the text of Article 1 of the Convention on the International Protection of Adults,[8] the term 'vulnerable adults' for the project was defined as 'adults who, by reason of an impairment or insufficiency of their personal faculties, are not in a position to protect their interests'.

This definition, therefore, also includes adults with a congenital injury resulting in impaired capacity. In order to clearly delineate this group of adults from adults who are not experiencing an impairment or insufficiency of their personal faculties, the term 'vulnerable' (which does not appear in the Convention on the International Protection of Adults) was chosen. Admittedly, the use of this phrase may appear somewhat arbitrary, as of course everyone can be considered vulnerable in one way or another. Furthermore, there is a growing body of literature that argues that using the term 'vulnerable' is problematic because it

[5] See https://www.who.int/news-room/fact-sheets/detail/ageing-and-health (last accessed 6.2.2025).

[6] See https://www.alzint.org/resource/numbers-of-people-with-dementia-worldwide/ (last accessed 6.2.2025).

[7] See, for example, the Netherlands, https://www.cbs.nl/nl-nl/visualisaties/dashboard-bevolking/leeftijd/ouderen (last accessed 6.2.2025).

[8] Convention of 13 January 2000 on the International Protection of Adults, available at https://www.hcch.net/en/instruments/conventions/full-text/?cid=71 (last accessed 6.2.2025).

can lead to (further) stigmatisation and exclusion of individuals and groups.[9] However, FL-EUR ultimately chose the term solely for clarity and without any intention to be disrespectful to those concerned.

Besides the societal challenge based on the increasing number of (older) people facing a decline in their cognitive abilities, there is also a challenge from a human rights perspective. The adoption of the UNCRPD has provided a major global paradigm shift in raising awareness of the need to empower adults in the exercise of their legal capacity, calling on states to move away from the paternalistic notion of protection through a deprivation or restriction of the adult's legal capacity. According to Article 1 UNCRPD, the aim of the convention is to 'promote, protect and ensure the full and equal enjoyment of all human rights and fundamental freedoms by all persons with disabilities, and to promote respect for their inherent dignity'.

Persons with disabilities are defined as including 'those who have long-term physical, mental, intellectual or sensory impairments which in interaction with various barriers may hinder their full and effective participation in society on an equal basis with others'.[10]

This means that the class of adults as defined in Article 1 of the Convention on the International Protection of Adults also falls within the scope of the UNCRPD. The UNCRPD definition emphasises what is known as a *social model of disability*, which focuses on the interaction between an impairment and barriers in society, including, for example, physical barriers such as buildings that are not accessible, but also attitudes in society, such as the assumption that an adult cannot do certain things, without checking whether this actually is the case. Such barriers are seen as hindering the full and equal enjoyment of human rights.

When it comes to the empowerment and protection of vulnerable adults, this call for a change of perspective is not surprising given the huge impact that traditional adult protection measures – involving a deprivation or restriction of the adult's legal capacity and the appointment of a representative to act on the adult's behalf – have on the adult's private life and ability to exercise his rights and duties. The UNCRPD therefore emphasises the adult's right to autonomy and to be recognised before the law as a full legal actor. This becomes apparent when looking at the general principles of Article 3 UNCRPD, which include 'respect for inherent dignity, individual autonomy including the freedom to make one's own choices, and independence of persons' with 'full and effective participation and inclusion in society'. In addition, Article 12 UNCRPD stresses that persons with disabilities have the right:

[9] See, for example, SC Munari, AN Wilson, NJ Blow, CSE Homer and JE Ward, 'Rethinking the use of "vulnerable"' (2023) *Australian New Zealand Journal of Public Health* 45(3), pp 197–99.

[10] Article 1, UNCRPD.

- to recognition everywhere as persons before the law (Article 12(1) UNCRPD);
- to enjoy legal capacity on an equal basis with others in all aspects of life (Article 12(2) UNCRPD); and
- to receive the support they need in the exercise of their legal capacity (Article 12(3) UNCRPD).

Moreover, besides the right to autonomy, adults also have the right to be protected from abuse. Article 16 UNCRPD requires states to take appropriate measures to protect persons with disabilities from all forms of exploitation, violence and abuse. In addition, Article 12(4) UNCRPD requires states to ensure that all measures relating to the exercise of legal capacity come with appropriate and effective safeguards to prevent abuse. Such safeguards must ensure that the rights, will and preferences of the adult are respected, and that conflicts of interest and undue influence are avoided.

When it comes to the right to autonomy and protection, there is no hierarchy where one right automatically takes precedence over the other and a proper balance must be struck between the two.[11] The question of how to balance these two rights, and the questions of what the precise meaning of Article 12 UNCRPD is and how far the requirements of this article actually go in practice have caused much debate internationally. Several countries made so-called reservations or interpretative declarations with regard to Article 12 UNCRPD upon the ratification of the convention, including Estonia, The Netherlands, Norway and Poland.[12] The discussion has been furthered by the stance of the Committee on the Rights of Persons with Disabilities – a body of independent experts monitoring the implementation of the UNCRPD by states – in General Comment No 1 on Article 12 UNCRPD. Closer examination of this General Comment No 1 shows that there are several issues regarding the interpretation of Article 12 UNCRPD that seem to give rise to debate. By way of example, below we discuss two of these issues, highlighting the complexities jurisdictions face in implementing Article 12 UNCRPD.

The first issue concerns the legitimacy of approaches that use the concept of mental capacity to determine when support and protection should be provided to the adult. The Committee defines the concept 'mental capacity' as referring to 'the decision-making skills of a person, which naturally vary from one person to another and may be different for a given person depending on many factors, including environmental and social factors'.[13]

[11] HN Stelma-Roorda, *In Anticipation of a Future Period of Incapacity. The Dutch 'Levenstestament' from a Legal, Empirical and Comparative Perspective* (The Hague: Eleven International Publishing 2024) 14.

[12] Galway, Centre for Disability Law and Policy, National University of Ireland (NUI), *A Study on the Equal Recognition before the Law. Contribution towards the Council of Europe Strategy on the Rights of Persons with Disabilities*, Council of Europe March 2017, 34–35.

[13] Committee on the Rights of Persons with Disabilities, *General Comment No 1. Article 12: Equal recognition before the law*, United Nations 2014, p 3.

According to the Committee, the use of this concept is highly problematic because:

> The concept of mental capacity is highly controversial in and of itself. Mental capacity is not, as is commonly presented, an objective, scientific and naturally occurring phenomenon. Mental capacity is contingent on social and political contexts, as are the disciplines, professions and practices which play a dominant role in assessing mental capacity.[14]

Consequently, the Committee also considers approaches that use the concept of mental capacity to assess whether a person needs support and protection to be problematic and not in line with Article 12 UNCRPD. These approaches include the so-called 'status approach', where a decision on whether a person has legal capacity or not is based on the diagnosis of an impairment, and the 'outcome approach', where a decision on whether a person has legal capacity or not is based on whether the person makes a decision that is deemed to have negative consequences.[15] More controversially, according to the Committee, the so-called 'functional approach' also falls under the approaches that are incompatible with Article 12 UNCRPD. An example of a jurisdiction with such an approach is England and Wales, where a person is deemed to lack capacity in relation to a specific decision, when, as a result of an impairment or disturbance in the functioning of the mind or brain, the adult is unable to understand, retain, use or weigh relevant information or to communicate his decision.[16] According to the Committee, the functional approach is flawed for two reasons:

> it is discriminatorily applied to people with disabilities and it presumes to be able to accurately assess the inner-working of the human mind and, when the person does not pass the assessment, it then denies him or her a core human right – the right to equal recognition before the law.[17]

The question then remains how to determine when a person needs support and protection.[18] The Committee confines itself to remarking that Article 12 UNCRPD does not allow a discriminatory denial of legal capacity, but rather requires the provision of support in the exercise of legal capacity.[19] In other

[14] Committee on the Rights of Persons with Disabilities, *General Comment No 1. Article 12: Equal recognition before the law*, United Nations 2014, p 4.

[15] Committee on the Rights of Persons with Disabilities, *General Comment No 1. Article 12: Equal recognition before the law*, United Nations 2014, p 4.

[16] See Mental Capacity Act 2005, ss 2 and 3. (The Mental Capacity Act 2005 of England and Wales.)

[17] Committee on the Rights of Persons with Disabilities, *General Comment No 1. Article 12: Equal recognition before the law*, United Nations 2014, p 4.

[18] W Martin, S Michalowski, J Stavert, A Ward, A Ruck Keene, C Caughey, A Hempsey, R McGregor, *The Essex Autonomy Project Three Jurisdictions Report. Towards Compliance with CRPD Art 12 in Capacity/Incapacity Legislation across the UK*, University of Essex 2016, 34.

[19] Committee on the Rights of Persons with Disabilities, *General Comment No 1. Article 12: Equal recognition before the law*, United Nations 2014, 4.

words, no clear answer to the question is given. But it is beyond the scope of this chapter to address this dilemma extensively. We therefore limit ourselves to mentioning two approaches to address this dilemma suggested in the literature. The first, by *Martin* et al, suggests an approach in which practical support is provided before a legal intervention is allowed.[20] In other words, an assessment of capacity is preceded or accompanied by efforts to support the adult's decision-making ability and to explore whether the adult – with support – is able to make a decision themself. The Mental Capacity Act 2005 Code of Practice provides examples of such support. These include guidance on how supporters can determine what information is most relevant to convey to the adult, so that the adult does not become overwhelmed, and guidance on how information can be communicated in such a way that the adult best understands the information.[21] The second, put forward by *Ruck Keene* et al, proposes that instead of debating the legitimacy of the concept of mental capacity and the functional approach, efforts ought to be focused on testing, probing and refining the functional approach to ensure that assessments in individual cases do as much justice to the adult as possible.[22]

Besides the question of how to determine *when* the adult needs support and protection, another question and point for discussion is *what* measures are allowed to support and protect the adult. As discussed above, measures to support and protect adults in many jurisdictions include so-called adult protection measures, which often involve deprivation or restriction of the adult's legal capacity and the appointment of a representative to act on the adult's behalf. The Committee considers these so-called measures of substitute decision-making incompatible with Article 12 UNCRPD and calls on states to abolish such measures.[23] According to the Committee, states should instead introduce measures of supported decision-making, that respect the autonomy, will and preference of the adult.[24] However, a definition of the term 'supported decision-making' is not provided in General Comment No 1, and the Committee notes that supported decision-making can take many forms. Examples listed include the possibility for adults to choose a support person to help them in exercising their legal capacity for certain types of decisions, banks and financial institutions providing information in an accessible and understandable format enabling adults

[20] W Martin, S Michalowski, J Stavert, A Ward, A Ruck Keene, C Caughey, A Hempsey, R McGregor, *The Essex Autonomy Project Three Jurisdictions Report. Towards Compliance with CRPD Art 12 in Capacity/Incapacity Legislation across the UK*, University of Essex 2016, 34–35.

[21] See chapter 3 of the Mental Capacity Act 2005 Code of Practice. Code of practice giving guidance for decisions made under the Mental Capacity Act 2005, https://www.gov.uk/government/publications/mental-capacity-act-code-of-practice (last accessed 6.2.2025).

[22] A Ruck Keene, NB Kane, SYH Kim and GS Owen, 'Mental Capacity – Why Look for a Paradigm Shift?' (2023) *Medical Law Review* 31, 340–57.

[23] Committee on the Rights of Persons with Disabilities, *General Comment No 1. Article 12: Equal recognition before the law*, United Nations 2014, 2.

[24] Committee on the Rights of Persons with Disabilities, *General Comment No 1. Article 12: Equal recognition before the law*, United Nations 2014, 6.

to, for example, open a bank account and advance planning mechanisms that enable adults to state their will and preferences for a time when they are no longer in a position to communicate those.[25] Moreover, the Committee lists a set of key provisions which supported decision-making measures should incorporate.[26] However, it is emphasised throughout General Comment No 1 that supported decision-making can never amount to a deprivation or restriction of legal capacity.

The latter is perhaps the issue that has generated the most discussion when it comes to the interpretation of Article 12 UNCRPD. While the premise that priority should be given to measures that support the adult in the exercise of legal capacity seems to be gaining ground, debate continues as to whether substitute decision-making measures could or should be abolished altogether, even as a last resort in so-called 'hard cases' such as comatose patients or adults in an advanced stage of dementia.[27] In the literature, there are several examples of a critical stance in this regard. *Lush*, for example, notes that 'some profoundly disabled individuals lack the ability to make any decisions at all, even with support, and for them there is no viable alternative to substitute decision-making'.[28]

As mentioned earlier, several jurisdictions have made a reservation or interpretative declaration regarding Article 12 UNCRPD, which in most cases amounts to an interpretation of Article 12 UNCRPD stating that measures of substitute decision-making and a deprivation or restriction of legal capacity are possible as a last resort. The European Court of Human Rights (ECtHR) also seems to accept that a deprivation or restriction of legal capacity and the appointment of a substitute decision-maker is sometimes necessary as a last resort. In the decision *Ivinović v Croatia* the ECtHR considered:

> [D]eprivation, even partial, of legal capacity should be a measure of last resort, applied only where the national authorities, after carrying out a careful consideration of possible alternatives, have concluded that no other, less restrictive measure would serve the purpose or where other, less restrictive measures, have been unsuccessfully attempted.[29]

An important point to stress in this context is that it should not be too easily assumed that a situation where an adult needs support and protection calls for a measure of 'last resort'. As socio-medical research increasingly shows, even in

[25] Committee on the Rights of Persons with Disabilities, *General Comment No 1. Article 12: Equal recognition before the law*, United Nations 2014, 4.

[26] Committee on the Rights of Persons with Disabilities, *General Comment No 1. Article 12: Equal recognition before the law*, United Nations 2014, 7.

[27] W Martin, S Michalowski, J Stavert, A Ward, A Ruck Keene, C Caughey, A Hempsey, R McGregor, *The Essex Autonomy Project Three Jurisdictions Report. Towards Compliance with CRPD Art 12 in Capacity/Incapacity Legislation across the UK*, University of Essex 2016, 35.

[28] D Lush, 'The Civil Law and the Common Law', in R Frimston, A Ruck Keene, C van Overdijk and AD Ward (eds), *The international Protection of Adults* (Oxford – New York: Oxford University Press 2015), 37–52.

[29] ECHR 18 September 2014 (*Ivinović v Croatia*), no 13006/13.

situations of severe intellectual impairments, adults are capable of more than is often assumed at first glance.[30]

In addition to these two points in the debate which have been discussed extensively above, another important issue that we cannot discuss at length here is what weight should be accorded to the adult's will and preferences. While in many jurisdictions decisions representatives make decisions in what is to be considered the best interests of the adult, the Committee argues that the 'best interest' standard does not comply with Article 12 UNCRPD. Measures of support should instead ensure respect for the adult's will and preferences.[31]

As these discussion points show, the roadmap to implement Article 12 UNCRPD is full of obstacles and question marks, making it difficult for countries to navigate which direction to take. The issue becomes even more complex when considering, for example, the challenge of Article 12 UNCRPD to provide tailored support in light of the societal challenge where demographic changes are putting increasing pressure on the availability and accessibility of care and support services. Through its national reports and subsequent analysis of these reports, FL-EUR aims to help national governments, supranational actors as well as professionals and their associations to address the human rights and societal challenges mentioned above in three ways:

- First, by providing information on the systems of support and protection of vulnerable adults in various jurisdictions.
- Secondly, by analysing how different jurisdictions have implemented Article 12 UNCRPD, looking at the degree of modernisation in FL-EUR jurisdictions with regard to systems of support and protection, the obstacles experienced in doing so and whether or not these can be overcome.
- Thirdly, based on this analysis of the common core, best practices and pitfalls, the aim is to compile a set of possible solutions to the challenges discussed in this chapter. In the next paragraph we will describe the methods used by FL-EUR to achieve these aims.

METHODS USED BY THE FL-EUR

The core aim of FL-EUR is to promote the harmonisation of family law by making it easier to learn from each other's experiences by identifying best

[30] See, for example, LM Miller, CJ Whitlatch and KS Lyons, 'Shared Decision-making in Dementia: A Review of Patient and Family Carer Involvement' (2016) *Dementia* 15, 1141–57.

[31] Committee on the Rights of Persons with Disabilities, *General Comment No 1. Article 12: Equal recognition before the law*, United Nations 2014, 5. See, for example, W Martin, S Michalowski, J Stavert, A Ward, A Ruck Keene, C Caughey, A Hempsey, R McGregor, *The Essex Autonomy Project Three Jurisdictions Report. Towards Compliance with CRPD Art 12 in Capacity/Incapacity Legislation across the UK*, University of Essex 2016 and HN Stelma-Roorda, C Blankman and MV Antokolskaia, 'A Changing Paradigm of Protection of Vulnerable Adults and its Implications for the Netherlands, *Family & Law* 2019, 1–18 for a more extensive discussion.

practices and pitfalls. Elaborating Principles or any other kind of model law are explicitly not among the objectives of FL-EUR. FL-EUR is committed to applying a problem-solving, multidisciplinary approach, combining the functional comparative law method with multidisciplinary methods. Legal solutions are described and analysed in their political and socio-economic context. Experts are asked to also describe the underlying policy considerations and political and academic debates behind legal solutions. When available, existing empirical evaluations of relevant legislation are included in the work in order to shed light on which national legal solutions work well and which work less well – and why. FL-EUR deliberately does not limit itself to looking for similarities, including functional equivalents, but also looks for differences, including functional de-equivalents.

The method employed by FL-EUR involves several phases as described below.

In the first phase for the current project, FL-EUR members were asked to make a quickscan of the relevant system of legal measures of empowerment and protection of vulnerable adults in their jurisdiction. These quickscans provided the basic information necessary for the development of a comprehensive questionnaire by FL-EUR's coordinating group.

In the second phase, a comprehensive questionnaire was drafted by the Coordinating Group with the continuous input of the entire FL-EUR membership. After some deliberations, the decision was made to draft a detailed questionnaire, with many specific sub-questions to ensure that all relevant aspects of the law and its context were captured. Members and additional country reporters (national experts in the relevant areas) then prepared country reports by answering the questionnaire.

The third phase, which is still ongoing, involves thorough analysis of the national reports aimed at uncovering similarities and differences between the jurisdictions. Three teams of FL-EUR members and several PhD students from different countries are currently engaged in this work. They are trying to identify which solutions meet the requirements of the UNCRPD and then, using the available empirical data, to consider which solutions seem to also work best in practice.

The fourth and final step will be aimed at making a list, describing the approaches found in various jurisdictions that appear to best implement the international obligations and protect those concerned, addressing their advantages and disadvantages.

CONCLUDING THOUGHTS

The UNCRPD has triggered legal reforms aimed at developing new systems of measures of legal protection and empowerment of vulnerable adults that can meet the requirements of the relevant human rights instruments. At the same time, these measures have to be implementable in practice as well as affordable, considering the financial and human resource constraints imposed by 'grey pressure'. As all European countries have ratified the UNCRPD, there is, at least in principle, a consensus on the direction in which reforms should proceed. However, in practice, the degree to which national systems have already been adapted to the UNCRPD requirements varies significantly. The initial findings of the FL-EUR project, along with other sources, indicate that there is considerable diversity among European jurisdictions in this regard. As there is a consensus on the general direction of these reforms, and all European jurisdictions basically face the same challenges, they can learn from each other and benefit from practical experiences with approaches implemented in other jurisdictions. FL-EUR's comparative project can therefore provide national and supranational lawmakers with reliable and detailed information on the existing systems of measures of legal protection and empowerment of vulnerable adults. In addition, the results of the comparative analysis of the national approaches conducted by the FL-EUR experts can provide national legislators with practical knowledge on which approaches appear to have worked best in achieving their policy aims (and why), and also provide a warning concerning approaches that have not done so. This, hopefully, will not only provide a basis for a more infirmed discussion but also save time as by building on the experiences of other jurisdictions, each individual jurisdictions does not have to reinvent the wheel(s) all over again.

4

Parents with Mental Incapacities – Risk Factor for Children or Persons with Rights to Support?

THOMAS MEYSEN

PARENTS WITH INCAPACITIES – AN ARENA FOR HUMAN RIGHTS

EQUALITY AND INCLUSION matter for parents with incapacities. Not being discriminated against because of disabilities is a human right of parents, as well as the requirement for the state to take effective measures to ensure this (Art 23 Convention on the Rights of Persons with Disabilities (CRPD)). This calls for a perspective that sees parents with disabilities as individuals with resources that may require supplementing by the state to provide for equal treatment. When, however, the focus rests on the child, the incapacities may turn the tide. Parental incapacities often bring up the right of the child to be protected against all forms of neglect or negligent behaviour, or physical or mental violence while in the care of the parents (Art 19 Convention of the Rights of the Child (CRC)). Due to their incapacities, parents might become a 'suspect case' and professionals may seek proof that their parenting is good enough to avoid the risk of harm for the child. Instead of focusing on responsibility as a state, its support system and on how parenting can be supported in such a way that it succeeds for the benefit of the child, the change in perspective can lead to parents being made responsible for proving themselves to be capable and willing carers.

This chapter will look into the German system. First, the tasks and roles in a system which differentiates between child and youth welfare, assistance for parents with disabilities, and the jurisdiction on parental rights of family courts are explained (see the following section). After sketching current knowledge about the interrelations between parental incapacities and the risk of harm for the child (see 'Parents with Mental Incapacity and Parenting – Flashlights from Human and Social Science' below), the approach towards parents with incapacities in published judgments on child protection cases will be explored and discussed (see 'Parents with Mental Incapacity or Mental Illness in Judgments by German Family Courts' below). The Conclusions reflect on implicit discrimination in the German family justice approach and propose a shift in perspective.

BEING A PARENT WITH DISABILITIES – THE GERMAN SUPPORT AND JUSTICE SYSTEM

Parents with disabilities face a fragmented German support system (Schönecker 2020). On the one hand, the child and youth welfare system has a comprehensive mandate to support families regardless of the specific circumstances and the parents' personal situation. On the other hand, the support system for people with disabilities – so-called 'integration assistance' – is responsible for supporting the removal of barriers and enabling participation, which also includes 'supported parenthood'. The healthcare system, with health insurance at its centre, is largely limited to cure and leaves care – in particular family systemic services – to other service providers.

Child and youth welfare under Social Code Book VIII provides a range of services. These include preventative early help programmes and general support for parenting in the family to outreach social pedagogical family support and residential settings for parents and children. The law does not address parental disabilities specifically, which results in patchy availability of services that explicitly address the needs of parents and their children (Düber/Remhof 2018).

The 'integration assistance' system under Social Code Book IX provides support for mothers and fathers with disabilities to support them in caring for and looking after their children. Assistance or supported parenthood services relate to the self-determined and independent management of everyday life, including structuring the day, and can include services for general everyday tasks such as housekeeping, organising social relationships, personal life planning, participation in community and cultural life, leisure activities including sports activities and ensuring the effectiveness of medical/medically prescribed services. The law differentiates between parental assistance and accompanied parenthood:

- so-called parental assistance as purely physical, practical everyday services that support parents with physical or sensory disabilities in particular in fulfilling their parental role in a self-determined manner, and according to their own educational ideas (eg nappy changing/feeding, and accompanying the child to the playground for parents with paralysis/visual impairments, and assistance with homework supervision for visually impaired parents); and

- so-called accompanied parenthood, especially for parents with mental and psychological disabilities in the form of 'educational guidance, counselling and support in performing the parental role' (von Boetticher 2018).

The absence of any provision that comprehensively regulates the delimitation of responsibilities between the two support systems in the context of parenthood with disabilities leads to negative conflicts of competence, and in effect more difficult access to support services (Schönecker 2022). Family support services are provided by the youth welfare office ('Jugendamt') which is also responsible for child protection. This leads to a reaction among parents with disabilities, which can prevent them from seeking help at an early stage (Sprung et al, 2021). If it is necessary to intervene in parental custody to protect the child because the risk of harm cannot be averted by voluntarily seeking support services, the youth welfare office must refer the matter to the family court.

Family courts must restrict or withdraw parental rights in the event of

- child endangerment ('Kindeswohlgefährdung'), which the jurisdiction defines as 'a present danger to such an extent that in further development considerable damage to the mental or physical well-being of the child can be foreseen with reasonable certainty' (fundamentally Supreme Court 14 July 1956 – IV ZB 32/56); or
- a lack of the will or ability to avert danger, while a separation of the child from its parental family is only admissible if the danger cannot be countered in another way, not even through support services (sec 1666 (1), 1666a Civil Code).

Taking into account the situation of parents with disabilities, a reform of sec 1666 Civil Code was introduced in 2008. The requirement to find evidence of abusive exercise of parental authority, neglect of the child or failure through no fault of their own has been removed. The intention was to shift the focus away from past-oriented findings of misconduct, often associated with accusations against the parents, towards current and future-oriented safeguarding of the child's welfare (Deutscher Bundestag 2007). When analysing legal literature, it can be doubted whether the legislative goal could be reached (Schönecker 2021). The framing of parents with mental incapacity and mental illness remains as 'deficient parents' (Cirullies 2025, no 23) or 'parental deficits' (Götz 2025, no 12). The cases are 'almost always' seen as including 'parental failure with no fault of the parent' (Ziegler 2019, nos 22, 29). A child-centred approach is still the exception (Coster 2021, nos 137 ff)

It is hoped that a look into published family court judgments will provide further insights in future (see below 'Parents with Mental Incapacity or Mental Illness in Judgments by German Family Courts'), but prior to that current human and social science knowledge about parentage with disabilities and child welfare will be considered (see the following section).

PARENTS WITH MENTAL INCAPACITY AND PARENTING – FLASHLIGHTS FROM HUMAN AND SOCIAL SCIENCE

Incapacity can be mental or physical. The first task is to differentiate between mental illness on the one hand and mental retardation or learning difficulty on the other. In this chapter, mental incapacity is understood as 'an inability through mental illness or significant cognitive impairment to carry on the everyday affairs of life or to care for one's person or property with reasonable discretion' (Merriam-Webster 2025).

For parents with intelligence impairment the adaptive skills and the overall life situation, characterised in particular by physical and mental health, family situation, biographical burdens, and social support, are more decisive for coping with parental tasks than the actual extent of the intellectual disability (Orthmann et al 2017; Pixa-Kettner/Bargfrede 2015).

Many parents with mental incapacities have significant difficulties in taking adequate care of their children's health and safety (Orthmann Bless 2021). Evidence shows that, when coping with parenting tasks, mothers with mental incapacities often experience severe stress (Aunos et al, 2008; Meppelder et al, 2015). When their children reach school age, this stress increases. Other stressors can add to that, in particular social isolation and socio-economic deprivation. The ability to influence parental skills through targeted training is limited and showed moderate effects. But the effectiveness of individually adapted, intensive, skill-based intervention at home could be demonstrated (Coren et al, 2011; Llewellyn et al, 2010; Wade et al, 2008).

For children, growing up with parents who are mentally disabled poses a variety of developmental risks, ranging from language and motor development to behavioural problems. Needs differ and shift in the various age groups. However, there are no automatisms either but major differences (overview at Orthmann Bless 2021). Often support services are required that provide for a permanent accompanied parenthood (Düber et al, 2020; Michel 2017; Vlasak 2006). Research on 'disabled parenthood' (Düber 2021) and the use of support services showed different types of parental self-concepts: the autonomous ('We handle all that ourselves'), the cooperative ('Because I cooperate so well here'), the strategist 'So that I do not stand there alone') or the reflecting user ('I get myself a lot of support').

For parents with mental illness, their ability to raise children can be so severely limited that they are no longer able to ensure the child's welfare, at least temporarily (Wiegand-Grefe 2020). Numerous studies have shown barriers with a significant impact on families' utilisation behaviour. Reasons are shame, excessive demands, silence (family secret), denial or fixation on illness, withdrawal/isolation, clinging, overreaction and resignation (eg Christiansen 2011). A lack of insight into the illness can relate to the concern of mentally ill parents regarding the well-being of their children without associating possible abnormalities in their children with their own illness (Festen et al, 2014).

With this brief overview over the knowledge base from human and social science research, the interest is how this is reflected in family court judgments regarding the restriction or withdrawal of parental rights (see the following section).

PARENTS WITH MENTAL INCAPACITY OR MENTAL ILLNESS IN JUDGMENTS BY GERMAN FAMILY COURTS

To explore how the German child protection system, in particular the family court system in interplay with the child and youth welfare system, handles (potential) risk of harm for children growing up with parents with mental incapacities, a qualitative content analysis has been conducted. Judgments in child protection proceedings with a connection to parents with mental incapacities, published between 2008 and 2023 (ie in the period since the revised definition of 'child endangerment' in sec 1666(1) Civil Code came into force (see 'Being a Parent with Disabilities – The German Support and Justice System' above)), have been searched via an online database (juris.de). The search included sec 1666 Civil Code and varying German terms for mental incapacity or disability. Judgments in which the mental incapacity did not relate to the mother, father or both parents have been excluded. In the end, 17 judgments relevant for the analysis could be identified. With regard to German courts' approach to publication, it should be noted that family courts have full discretion as to whether to publish judgments and, if so, which to publish. This poses limitations on the following findings, as they are not at all representative since it can be assumed that family courts only publish judgments of which they are particularly convinced. Hence, this highly selective publication practice is clearly an issue of accountability for the German family justice system (Burns et al, 2019).

Court decisions were not analysed with regard to their interpretation of the law. Instead, a qualitative content analysis of the 17 judgments (Kuckartz/Rädiker 2022; Meysen 2022) was used, after a brief general overview of the body of judgments, to analyse the linguistic and content-related introduction as well as framing of the parents' restrictions (a), the significance of the disabilities for parenting (b), the description of the situation of the children concerned (c), the justification that support services are sufficient or not (d) and the assignment of responsibility for adequate care (e).

Of the 17 judgments that could be included in the qualitative content analysis two are issued by the Federal Constitutional Supreme Court, 15 by 8 of the 24 higher regional courts (family senates) and none by first-instance family courts (for a list, see 'judgments' in the annex). None of the proceedings had to deal with judgments in which restrictions or withdrawal of parental rights had been rejected. Hence, all had to deal with the question of upholding interventions in parental rights or restoring them. In 13 cases the appeal was rejected; in three it was successful; and in one case the appeal by the mother was dismissed but the decision against the father overturned. In total, eight appeals were submitted by the mother, two by the father, six by both parents and one by the guardian ad litem on behalf of the child.

(a) framing of mental incapacity

All judgments explicitly mentioned mental incapacity in one way or another. About half reproduced the content of a medical or psychological examination (1, 2, 3, 5, 6, 7, 8, 10, 11, 14, 15, 16, 17) or, indirectly, by citing a judgment in which a legal custodian had been appointed by the custodianship court which required a medical examination (1, 6, 7, 14). However, two courts limit the basis of their categorisation to mental incapacity on attendance at a special school (9, 10). A few courts do not explain where their classification has been derived (4, 12, 13).

If available, the courts name the clinical picture and the diagnosis under the International Statistical Classification of Diseases and Related Health Problems (ICD). Mental impairment is framed as intelligence impairment, intelligence disability, learning difficulties, learning disability, cognitive impairments or cognitive deficits. Concerning mental illnesses, in some cases combined with mental impairment, the comorbidities show a wide range including depression, schizoaffective disorder, borderline disorder or agoraphobia. Others remain more general and refer to stress due to trauma or mention anxiety disorder, combined personality disorder, psycho-emotional limitations, maturity and development disorder, or severe dissocial disorder. Suicidality and illiteracy are also cited to describe the personal disposition of the parent.

Overall, it can be stated that the courts name parents' mental incapacities pretty straightforwardly and that the courts rely on medical or psychological expertise – with a few exceptions where the reasons for the classification remain unclear. The reasoning of the judgments does not dwell too long on the personality traits of the parents as adults, but instead focuses primarily on parenting and the situation of the child.

(b) significance of mental incapacity for parenting

The Federal Constitutional Court has set the stage for child protection proceedings at the family courts and repeated its established rulings in 2019: 'A court decision on the withdrawal of parental custody meets with constitutional objections if it is not based on sufficiently concrete findings on the restrictions of the parents with regard to their parenting skills and on the nature, severity and probability of the feared impairments to the child' (1). In another judgment it was critical of the fact that an expert witness declared a parent 'incapable of parenting due to illness' (2), a reasoning used in one of the high regional court judgments (8). However, the positioning of the Constitutional Supreme Court is reflected in clear statements by high regional courts that no conclusions should be drawn about parenting ability from an IQ test (8) or the assignment of a legal curatorship (14).

In consequence, some family courts refer to excessive demands and overload the parenting duties pose (4, 10, 11). Quite a few others focus on satisfying the child's needs and/or interests (4, 5, 6, 7, 9, 10, 12). Problems have been identified in recognising the child's needs or risks for the child (6, 7, 10, 15), understanding them (10) or adequately reacting to them (7). A lack of sensitivity and competence in mentalisation has been lamented (10), hindering child-oriented interaction (7). An uncertain distanced relationship to the child caused deficits in emotional care (9). The parents were denied the ability to offer their children a stable relationship (17) or everyday framework (4), at least in phases (5, 8), which created a level of emotional and physical deficiency for the child (6). The cognition and reflection on their own actions towards the child has been assessed as insufficient (15). Some parents always attributed the reasons for their problems to others, which hindered them in achieving the necessary changes (6). In one judgment, cognitive and parenting deficits were deemed to be very pronounced in terms of both extent and intensity, so that caring for four children was regarded as being too much (3). Another saw a relationship between the mental incapacities and the special needs of a child with a chronic illness (9).

With one exception, the published judgments avoided direct links between mental incapacities and parenting abilities. Actions were assessed, and the mental impairment or illness in most cases only reflected in relation to the capacities to bring about the needed improvements in parenting skills. The problems of parents with intellectual disabilities in contact with the child protection system described in social science research which indicates a one sided deficit-orientated focus (Düber 2021; More 2021) are thus contrasted with the court decisions selectively chosen for publication which give the impression of almost exclusively good practice.

(c) situation of the child

The courts' examination of the child's development and the damage that is almost certainly to be expected if things continue unhindered is described in much less detail than that of the parents' ability to raise the child. Accordingly, the courts take a forward-looking view of children's development (4, 6, 9, 10, 12, 17) and the long-term consequences (12), even if the harm is not yet evident (4). Parents are a 'fate and life risk', the state has no obligation to provide for the 'best possible care of children' (6, 9, 12).

Four judgments described a pattern of parentification (ie a reversal of parental responsibility for the child). The child assumes inappropriate responsibility for the well-being of its parents (4, 6, 10, 12). Justifications for this related to the child assuming a protective role or being assessed with emotional neediness, disorientation, cognitive parity. In other proceedings the expert witness examined an attachment disorder (9, 10, 17). Serious motorical, language, social-emotional and cognitive developmental deficits were identified (10, 17). One child had been exposed to dangerous situations (9).

It is striking that around half of the decisions do not explicitly deal with the child's situation and development, but instead are based on parental behaviour and the potential of support services. This could indicate a responsibilisation of parents with mental incapacities or of an adult-oriented practice in some of the family courts.

(d) support services suffice?

In a next step, family courts are required to assess whether the risk of harm can be averted by support services for parents with disabilities (a system of integration assistance for people with disabilities), or for parents with the need of support in their parenting (a system of child and youth welfare). As support services within the family are a milder means than an out-of-home placement of the child they are to be prioritised (1). The insight and co-operation of the parents are necessary here (1).

Most of the judgments on restrictions and withdrawals of rights of parents with incapacities report on a long history of efforts to assist (7). Home visits are the most common service (3, 4, 6, 9, 16, 17). The placement in a mother/father-child facility is one option often discussed or utilised without success (4, 7, 12, 14), therapy another (3, 4, 17).

One of the conclusions has been that 'despite maximum support services' over a long period of time 'the relationship between mother and child only reached a level which is characterised by risk of harm' (4, 9, 16). Support services have been deemed to be inadequate (7, 10, 12, 17), or at least doubted (14). There has been a lack of voluntary utilisation (4). Support services have been perceived as tantamount to control (6). Therefore, parents have not been 'able to accept and use support services', or to cooperate with them (8, 10, 11, 12), or have at least shown ambivalent behaviour and a lack of awareness of the problems (11). Illness has meant that support cannot alleviate stresses and risks for the child (8). Learning disabilities have been presumed to be an obstacle to problem awareness (10). No positive changes could be recorded (9).

The acceptance of support services has never been an issue for the services providers, youth welfare offices or family courts. It is always the parents who bear the responsibility. Trust seems to be a one-way street. Helpers' interactions within the family naturally create a 'competition' with the parents from which frictions can arise. The family courts have not considered how to address this catch-22 situation. There are indications that the approaches to support services need to be scrutinised in terms of how to increase acceptability (Meysen/Rixen 2023).

(e) assignment of responsibilities

The question of courts dealing with the issue of responsibility for averting risks of harm to the child provides a bird's-eye view on the relationship between the state and parents with incapacities. Do family courts solely assign responsibility to the parents, or do they hold the state accountable as well? The body of judgments gives an anecdotal, but nonetheless valuable insight into practice.

The Federal Constitutional Supreme Court and several high regional courts have firmly pointed out that a reversal of the burden of proof is inappropriate and not acceptable. At least in principle, the state bears the burden of proof in child-protection proceedings with its *ex officio* assessment. Parents do not have to prove their parenting skills (1, 2, 14) and, in consequence, do not necessarily have to activate support themselves; but the state has to proactively offer services and assistance. The individuality of the family is protected, and the state is not allowed to develop its own educational ideas to replace those of the parents (1). Several courts stress that the failure is not the fault of the parents with incapacities (4, 7, 14, 15), for example if a mother could not even care for herself without support (11). The cause is not to be equated with fault (4, 5, 11). The decisive factor is whether it is possible to interrupt or redirect the child's harmful development with support services (4). Ultimately, parents were recognised as having a sense of responsibility if they agreed to a placement (10), or a seriously damaging parenting failure if the risks of harm could not be averted (14).

Judgments are strictly based on single case assessment and normative generalisation is avoided. Again, the family courts make clear that only actions are relevant and not predispositions or state of health. Nevertheless, identifying parents as a parenting failure and at the same time deeming this no-fault strikes a contradictory note.

CONCLUSIONS

Judges in Germany know how to use language and are trained to conceal personal beliefs and biographical influences behind an objectively distanced approach. The qualitative content analysis of the 17 judgments has, for the most part, shown politically and ethically correct reasoning. It confirms the difficulty as well as the necessity of a distinction between assumption and presumption (Barcham & Bogg 2019, p 13 f). An assumption, as a belief without evidence, should be the starting point for approaching parenting by all parents with or without mental incapacities. Presumptions should be a probabilistic belief, reached with evidence.

Hence, a parent should be assumed to be capable of caring for a child unless it is established that the parent lacks the capacity to do so.

REFERENCES

Aunos, Marjorie, Feldman, Maurice A, Goupil, Georgette (2008). 'Mothering with Intellectual Disabilities: Relationship Between Social Support, Health and Well-Being, Parenting and Child Behaviour Outcomes', *Journal of Applied Research in Intellectual Disabilities: JARID,* 21(4), 320–30.

Barcham, Claire and Bogg, Daisy, *The Pocketbook Guide to Mental Capacity Act Assessment* (New York, McGraw-Hill Education 2019).

Boetticher, Arne von *Das neue Teilhaberecht* (Baden-Baden, Nomos, 2018).

Burns, Kenneth, Kriz, Katrin, Krutzinna, Jenny, Luhamaa, Katre, Meysen, Thomas; Pösö, Tarja; Segado, Sagrario, Skivenes, Marit, Thoburn, June (2019) 'The Hidden Proceedings – An Analysis of Accountability of Child Protection Adoption Proceedings in Eight European Jurisdictions' in *European Journal of Comparative Law and Governance*, H. 6, S. 339–71.

Christiansen, Hanna, Mattejat, Fritz; Röhrle, Bernd, 'Wirksamkeitsbefunde von Interventionen bei Kindern und Familien psychisch kranker Eltern – ein meta-analytisch fundierter Überblick', in Wiegand-Grefe, Silke, Mattejat, Fritz, Lenz, Albert (eds), *Kinder mit Psychisch Kranken Eltern. Klinik und Forschung* (Göttingen: Vandenhoeck and Ruprecht, 2011), 458–81.

Cirullies, Jan, '§ 1666 BGB Gerichtliche Maßnahmen bei Gefährdung des Kindeswohls', in Heilmann, Stefan (ed), *Praxiskommentar Kindschaftsrecht*, 3rd edn (Cologne, Reguvis, 2025).

Coester, Michael, '§ 1666 BGB Gerichtliche Maßnahmen bei Gefährdung des Kindeswohls', in Staudinger, Julius von (ed), *Kommentar zum Bürgerlichen Gesetzbuch mit Einführungsgesetz und Nebengesetzen.* Buch 4 Familienrecht §§ 1638–83 (Elterliche Sorge 2 – Vermögenssorge, Kindesschutz, Sorgerechtswechsel), (Berlin, Sellier-de Gruyter, 2021).

Coren, Esther, Thomae, Manuela, Hutchfield, Jemeela (2011) 'Parenting Training for Intellectually Disabled Parents: A Cochrane Systematic Review', *Research on Social Work Practice*, 21(4), 432–41.

Deutscher Bundestag *Entwurf eines Gesetzes zur Erleichterung familiengerichtlicher Maßnahmen bei Gefährdung des Kindeswohls. Gesetzentwurf der Bundesregierung* (Bundestags-Drucksache 16/6815, Berlin, 2007).

Düber, Miriam *Behinderte Elternschaft und ihre Bewältigung. Perspektiven von Eltern mit Lernschwierigkeiten auf (nicht) professionelle Unterstützungsnetzwerke und allgemeine familienspezifische Angebote* (Weinheim/Basel, Beltz Juventa, 2021).

Düber, Miriam (2019). 'Die Balance halten. Pädagogische Spannungsfelder bei der professionellen Begleitung von Eltern mit Lernschwierigkeiten', in *FORUM Jugendhilfe*, 62–72.

Düber, Miriam, Remhof, Constance (2018). Ergebnisse der Gruppendiskussionen. Bericht im Rahmen des Modellprojektes, Entwicklung von Leitlinien zu Qualitätsmerkmalen Begleitete Elternschaft zu Nordrhein-Westfalen, hrsg. von MOBILE Selbstbestimmtes Leben Behinderter. Siegen.

Festen, Helma, Schipper, Karen, de Vries, Sybolt O, Reichart, Catrien G, Abma, Tineke A, Nauta, Maaike H (2014). 'Parents' Perceptions on Offspring Risk and Prevention of Anxiety and Depression: A Qualitative Study', *BMC Psychol*, 2(1), 17.

Götz, Isabell, '§ 1666 BGB Gerichtliche Maßnahmen bei Gefährdung des Kindeswohls', in Grüneberg, Christian (ed), Bürgerliches Gesetzbuch mit Nebengesetzen, 84th edn (Munich, C.H. Beck, 2025).

Kuckartz, Uwe/Rädiker, Stefan, *Qualitative Inhaltsanalyse. Methoden, Praxis, Computerunterstützung* 5th edn (Weinheim Basel, Beltz Juventa, 2025).

Llewellyn, Gwynnyth, Traustadttir, Ranveig, McConnell, David, Bjørg Sigurjnsdttir, Hanna, *Parents with Intellectual Disabilities* (Chichester, UK, John Wiley & Sons, 2010).

Meppelder, M, Hodes, M, Kef, S and Schuengel, C (2015) 'Parenting Stress and Child Behaviour Problems among Parents with Intellectual Disabilities: The Buffering Role of Resources', *Journal of Intellectual Disability Research*, 59(7), 664–77.

Merriam-Webster (2025), 'Mental incapacity', Merriam-Webster.com Medical Dictionary, www.merriam-webster.com/medical/mental%20incapacity. Accessed 21 March 2025.

Meysen, Thomas, 'Familiengerichte und Elternschaft bei Getrenntleben: Eine qualitative Inhaltsanalyse zu persönlichen Einstellungen und deren Objektivierung am Beispiel des Wechselmodells', in Doll, Daniel, Kavemann, Barbara, Nagel, Bianca, Etzel, Adrian (eds), *Beiträge zur Forschung zu Geschlechterbeziehungen, Gewalt und privaten Lebensformen. Disziplinäres, Interdisziplinäres und Essays* (Opladen, Verlag Barbara Budrich, 2022), 279–91.

Meysen, Thomas, Rixen, Stephan (2023), Elternberatung in Familien mit Kind mit Behinderung. Rechtsexpertise zur psychologischen Beratung KOMPASS des Bunten Kreises Münsterland e.V. für Eltern von zu frühgeborenen, schwer und chronisch kranken Kindern. Erstellt im Auftrag des Ministeriums für Kinder, Jugend, Familie, Gleichstellung, Flucht und Integration des Landes Nordrhein-Westfalen (MKJFGFI) und des Ministeriums für Arbeit, Gesundheit und Soziales des Landes Nordrhein-Westfalen (MAGS). Heidelberg.

Michel, Marion, Conrad, Ines, Müller, Martina, Pantenburg, Birte (2017): Unterstützte Elternschaft – Angebote für behinderte und chronisch kranke Eltern – Analyse zur Umsetzung des Artikels 23 der UN-BRK (Abschlussbericht, Berlin).

More, Rahel, *Disability, Elternschaft und Soziale Arbeit. Zur Bedeutung von Zuschreibungen, Fremdwahrnehmungen und Selbstverständnissen für Eltern mit Lernschwierigkeiten* (Opladen, Berlin, Toronto. Barbara Budrich 2021).

Orthmann Bless, Dagmar, Hinni, Chantal, Hellfritz, Karina-Linnéa (2017). 'Fachbeitrag: Zwei Mütter ± zwei Kinder. Eine vergleichende Fallstudie zur Entwicklung von Kindern intellektuell beeinträchtigter Eltern'. *Vierteljahresschrift für Heilpädagogik und ihre Nachbargebiete*, 87(1), 27.

Pixa-Kettner, Ursula, *Tabu oder Normalität? Eltern mit geistiger Behinderung und ihre Kinder*, 3rd edn (Winter, Heidelberg 2015).

Schönecker, Lydia (2020) 'Familien- und sozialrechtliche Situation von Eltern mit Behinderungen', in *Bundesministerium für Familie, Senioren, Frauen und Jugend* (ed): Neunter Familienbericht. Eltern sein in Deutschland. Berlin, S. 666–709.

Schönecker, Lydia (2022): '§ 10 SGB VIII Verhältnis zu anderen Leistungen und Verpflichtungen', in Münder, Johannes, Meysen, Thomas, Trenczek, Thomas (eds) *Frankfurter Kommentar SGB VIII*, 9th ed, Baden-Baden, Nomos, 180–97.

Sprung, Christiane, Remhof, Constance, Düber, Miriam, Riesberg, Ulla (2021): 'Wir müssen Gutes unterstellen und wir müssen den Beweis dafür erbringen, dass es mit Hilfe gut bleibt', in *Das Jugendamt*, 75–78.

Vlasak, Annette, *Möglichkeiten und Grenzen des Zusammenlebens von Eltern mit geistiger Behinderung und ihren Kindern in Einrichtungen der Eingliederungshilfe / Jugendhilfe im Land* (Brandenburg. Oranienburg, 2006).

Wade, Catherine, Llewellyn, Gwynnyth, Matthews, Jan (2008). 'Review of Parent Training Interventions for Parents with Intellectual Disability', *Journal of Applied Research in Intellectual Disabilities: JARID*, 21(4), 351–66.

Wiegand-Grefe, Silke, Klein, Michael, Kölch, Michael, Lenz, Albert, Seckinger, Mike, Thomasius, Rainer, Ziegenhain, Ute, *Kinder psychisch kranker ‚Eltern Forschung'. IST-Analyse zur Situation von Kindern psychisch kranker Eltern* (Berlin, 2020).

Ziegler, Eberhard, '§ 1666 BGB Gerichtliche Maßnahmen bei Gefährdung des Kindeswohls', in Klein, Michael, Weinreich, Gerd (eds). *Familienrecht Kommentar*, 7th edn (Luchterhand, Munich 2021).

JUDGMENTS

(1) BVerfG 10 Dec 2019 – 1 BvR 2214/19

(2) BVerfG 19 Nov 2014 – 1 BvR 1178/14

(3) OLG Brandenburg 1 Feb 2022 – 9 WF 282/21
(4) OLG Brandenburg 4 Dec 2015 – 13 UF 95/15
(5) OLG Brandenburg 17 Dec 2012 – 3 UF 84/12
(6) OLG Brandenburg 15 Jan 2009 – 9 UF 51/07
(7) OLG Celle 8 Oct 2018 – 10 UF 91/18
(8) OLG Düsseldorf 5 Jun 2009 – 6 UF 130/07
(9) OLG Hamm 9 Mar 2015 – 8 UF 156/14
(10) OLG Hamm 26 Feb 2014 – 3 UF 184/13
(11) OLG Hamm 25 Nov 2013 – 8 UF 114/12
(12) OLG Karlsruhe 16 Oct 2017 – 18 UF 154/17
(13) OLG Köln 16 Mar 2016– 10 UF 173/15
(14) OLG Köln 25 Feb 2015– 26 UF 156/14
(15) OLG Saarbrücken 18 Jun 2018 – 6 UF 20/15
(16) OLG Saarbrücken 18 Feb 2010 – 6 UF 96/09
(17) OLG Schleswig 31 May 2019 – 13 UF 13/19

Part II

Legislative Change

5

Protecting whose Interests? Exploring the Operation of the Guardianship and Administration Act 2019 (Vic)

RICHARD INGLEBY AND BELINDA FEHLBERG

INTRODUCTION

In Australia, it is the State governments[1] who have power to make laws to support people with disabilities that reduce or remove their capacity to make their own decisions. State laws are intended to operate as a safety net in the absence of private ordering or where there are complaints about private ordering, and in a manner least restrictive of a person's ability to decide and act. Even so, these laws, and decisions made pursuant to them, affect many vulnerable people and their families. Yet they have not so far been the focus of systematic empirical analysis.[2]

In this chapter, after first providing context, we analyse decisions made in one state of Australia – Victoria[3] – under the current Victorian guardianship and administration legislation[4] and its predecessor[5] by analysing all cases reported

[1] Rather than the Federal Government, which only has the powers afforded by the Constitution or referrals of power.

[2] With the exception of a recent analysis by the Office of the Public Advocate on how long a represented person spends under its guardianship and what factors might influence length of time under its guardianship: Office of the Public Advocate, *Reflections on Guardianship: The Law and Practice in Victoria*, 28 February 2023, section 1 (pages not numbered), available at: https://www.publicadvocate.vic.gov.au/opa-s-work/research/580-reflections-on-guardianship-the-law-and-practice-in-victoria.

[3] For analysis of guardianship and administration laws in other Australian states, see: Nick O'Neill and Carmell Peisah, *Capacity and the Law*, 2021 edition, AustLII Communities, available at: https://austlii.community/wiki/Books/CapacityAndTheLaw/.

[4] Guardianship and Administration Act 2019 (Vic).

[5] Guardianship and Administration Act 1986 (Vic) (originally the Guardianship and Administration Board Act 1986 (Vic)); the Act was renamed when Victoria's Guardianship and Administration Board was abolished in 1998 when VCAT was established. See further: Nick O'Neill and Carmell Peisah, *Capacity and the Law*, 2021 edition, AustLII Communities, available at: https://austlii.community/wiki/Books/CapacityAndTheLaw/.

on the Australian Legal Information Institute's (AustLII's) website[6] in the years 2018 (the last year before legislative reform in 2019) and 2022 (the first year after the current legislation came into effect on 1 March 2020).

The two questions addressed in our analysis are:

(i) Did the 2019 legislative change, which was viewed as by the Victorian Government as 'a milestone in the way that Victoria upholds the rights and meets the needs of people with disability whose decision-making capacity is impaired',[7] result in any changed outcomes or approaches?
(ii) More broadly, what are the issues most commonly arising in the reported cases?

CONTEXT

Definition of key terms and a brief overview of the relevant legislative framework are needed to provide context for our analysis.

Key Terms

In Australia orders to support adults with disabilities and who lack legal capacity to make their own decisions are called 'guardianship and administration orders'.

In Victoria, such orders are made under the Guardianship and Administration Act 2019 (Vic) (the 2019 Act) by the Victorian Civil and Administrative Appeals Tribunal (the Tribunal).

Guardianship orders typically cover decisions such as where the person subject to the orders (the represented person) lives, their health care and their access to services and access to people.[8] A guardian must be a 'suitable person' whose interests do not conflict with those of the represented person.[9] They may be a friend or relative of the represented person, or the Office of the Public Advocate (OPA).[10]

The OPA is an independent statutory officer, with significant legislative power to protect the rights and interests of people with disability,[11] including investigative powers.[12] One aspect of these powers, frequently seen in our sample, is that at the Tribunal's request, the OPA conducts investigations to assist the Tribunal's determination of applications for guardianship, administration, or

[6] See https://www.austlii.edu.au/.

[7] Parliament of Victoria, *Parliamentary Debates*, Legislative Assembly, 19 December 2018, 63 (Jill Hennessy, Attorney-General).

[8] Victorian Civil and Administrative Appeals Tribunal (VCAT), 'Types of guardianship and administration orders', https://www.vcat.vic.gov.au/case-types/guardians-and-administrators/types-of-orders.

[9] Guardianship and Administration Act 2019 (Vic), s 32(1).

[10] VCAT, 'Guardians', https://www.vcat.vic.gov.au/case-types/guardians-and-administrators/guardians, Guardianship and Administration Act 2019 (Vic), ss 33(1), 16(1)(a).

[11] Guardianship and Administration Act 2019 (Vic), s 15.

[12] Guardianship and Administration Act 2019 (Vic), s 17.

about powers of attorney.[13] The OPA can also of its own motion apply to the Tribunal for the appointment of a guardian and/or an administrator, for the rehearing or reassessment of a guardianship and/or an administration order, may join existing proceedings, and has broad powers to advocate for the human rights and interests of a person with a disability.[14] The OPA is thus 'in the unusual position of being substitute decision-maker of last resort, while hoping to see that role played less, by OPA and others, over time'.[15]

Administration orders typically cover financial decisions of the represented person. An administrator must be a 'suitable person' whose interests do not conflict with those of the represented person and who 'has sufficient expertise to make decisions about any financial matter to be specified in the administration order'.[16] An administrator may be a friend or relative of the represented person, a solicitor, an accountant, a private trustee company, or State Trustees Limited.[17] State Trustees Limited, a company owned by the Victorian Government, is the Public Trustee for Victoria, providing administration, trustee and estate-related services, often in cases where those services cannot be accessed elsewhere.[18]

Guardianship and administration orders are only made when, due to disability, a person lacks legal capacity to make their own decisions and is in need of a guardian or administrator.[19] As part of the broader law and policy context that supports individuals' continued involvement in making their own decisions, any adult with legal capacity who wishes to plan ahead can appoint someone to make decisions for them if they become unable to do so by entering an Enduring Power of Attorney, under the Powers of Attorney Act 2014 (Vic).[20] An attorney will often be a spouse, de facto partner, child, relative or close friend of the grantor. The attorney can be appointed to make decisions about personal matters (such as where the person lives) or financial matters (such as paying bills) or both.[21] The grantor can limit the attorney's power to cover only specific matters and can choose when the attorney's powers start.[22]

The attorney cannot, however, make medical treatment decisions for the person unless they are also the person's medical treatment decision maker.[23]

[13] Office of the Public Advocate (OPA), 'OPA investigations', https://www.publicadvocate.vic.gov.au/guardianship-and-administration/opa-investigations.

[14] Guardianship and Administration Act 2019 (Vic), s 16.

[15] Office of the Public Advocate, *Reflections on Guardianship: The Law and Practice in Victoria*, 28 February 2023, section 1 (pages not numbered), available at: https://www.publicadvocate.vic.gov.au/opa-s-work/research/580-reflections-on-guardianship-the-law-and-practice-in-victoria.

[16] Guardianship and Administration Act 2019 (Vic), s 32(2).

[17] VCAT, 'What it means to be an administrator', https://www.vcat.vic.gov.au/case-types/guardians-and-administrators/administrators.

[18] State Trustees (Victoria), 'About us', https://www.statetrustees.com.au/about-us/, State Trustees (State Owned Company) Act 1994 (Vic).

[19] Guardianship and Administration Act 2019 (Vic), s 30(2).

[20] Powers of Attorney Act 2014 (Vic), Part 3.

[21] Powers of Attorney Act 2014 (Vic), s 22(2).

[22] Powers of Attorney Act 2014 (Vic), s 39.

[23] Powers of Attorney Act 2014 (Vic), s 3(1), 'personal matter'.

Medical treatment decision making is covered by the Medical Treatment Planning and Decisions Act 2016 (Vic). The Act specifies who has legal authority by default to make a person's medical treatment decisions (namely, their guardian if a guardian has been appointed by the Tribunal, and otherwise their next of kin).[24] The Act, however, also provides that a person with decision-making capacity can override the default position by appointing someone of their choosing to be their medical treatment decision maker.[25]

The Tribunal

The Tribunal (known colloquially as 'VCAT') makes guardianship and administration orders for adults who are unable to make those decisions because of their disability and who have not appointed a decision maker. The Tribunal also has power to resolve questions and disputes that arise regarding the exercise of powers by attorneys, medical treatment decision makers, guardians, and administrators.

More broadly, the Tribunal offers a low-cost, accessible, and independent dispute-resolution process in relation to a range of matters under more than 150 pieces of Victorian legislation,[26] from residential tenancies to voluntary assisted dying. Although part of Victoria's justice system, as the Tribunal is not a court, an application must be made to a court to enforce its orders.[27]

Appeals from the Tribunal's decisions are usually to the Supreme Court of Victoria,[28] Victoria's most senior court. The President of the Tribunal is a Supreme Court Judge, County Court Judges serve as Vice-Presidents, and applications are heard and determined by Deputy Presidents (appointed full time), as well as Senior Members and ordinary Members.[29] Members have a broad range of specialist skills and qualifications and can be appointed on a full-time, part time or sessional basis.

Charter of Human Rights and Responsibilities Act 2006 (Vic)

In performing its role, the Tribunal must act in accordance with the Charter of Human Rights and Responsibilities Act 2006 (Vic) (the Charter), which came into effect on 1 January 2008.

[24] Medical Treatment Planning and Decisions Act 2016 (Vic), s 55.

[25] Medical Treatment Planning and Decisions Act 2016 (Vic), s 55(1) and Div 2, Pt 3.

[26] VCAT Annual Report 2021–22 (accessible version), p 4, available at: https://www.vcat.vic.gov.au/about-vcat/annual-reports-and-strategic-directions#annual-report.

[27] VCAT, 'Enforce and order through the Court', https://www.vcat.vic.gov.au/the-vcat-process/decisions/enforce-a-vcat-order; Victorian Civil and Administrative Tribunal Act 1998 (Vic), ss 122, 123.

[28] Victorian Civil and Administrative Tribunal Act 1998 (Vic), s 148.

[29] Victorian Civil and Administrative Tribunal Act 1998 (Vic), Pt 2, Div 1-3.

The Charter was enacted by the Victorian Parliament in 2006 to address for Victoria the absence of a Bill of Rights in Australia. It sets out 20 human rights of all Victorians,[30] largely based on those in the International Covenant on Civil and Political Rights,[31] including 'recognition and equality before the law'[32] and provides that, '[s]o far as it is possible to do so consistently with their purpose, all statutory provisions must be interpreted in a way that is compatible with human rights'.[33]

Importantly, the Charter applies to all the work of the Victorian Government and public service: 'It is about the relationship between government and the people it serves'.[34] It 'requires public authorities, such as Victorian state and local government departments and agencies, and people delivering services on behalf of government, to act consistently with the human rights in the Charter',[35] and for policies and legislation to take into account human rights.

In the view of Victoria Legal Aid, which plays an important role in supporting and representing vulnerable individuals in legal matters:

> The Victorian Charter has substantially contributed to a more rights-respecting culture within the Victorian Government, including the public service, through embedding consideration of human rights during the development of new laws, policies and guidelines, and as part of government decision-making. The Victorian Charter has also provided a helpful framework for decision-makers without placing unreasonable constraints on decision-making.[36]

United Nations Convention on the Rights of Persons with Disabilities

A further important influence on the development of law and policy on disability in Australia is the United Nations Convention on the Rights of Persons with Disabilities.[37] As the Victorian Attorney-General observed when the 2019 Act was introduced into the Victorian Parliament:

> Australian legislation increasingly seeks to fully recognise the dignity, equality and autonomy of people with disability, whose fundamental rights have been enshrined in

[30] Human Rights and Responsibilities Act 2006 (Vic), Part 2.

[31] International Covenant on Civil and Political Rights, opened for signature 19 December 1966, 999 UNTS 171 (entered into force 23 March 1976), signed by Australia in 1972 and ratified in 1980 but never adopted into domestic law, available at: https://www.ohchr.org/en/instruments-mechanisms/instruments/international-covenant-civil-and-political-rights.

[32] Human Rights and Responsibilities Act 2006 (Vic), s 8.

[33] Human Rights and Responsibilities Act 2006 (Vic), s 32(1).

[34] Victorian Equal Opportunity and Human Rights Commission, 'About the Charter', available at: https://www.humanrights.vic.gov.au/legal-and-policy/victorias-human-rights-laws/the-charter/.

[35] Ibid.

[36] Victoria Legal Aid, *Submission to the Australian Human Rights Commission's Free and Equal Inquiry Discussion Paper: A Model for Positive Human Rights Reform in Australia*.

[37] Convention on the Rights of Persons with Disabilities, opened for signature 30 March 2007, 2515 UNTS 3 (entered into force 3 May 2008).

the United Nations Convention on the Rights of Persons with Disabilities. Australia was an original signatory to the Convention in 2008.[38]

The Convention's provisions include that States Parties shall 'recognize that persons with disabilities enjoy legal capacity on an equal basis with others in all aspects of life'[39] and ensure 'that measures relating to the exercise of legal capacity respect the rights, will and preferences of the person'.[40]

The Guardianship and Administration Act 2019 (Vic) ('2019 Act')

The 2019 Act came into effect on 1 March 2020. It repealed the former Guardianship and Administration Act 1986 (Vic) ('1986 Act').[41]

Introducing the bill into the Victorian parliament, the Attorney-General made clear that the bill complied with the requirement of being 'compatible with human rights as set out in the Charter', and 'reflect[ed] the paradigm shift signalled in the United Nations Convention on the Rights of Persons with Disabilities':[42]

Accordingly, the primary object of the 2019 Act is 'to protect and promote the human rights and dignity of persons with a disability' by:

(a) having regard to the Convention on the Rights of Persons with Disabilities, recognising the need to support persons with a disability to make, participate in and implement decisions that affect their lives; and
(b) if a guardianship order or administration order is made for such persons –
   (i) enabling the Tribunal to set safeguards and appropriate limitations on the powers of guardians and administrators when making such orders; and
   (ii) requiring the Tribunal to review regularly such orders; and
   (iii) providing guidance for guardians and administrators when making decisions for represented persons, as the case requires.[43]

[38] Parliament of Victoria, *Parliamentary Debates*, Legislative Assembly, 19 December 2018, 60 (Jill Hennessy, Attorney-General). In addition, the Attorney-General referred to the influence of 'the 2012 Report of the Victorian Law Reform Commission on Guardianship, the 2015 Report of the Australian Law Reform Commission on Equality, Capacity and Disability in Commonwealth Laws, and recent Victorian legislation, such as the Powers of Attorney Act 2014 (POA Act), the Mental Health Act 2014 and the Medical Treatment Planning and Decisions Act 2016 (MTPD Act)' (60).

[39] Convention on the Rights of Persons with Disabilities, opened for signature 30 March 2007, 2515 UNTS 3 (entered into force 3 May 2008) art 12(2).

[40] Convention on the Rights of Persons with Disabilities, opened for signature 30 March 2007, 2515 UNTS 3 (entered into force 3 May 2008) art 12(4).

[41] For a history of guardianship and administration in Australia, see Nick O'Neill and Carmell Peisah, *Capacity and the Law*, 2021 edition, AustLII Communities, available at: https://austlii.community/wiki/Books/CapacityAndTheLaw/.

[42] Parliament of Victoria, *Parliamentary Debates*, Legislative Assembly, 19 December 2018, 49 (Jill Hennessy, Attorney-General).

[43] Guardianship and Administration Act 2019 (Vic), s 7.

The 2019 Act's general principles, which apply to those exercising powers under the Act, now include that a person with a disability who requires support to make decisions should be provided with practicable and appropriate support to do so,[44] and the principle that 'the will and preferences of a person with a disability should direct, as far as practicable, decisions made for that person'.[45]

The 2019 Act was viewed by the Victorian Government as recognising to a greater extent than the previous Act the human rights of people with disabilities, including the importance of supporting them to make or be involved in decisions that are made about them:

> [It] represents a milestone in the way that Victoria upholds the rights and meets the needs of people with disability whose decision-making capacity is impaired. It moves away from the old 'best interests' principle that underpinned a paternalistic approach to disability, to a position of promoting the dignity, equality and autonomy of people living with disability, while retaining the safeguards necessary for them to most fully realise their potential.[46]

However, in considering the enormity (or otherwise) of the 2019 reforms, it is important to note that that the 1986 legislation was also a major reform measure, reflecting growing policy and community understanding of disability and decision-making, and a shift away deinstitutionisation.[47] Most relevant for our analysis,[48] objects of the 1986 Act had included that powers under the Act be exercised in a way that was 'the least restrictive of a person's freedom of decision and action as is possible in the circumstances':

> It is the intention of Parliament that the provisions of this Act be interpreted and that every function, power, authority, discretion, jurisdiction and duty conferred or imposed by this Act is to be exercised or performed so that—
> (a) the means which is the least restrictive of a person's freedom of decision and action as is possible in the circumstances is adopted; and
> (b) the best interests of a person with a disability are promoted; and
> (c) the wishes of a person with a disability are wherever possible given effect to.[49]

[44] Guardianship and Administration Act 2019 (Vic), s 8(1)(a).

[45] Guardianship and Administration Act 2019 (Vic), s 8(1)(b). The Act also introduced the new option of VCAT appointing a supportive guardian or supportive administrator as an alternative to, or in addition to, a guardian or administrator where VCAT determines that 'if the person is given practicable and appropriate support, the person will have decision-making capacity': Guardianship and Administration Act 1986 (Vic), s 87. This is a less restrictive option than appointing a guardian or administrator.

[46] Parliament of Victoria, *Parliamentary Debates*, Legislative Assembly, 19 December 2018, 63 (Jill Hennessy, Attorney-General).

[47] Nick O'Neill and Carmell Peisah, *Capacity and the Law*, 2021 edition, 5.4.1, AustLII Communities, available at: https://austlii.community/wiki/Books/CapacityAndTheLaw/.

[48] The 1986 Act also introduced a Guardianship Board as an independent tribunal empowered to appoint guardians and administrators, which was 'the first of the modern, independent guardianship tribunals in Australia' (Nick O'Neill and Carmell Peisah, *Capacity and the Law*, 2021 edition, 5.4.3.1, AustLII Communities, available at: https://austlii.community/wiki/Books/CapacityAndTheLaw/), replacing the Supreme Court based system. It also established the OPA.

[49] Guardianship and Administration Board Act 1986 (Vic), s 4(2).

The 'least restrictive' provision in the 1986 Act was carried over into the 2019 Act[50] and expanded upon, in a broader law and policy context where, '[t]he challenges have shifted from de-institutionalising the many people whose disability was treated as a condition best managed behind secure walls, to managing the increasing numbers of people living in the community who lose their capacity through the onset of dementia or an acquired brain injury'.[51]

AIMS AND METHODOLOGY

To explore whether there had been any discernible change to approach and outcomes in cases decided under the 2019 Act and the 1986 Act, we compared two datasets, each of about 30 cases, all being decisions available on the AustLii website (austlii.edu.au) from the Tribunal, the relevant decision-making authority:

(i) in 2022 which refer to the 2019 Act; and
(ii) in 2018 which refer to the 1986 Act.

We did not find a decision where an appeal had been made to the Supreme Court of Victoria on a point of law directly arising from the change in legislative provision.

The decisions are publicly available on AustLII, a free access website. The decisions are not, however, necessarily representative of the totality of the day-to-day work of the Tribunal because:

(i) many decisions are made without formal rulings; and
(ii) it is not known how many formal rulings find their way to the AustLII website.

RESULTS

Impacts of Legislative Amendment?

We did not find any decisions where the distinction between 'rights' (2019 Act) and 'best interests' (1986 Act) made any difference to the outcome, as opposed to the language used to reach the outcome.

We suggest that there are four reasons why there was no discernible difference in the outcomes as between the two datasets:

[50] Guardianship and Administration Act 2019 (Vic), s 8(1)(c).

[51] Parliament of Victoria, *Parliamentary Debates*, Legislative Assembly, 19 December 2018, 60 (Jill Hennessy, Attorney-General).

(i) The 1986 legislation already contained reference to the need for 'least restrictive' outcomes.
(ii) The Charter of Human Rights and Responsibilities Act 2006 (Vic) was a well-established part of the legal framework before the 2019 Act.
(iii) The distinction between 'rights' and 'best interests' in most cases is one of semantics.
(iv) The laws relating to guardianship and administration are not an autonomous area of law. In addition to the omnipresence of the Charter, there is:

    (a) the Medical Treatment Planning and Decisions Act 2016 (Vic) which, as noted earlier, makes specific provision (s 55) as to who is a person's medical treatment decision maker in the absence of that person having made specific provision in advance; and
    (b) the unambiguously titled Powers of Attorney Act 2014 (Vic) which, as also mentioned earlier, allows those with legal capacity to appoint a decision maker in advance to made decisions on the grantor's behalf.

The combination of the 'least restrictive' principle and the capacity of individuals to make provision for what is to happen in advance of incapacity (whether such incapacity is an emergency situation or general decline), means that guardianship and administration become 'last resort' measures, which are preferable by reference to the legislative restrictions on when resort should be made to guardianship and administration orders. The incidence of 'last resort' measures would thus seem less likely to change significantly following law reform.

Yet the absence of any discernible difference in the outcomes following reform also appears consistent with the OPA's 'growing concerns about whether the intention of the [2019] Act is being fully realised', and particularly regarding 'the growing number of OPA clients under 65 who are under guardianship, and the increased time that people in this cohort are spending under guardianship. This statistic seems at odds with the intention of the legislation.'[52] The OPA had suggested several reasons for this, including 'over-reliance on guardianship to fill service gaps', inadequate 'resourcing of services and initiatives that will help realise the intention of the Act' such as funding for advocacy and supported decision-making services, and '[i]ncreased community understanding of supported decision-making and its value in promoting the dignity, equality and autonomy of people with disability'.[53] The OPA's observations underline that we are only looking at the tip of the iceberg when we focus on reported cases: the Tribunal is part of a much wider context of supports and services available (or not available) to people with disabilities, and which have an impact on outcomes.

[52] Office of the Public Advocate, *Reflections on Guardianship: The Law and Practice in Victoria*, 28 February 2023, section 1 (pages not numbered), available at: https://www.publicadvocate.vic.gov.au/opa-s-work/research/580-reflections-on-guardianship-the-law-and-practice-in-victoria.

[53] Office of the Public Advocate, *Reflections on Guardianship: The Law and Practice in Victoria*, 28 February 2023, section 1 (pages not numbered), available at: https://www.publicadvocate.vic.gov.au/opa-s-work/research/580-reflections-on-guardianship-the-law-and-practice-in-victoria.

Taxonomy

The broader legislative regime for medical treatment decision makers and powers of attorney also provides a framework with which to generate a taxonomy of the issues most commonly arising in the reported cases.

First, each of the 58 cases falls within one of three major categories:

1. orders had previously been made for guardianship and/or administration: n = 28;
2. provision had previously been made by way of power of attorney and/or provision for medical treatment decision maker: n= 24; or
3. no provision at all had been made: n = 6.

Within these three categories, we identified sub-categories:

In group 1, the 28 cases where orders for guardianship and/or administration had previously been made, there were three subcategories:

1.1 an application was made for a specific purpose, typically where required by the relevant legal rules: n = 11;
1.2 a challenge was made to the existing regime and no change was made: n = 8; or
1.3 a challenge was made (or required) to the existing regime and something changed: n = 9.

In group 2, the 24 cases where provision had previously been made by way of Power of Attorney and/or medical treatment decision maker), there were two subcategories:

2.1 the existing provision remained with no changes: n = 14; or
2.2 a change was ordered: n = 10.

In group 3, the six cases where applications are made absent any orders or provision, typically (and understandably) by hospital social workers or case managers due to the absence of next of kin, there were two subcategories:

3.1 orders were made: n = 3; or
3.2 no orders were made: n = 3.

1.1: Orders for guardianship and/or administration previously been made: application made for a specific purpose

Once orders for guardianship and/or administration have been made, the orders themselves create the basis for further applications, which we found were made for a wide range of reasons.

For example, the represented person sought that the Tribunal provide reasons for a decision which at face value seems so routine that it does not require explanation, being the reappointment of State Trustees, in *XEZ (Guardianship)*

[2018] VCAT 8. In *LWJ (Guardianship)* [2018] VCAT 775, the professional administrator's application for approval to sell the represented person's home led to a new order appointing another professional administrator. It appeared that the contentious issue was the sale of the home, in relation to which there was also a specific ruling, but that during the hearing the Tribunal formed the view that the existing administrator was not acting in the represented person's best financial interests.

Because of the rules relating to the confidentiality of the Tribunal's proceedings, a formerly represented person made specific (and successful) applications to publish details for a documentary in *Kaplan* [2022] VCAT 6 and to give evidence before a Royal Commission in *Cartwright* [2022] VCAT 1089.[54]

Specific orders about the administrator's remuneration were made in *VVA (Guardianship)* [2018] 1220 and an application for costs against the administrator relating to the conduct of a testamentary dispute was dismissed in *GKM (Guardianship)* [2022] VCAT 1362.

A 'one case' group within this category, *HYY (Guardianship)* [2022] VCAT 97, was a 'specific purpose' guardianship application as to whether a guardian's power to make decisions about medical treatment including decisions about physical restraints required for the treatment and related matters. The OPA, the Attorney-General, the Victorian Equal Opportunity and Human Rights Commission and the Department of Health were each represented by counsel. There was extensive discussion of the principles under the legislation and the Charter before deciding that the guardian's power did not extend to restraint, and that a specific application required to be made for the represented person to comply with the guardian's decision. This is clearly a decision which confines the scope of the guardian's powers and the regulatory control of the Tribunal. The Charter loomed large throughout the lengthy reasons.

The precise scope of the guardianship order was also at issue in *THD (Guardianship)* [2018] VCAT 1588. The wishes of the represented person were crucial in the determination that the scope of the guardianship order in favour of the OPA extend to the represented person's contact with his parents, the parents seeking that they be guardians in relation to this issue.

There was a sub-group of cases where there were existing orders, and either the expiry of fixed terms required reassessment[55] or the administrator sought to protect their position by authorising a particular transaction or action.

Another sub-group, important for the context of the closing discussion in this chapter, was where an administrator sought specific permission in relation to the conduct of litigation in another setting. An order was made on the application of a relative of the represented person for the professional trustee to discontinue a challenge to testamentary provision in *EBG (Guardianship)* [2018]

[54] See also the successful application to revoke a suppression order in *EQY (Human Rights)* [2018] VCAT 709.

[55] *XEZ (Guardianship)* [2018] VCAT 8, 470.

VCAT 2064, but was not allowed for the pursuit of a claim for property settlement under the Family Law Act in *LNA (Guardianship)* [2018] VCAT 1578.

1.2 Orders for guardianship and/or administration previously been made: the Tribunal rejects challenge to the existing regime

Unsuccessful challenges to existing guardianship and/or administration orders by a protected person or their family often involved an existing professional guardian or administrator, or sometimes a family member acting in this capacity, who was considered by the Tribunal to be the best option in the context of ongoing family conflict.

An adult child challenged the identity of the guardian (the OPA), rather than the need for a guardianship order in *WAI (Guardianship)* [2018 VCAT 114. The Tribunal maintained the current position because the independent OPA was the best option in the context of 'long standing animosity' between family members. There was a more spectacular fail to the challenge to the administrator's conduct in *RPR (Guardianship)* [2022] VCAT 54. The audit commissioned in response to the complaint about the administrator's conduct revealed that the greatest beneficiary of the mismanagement was the complainant herself!

In *LPF (Guardianship)* [2022] VCAT 294, the Tribunal (in circumstances where there was an order for administration) dismissed an application for guardianship because the applicant already had the power to make medical decisions under the medical treatment legislation discussed above.

The represented person challenged the administration order in *VIP (Guardianship)* [2018] VCAT 201 on two bases. He alleged that he was not a person under a disability,[56] and also that the professional trustees (State Trustees Limited) had mismanaged assets. The Tribunal considered the medical evidence and a report from the administrator before confirming the existing orders. Challenges to the conduct of the professional administrator were also heard and dismissed in *FPZ (Guardianship)* [2018] VCAT 408 and difficulties in the appointment of a guardian were insufficient to discharge the order for guardianship in *HVJ (Guardianship)* [2022] VCAT 766. In addition to VCAT rejecting the complaints against the professional administrators, they also saw them as preferable to 'unworkable' arrangements between siblings.

1.3 Orders for guardianship and/or administration previously made: change made to the existing regime

Successful challenges to existing guardianship and/or administration orders often involved family members (usually siblings) who were concerned about their contact with, or the care, safety and/or the financial wellbeing of, an elderly relative (usually a parent).

[56] The first of these challenges was dismissed in *KSJ (Guardianship)* [2018] VCAT 1275.

In *ZFN (Guardianship)* [2022] VCAT 262, the prior appointment of the OPA as guardian was discharged on the basis that the (soon not to be) represented person's psychologist was now acting as a mediator in relation to the intra-sibling disputes about contact with her and an earlier intervention order was no longer current. There was therefore no need for a guardian.

The 'no longer any need for a guardian' argument also prevailed when a temporary order of OPA as guardian was discharged, and an administration order made, in *PCP (Guardianship)* [2022] VCAT 364.[57] In the context of adult children securing their mother's separation from a violent relationship, there was no longer any need for arrangements to be made for housing, but there was now a need for financial decisions to be in the hands of a third party, that third party being, in accordance with the represented person's wishes, her adult children.

The OPA was a safer choice than a friend to replace a solicitor who had been acting as guardian for the purposes of securing disability funding in *NCX (Guardianship)* [2018] VCAT 520. In a common theme in the decisions, the Tribunal was not inclined to appoint people who had a confrontational approach to bureaucrats or professionals more generally.[58]

In *YPO* [2022] VCAT 377, key findings leading, on application of the protected person's children, to administration being ordered and the revocation of the power of attorney (who was a close friend of the grantor's) included the lack of detail in the accounts provided, a personal advantage being derived from the control of the grantor's funds, and a conflict of interest caused by the mingling of funds. This decision falls within this group because of an existing guardianship order which was not challenged. A change to a professional administrator was made in *STY* [2018] VCAT 282 when one of two siblings passed away, and it was agreed that the remaining sibling should not have this duty alone.

In the context of an existing administration order, guardianship was ordered in favour of a sibling and co-operative accountant in *WLH (Guardianship)* [2022] after a decline in the represented person's capacity, but consistently with her wishes. In the same context, but where there was disagreement between the potential guardians, being three daughters of the protected person, the OPA was made guardian in *VIJ (Guardianship)* [2022] VCAT 1310.

2.1 Provision previously made by way of Power of Attorney and/or medical treatment decision maker): no change ordered

This group of cases usually involved a challenge to the appointment by an elderly family member as their decision maker by another family member who was not happy with the grant of power and/or how it was being exercised.

[57] Likewise, where the represented person had moved overseas in *VQL (Guardianship)* [2018] VCAT 1797.

[58] See also *YXG (Guardianship)* [2022] VCAT 900.

Within this category there was a sub-group where a child of the grantor challenged the exercises of power by the holder of a power of attorney. The challenge usually manifested itself in a double-barrelled application to revoke the power of attorney and/or make orders for administration (which suspend the power). The Tribunal often referred these concerns to the OPA for investigation and/or ordered the attorneys to file a report on the exercise of their powers, and the outcome of these processes then informed the decision.

For example, in *REX* [2022] VCAT 396,[59] no change was ordered where there was a clean bill of health, because the absence of impropriety means that there is no need for an order within section 31 of the 2019 Act and/or the least restrictive approach has already been chosen. The cases in this sub-group are the converse of those below. There are found to be no concerns about the existing provision and therefore no need to change it because it is definitionally less restrictive to have powers of attorney than Tribunal orders.

The Tribunal refused to revoke the power of attorney in *OME* [2018] VCAT 1651 despite the acrimony between the grantor's adult child and partner, because the relevant issues were the subject of proceedings in the Federal Circuit Court and, in addition to the costs of an independent administrator, there was no basis for any complaint against the attorney's conduct.

The application to revoke a power of attorney, and then for guardianship and administration orders, was cut off at the pass in *DOA (Guardianship)* [2018] VCAT 1373 because, as also discussed in 3.1 below, there was no basis for a finding that there was a lack of decision-making capacity.[60]

2.2 Provision previously made by way of Power of Attorney and/or medical treatment decision maker): change ordered

This group of cases also usually involved a challenge to the appointment by an elderly family member as their decision maker by another family member who was not happy with the grant of power and/or how it was being exercised. The 'least restrictive' approach was evident in the changes made, and the OPA was often appointed as a guardian 'tiebreaker' in the context of ongoing family conflict.

By way of contrast to the previous subsection, in *LWW (Guardianship)* [2022] VCAT 221 the power of attorney was suspended and orders made appointing the daughter who had been the attorney as administrator with some monitoring by the Tribunal, and the OPA as guardian, because conflict between family members required someone to be accountable for financial decisions and for the

[59] This was the largest sub-group, cases where complaints which seemed innocuous and were clearly triggered by sibling disagreement. The sub-group comprises in addition to *REX, MGL (Guardianship)* [2022] VCAT 468; *VNH* [2022] VCAT 379; *WHS (Guardianship)* [2022] VCAT 589; *OQQ (Guardianship)* [2018] VCAT 286; *IVH (Guardianship)* [2018] VCAT 1839; *QJB (Guardianship)* [2018] VCAT 531; *DMY (Guardianship)* [2018] VCAT 721; *EML (Guardianship)* [2018] VCAT 766; *UXM (Guardianship)* [2022] VCAT 818.

[60] As in *LPS (Guardianship)* [2022] VCAT 1370 and *VQV (Guardianship)* [2022] VCAT 1369.

OPA to make decisions regarding access by the mother to family and friends.[61] Interestingly, a family member was appointed for administration, and the OPA as the guardian, in *EPM* [2022] VCAT 521. It was the hospital social worker who applied for the orders and the adult child most acceptable to the represented person who was made administrator and guardian for living arrangements, but not for medical treatment, where the answer was in the legislation. Again, the least restrictive approach led to the guardianship order being confined as much as possible.

Conflict between family members which goes beyond quibbles about the exercise of decision-making and requires a 'tiebreaker' administrator is one sub-category. Another is justifiable concerns about the exercise of power by the attorney. A change to the existing financial regime was ordered in *NKT* [2022] VCAT 362 because of the Tribunal's finding that the power of attorney, the grantor's son, was not acting in the best interests of the grantor. This finding was based on a substantial body of evidence from the grantor's other family members and health-care professionals. Family members who supported the changes were made guardian and administrator, rather than the professional alternatives.[62]

In *DQU (Guardianship)* [2018] VCAT 1953 the OPA was made guardian on the application of a hospital social worker where the children of the represented person disagreed as to whether she should be cared for at home, but the medical professionals were clear that she required access to services and a safe environment, in circumstances where one of her sons, who said he wished to care for her, was the subject of a family violence intervention order for her protection due to concerns about his past financial and physical abuse of her.[63] This overrode the wishes of the represented person. The OPA was also the tiebreaker where the family members had different views about access to services for dementia in *TBV (Guardianship)* [2018] VCAT 1506. The OPA was made a guardian to deal with accommodation and services because of family conflict in *ILW (Guardianship)* [2018] VCAT 1271, but the power of attorney arrangements remained untouched.

In the extreme circumstances of *FNJ (Guardianship)* [2022] VCAT 269 the adult child was made a guardian so that they would have the authority to commence legal proceedings against a hospital which had indicated its intention to turn off a life support machine.

3.1 No existing orders or provision: no orders made

Both 3.1 and 3.2 usually involved applications made by hospital social workers in relation to a person in their care who had no next of kin. In this first subcategory

[61] As in *XXH (Guardianship)* [2022] VCAT 1410 as to an administrator.

[62] Who were appointed in (re administration) in *WRU (Guardianship)* [2018] VCAT 1171 where a power of attorney was revoked because of conflict of interest.

[63] *IEX (Guardianship)* is a related example of a particular guardian being appointed on the basis that they could best guarantee access to required medical supports.

of cases, the Tribunal did not agree with the applicant that the order sought was needed, again demonstrating the 'least restrictive' approach.

On a rehearing,[64] the Tribunal discharged a recent administration order in *OKY (Guardianship)* [2018] VCAT 892 and refused to make a guardianship order on the application of a case manager. There was insufficient evidence of the threshold issue of a disability. Past difficulties with alcohol (even if present non-consumption was related to absence of funds) did not meet the disability test, and there was (unusually) reference to precedent in addition to the statutory requirements.[65] Likewise in *UWJ (Guardianship)* [2018] VCAT 1063 the Tribunal refused to make a finding as to disability when the basis for the social worker's application was to prevent the potentially represented person's gender reassignment. In *UWC (Guardianship)* [2022] VCAT 1207 the Tribunal was satisfied that the potentially represented person had no need for a guardian.[66]

3.2 No existing orders or provision: orders made

In this subcategory, orders were made, but the 'least restrictive' approach remained evident.

The trigger for the Case Manager's application in *DZZ* [2018] VCAT 194 was the life-threatening consequences of the proposed represented person's refusal to follow medical advice. There had been an investigation by the OPA which recommended the option of using family members to influence DZZ. The Tribunal carefully analysed DZZ's specific requirements and found that a guardianship order was not required in relation to medical, health care and accommodation decisions, and an administration order was not required in relation to finances, but a guardianship order, in favour of the OPA, was required in relation to service needs. This decision is a clear example of orders as a last resort: it shows the Tribunal being careful to limit the application of orders as much as it can.

The OPA was also made a guardian with limited powers in *SPY* [2018] VCAT 411 because medical decisions needed to be made in the context of severe brain injury and there was too much conflict between the represented person's mother and partner for either of them to be the guardian. Similarly, in *UEV (Guardianship)* [2018] VCAT 1384, the hospital social worker's application for administration and guardianship was only successful as to administration because proper arrangements for the care of the represented person were in place.

[64] Arguably this case should be in 1.3 because of the existing order, but it is included here because of the interim nature of the existing order and the reported decision being the first proper examination.

[65] At [8]: 'In the decision of XYZ v State Trustees Ltd (XYZ), Justice Cavanough stressed the essential task of addressing the statutory standard as precisely as possible, the jurisdiction being one of public law rather than private law, affecting 'civil liberties and . . . dignity'.

[66] This may have been due to change of circumstances since the original application.

DISCUSSION AND CONCLUSION

In summary, we found that apart from the cases in categories 1.1 and 3, the cases involved sibling squabbles manifesting in contests over the appropriate orders, resulting from disagreement about care of an elderly family member (usually a parent). While the reasons for disagreement were not always evident, concerns about the welfare of that family member (eg *DQU (Guardianship)* [2018] VCAT 1953, involving reports of an ongoing history of financial and physical abuse of a mother by the son who sought to be her carer) and inheritance concerns (eg *LWW (Guardianship)* [2022] VCAT 221, in which one sibling saw the other as affected by 'inheritance impatience' and as a 'predator' ([11]) were evident. When something changed, the change was as to the identity of the guardian rather than to a position of not having a guardian. There was real effort by the Tribunal to opt for the alternative that was least restrictive of the right of the person with disability to make their own decisions. Our analysis also shows that the role played by the Tribunal was often to protect authorised decision makers from being in breach of their responsibilities (eg *HYY (Guardianship)* [2022] VCAT 97).

In its 'least restrictive' approach, management of family squabbles, and protection of authorised decision makers from being in breach, the role of the Tribunal at state level mirrors that played by the High Court of Australia when determining two appeals involving applications made by legal representatives of parties who lacked legal capacity under the federal Family Law Act 1975 (Cth) for financial (property and maintenance) orders between spouses, or between de facto partners on relationship breakdown.

In *Stanford v Stanford* [2012] HCA 52 the parties were married and the wife had no capacity. The wife's case guardian, her daughter, sought that the home in which the husband now resided alone be sold, claiming that the wife's nursing care needs were not being adequately met. The daughter also stood to gain more from FLA orders than she would under the wife's will. The High Court's decision that it would not be just and equitable to make a property settlement order protected the husband from the daughter, the wife having died by the time the orders were made.

In *Fairbairn v Radecki* [2022] HCA 18 Ms Fairbairn's guardian and administrator, the NSW State Trustee and Guardian, applied to the Family Court for orders to sell her property to pay for her care. The application was opposed by her de facto partner who argued that as their relationship had not broken down the court had no jurisdiction to make the orders sought. The High Court held that due to the male partner's self-interested conduct, the de facto relationship had broken down even though neither party had decided to end it. As a result, the Family Court had jurisdiction to make the orders sought by the State Trustee and Guardian, and Ms Fairbairn (and her children, as the main beneficiaries of her will) were protected from Mr Radecki's self-interested behaviour, and the State Trustee and Guardian was protected in its proposed action.

It further appeared that in the High Court, similar to the Tribunal, the greatest risk to those lacking legal capacity was likely to be members of the family of the represented person who act self-interestedly. Our analysis suggests that tribunals and courts are well aware of this risk and act protectively of the represented person in the minority of cases where an application is made. However, a more systematic analysis of the Family Law Act cases, and the decisions of tribunals in other Australian states, is needed to test these conclusions.

6

The Implementation of the Convention on the Rights of Persons with Disabilities in Spain: The State Law 8/2021 with Special Reference to the Aragon Regional Law

TERESA PICONTÓ NOVALES*

SPANISH STATE LAW 8/2021 WITHIN THE FRAMEWORK OF THE UNITED NATIONS CONVENTION ON THE RIGHTS OF PERSONS WITH DISABILITIES (2006)

IN RECENT YEARS there has been a radical change in Spain in the conception of people with disabilities. An important element in this change has been the introduction of a new state law (8/2021) on the protection of persons with disabilities. The new law represents a change of model from the previous law in Spain and is based on equal conditions for people with disabilities with those of other people in the exercise of rights such as dignity, individual autonomy and the freedom to make their own decisions, among others. Specifically, the measures envisaged are intended to ensure that the rights and preferences of people with disabilities are respected.

Law 8/2021 is very ambitious because it has changed the way various previous laws have addressed disability. The main objective now is to provide support for the disabled. The basis for the recognition of the legal capacity of persons with disabilities is their dignity and respect for their autonomy on an equal footing with other persons. However, persons with disabilities continue to be vulnerable, so that the application of this new legal model will have to be carried

* This chapter is part of the Research Project, The Right to Care in the Digital Society: Analysis of the Effectiveness of Rights Related to Long-term Care in the Context of their Increasing Digitalization (e-CARE). Grant PID2023-152437NB-I00/Generación de Conocimiento funded by MICIU/AEI/10.13039/501100011033 by ERDF A way of making Europe.

out very carefully to avoid abuses by people who could take advantage of such vulnerability, given that this legal reform has greatly reduced the protection of the vulnerability and specific needs of disabled people in favour of their autonomy and preferences.

Specifically, under the new law nobody can be deprived of their 'capacity' or deprived of their rights. The law is designed only to adopt the necessary measures of support which a disabled person needs to exercise their rights.[1] In this respect, the Spanish law follows the New York Convention (2006). The Convention understands that disability encompasses not only personal and medical factors, but also external or social factors. There is a clear presence of a social model in the conception of disability, especially in terms of dignity and autonomy, participation in society, and respect for diversity.

It is significant that the Convention replaced the word 'protection' with 'support', given that the idea is to provide support, not protection, aimed exclusively at respecting the will and preferences of the disabled.

There is only one concept of 'legal capacity' in the Convention, because this capacity is the same for everybody, without distinction or discrimination between people. With this concept of 'legal capacity', the Convention aims to place disabled people on exactly the same level as people without disability. We are all equal and subject to equal conditions. The Convention establishes that support is aimed at enabling disabled people to exercise their rights when their mental or psychological capacity to do so is limited, respecting their wishes.[2]

The Convention, which has been integrated into Spanish law since May 2008, represented a significant change in the treatment of disabled people in Spain. Before state Law 8/2021, the Spanish Supreme Court played an important role in adapting Spanish law to the principles of the Convention. However, despite the significant progress made by the Supreme Court in adapting existing civil law to the principles and rights of people with disabilities in accordance with the New York Convention, its efforts were not enough and a profound change in the legal basis of guardianship institutions was necessary to comply with the requirements of the Convention. In fact, a radical legal change was needed to adapt the law to the model set out in the Convention (ie that persons with disabilities have the same rights as other persons and that no prior distinction can be made

[1] See MA Parra Lucán, 'Hacia una reforma del régimen de la discapacidad: La doctrina del Tribunal Supremo y la Convención de Nueva York', in MC Gete-Alonso Calera (coord), *Jornadas sobre el nuevo modelo de discapacidad*, Marcial Pons, 2020, 119–148; E Diaz Velázquez, 'Disability Law in Spain. Moving Forward Towards Full Citizenship and Inclusion?', in C Spivakovsky, L Steele and P Weller, *The Legacies of Institutionalisation: Disability, Law and Policy in the 'Deinstitutionalised' Community*, (Oxford, Hart Publishing, 2020), 59–72.

[2] See Martínez-Pujalte, AL (2020) 'A propósito de la reforma de la legislación española en materia de capacidad jurídica: la voluntariedad como nota esencial del apoyo', in *Cuadernos Electrónicos de Filosofía del Derecho* 42, 240–62.

regarding limitations in the exercise of their capacity). The enactment of state Law 8/2021 had been overdue for years in Spain.

The main axis of this state Law is the principle of respect for the will and preferences of the disabled person, with the aim of giving a leading role to disabled people both in the design of the support system they may need in the future and also in decision-making in general. Therefore, respect for the will and preferences of the disabled person underpins the whole law.

With this new state Law, people with disabilities become the actors in their own legal lives. Previously, a person with a disability had a legal guardian appointed who acted on his or her behalf. The new law requires that they receive support consisting of the assistance of a person who instead of substituting for them, must act together with them and follow their will, wishes and preferences. The aim of the law is for the person with a disability to be able to 'develop his or her own decision-making process'.

In relation to this, one of the key aspects of this law is the relevance that it gives to the will of the person with a disability in planning support measures. The law establishes that the person with a disability may, by means of a public deed, have support measures put in place for the care of their person or the administration of their assets, in anticipation of future circumstances that may hinder the exercise of their legal capacity, and it must be indicated in this document who will be the person responsible for this support.

Therefore, the relevance of the will of the person with a disability arises not just from the fact that the voluntary support measure prevails over all others, but also because of the wide range of autonomy that the law grants to the disabled person to establish the content of such a support measure. In other words, this law allows the disabled person to construct the support measure in the way he or she considers most appropriate according to his or her needs.

In short, the law aims to ensure that the will of the disabled person is respected as much as possible with the support measures, so that the previous model based on the 'best interests of the disabled person' has been replaced, at least in part, by a system based on their preferences and will or, where appropriate, on the best possible interpretation of their will, wishes and preferences.

The law states that there may be exceptional cases in which it is not possible for the person with a disability, even with all the help that can be given, to make decisions independently. In these exceptional cases the appointment of a representative is possible.

In cases where the intellectual faculties are impaired to such a degree that the person with a disability needs a representative rather than mere assistance, state Law 8/2021 states that 'the representative shall take into account the life history, values and beliefs of the person with a disability and shall seek to determine the decision that would have been made had the person with a disability not needed representation'.

Given that representation is an extreme option, support for the person with a disability will be provided by what may be called a 'curator' and no longer by a 'guardian'. In Spanish law, the so-called 'curatela' or partial guardianship is a more flexible system which adapts more easily to the needs of the person with disabilities.[3] The objective of the law is to provide a closer correlation between the help and the need for help, the degree of disability and the degree of assistance, with the aim of safeguarding as much as possible the autonomy and the will of the person with disability.

Under this law, voluntary support measures take precedence over legal and judicial measures. Therefore, a judicial measure can only be adopted in the absence or failure of a voluntary support measure. Specifically, these voluntary measures can give the person with disability the opportunity to take his or her own decisions relating to his or her person or property before reaching a stage of disability under which the court would formally need to appoint a 'curator'.

This profound legal change has required a change in the mentality of legal operators accustomed to working with the idea of 'legal incapacity'. The legal capacity of persons with disabilities cannot be taken away or reduced. Therefore, the person with a disability has full legal capacity and its exercise will require more or less support or assistance depending on their degree of autonomy. If a representative who acts in their name is necessary (to a degree depending on their level of disability and their needs), any actions taken must be based on the wishes and will of the disabled person in question.

It is important to realise that state Law 8/2021 does not take into account the plurality of civil laws existing within Spain ('foral' or regional laws), for example in Aragon, Catalunya and Navarre which have their own civil laws relating to people with disabilities. For this reason, the coming into force of state Law 8/2021 has generated some debate and difficulties.[4] This will be briefly commented on in the conclusions of this chapter.

The second part of this chapter addresses the situation in the autonomous region of Aragon where the regional law 3/2024 of 13 June was recently passed, modifying the regional Legal Code of Aragon in relation to legal capacity. From the coming into effect of this law on 15 July 2024, the courts cannot deprive any person with mental disability of their legal capacity and are required to provide any necessary support in order for such capacity to be exercised. From now on, no person with a disability can be deprived of their legal capacity as this goes against their dignity. However, in order that the person can exercise their legal capacity in practice despite their difficulties or disability, the court must

[3] For more information about the new system of support in the exercise of legal capacity under State Law 8/2021, see C Guilarte Martín-Calero, 'De las medidas de apoyo a las personas con discapacidad para el ejercicio de su capacidad jurídica', in C Guilarte Martín-Calero (dir), *Comentarios a la Ley 8/2021 por la que se reforma la legislación civil y procesal en materia de discapacidad*, vol III (1st edn) (Pamplona, Aranzadi, 2021), 528–52.

[4] See A López Azcona, 'El sistema de apoyos a las personas con discapacidad en Derecho Aragonés', in *Actualidad Jurídica iberoamericana* (2022) nº 17, 48–79. A López Azcona, 'La modificación del Código del Derecho Foral de Aragón en materia de ejercicio de la capacidad jurídica de las personas con discapacidad por la Ley 3/2024, de 13 de junio' (2025) *Anuario de Derecho Civil*, 78:3.

provide them with the necessary support measures depending on the degree of such disability.

THE RIGHTS OF PEOPLE WITH MENTAL DISABILITY IN ARAGON WITHIN THE FRAMEWORK OF THE UNITED NATIONS CONVENTION (2006) AND STATE LAW 8/2021

In the autonomous region of Aragon, Spanish state Law 8/2021 to support people with disabilities in the exercise of their rights was only partially applied because of the existence of its own regional law relating to people with disabilities. However, as mentioned above, regional law 3/2024 was passed three years after the state law, modifying the regional Legal Code of Aragon in respect of legal capacity. This came into effect on 15 July 2024.

Until July 2024, Aragon Law 5/2019 was applied. This law was not totally consistent with the New York Convention of the United Nations (2006) which developed a social model of rights for persons with disabilities. In practice, the professionals (judges, prosecutors, notaries, social workers in the social services), and also the public *Foundation Supporting Disabled People in Aragon* and private associations working with disabled people, tried to apply the Aragonese 5/2019 Law according to the principles and rights established by the New York Convention and the Spanish state Law 8/2021. This created some practical difficulties and uncertainties for the courts and professionals working with disabled people.

During this transitional period, the author carried out some exploratory research (in the period March–May 2023) to find out which model was being applied, the old or the new, in which cases and why this was so, and other specific questions such as: what are the practical advantages and disadvantages of the new social model in terms of the rights and needs of disabled people? To what extent was state Law 8/2021 being applied in Aragon? Since state Law 8/2021 came into force, did the judges in Aragon give rulings of legal incapacity and, if so, until when and in what cases? Since the introduction of the state law, were the courts still appointing full guardianship ('tutelas')? To what extent were they applying partial guardianship ('curatelas asistenciales') and partial guardianship with representation in specified circumstances? How should the Aragonese law in force at the time be modified in the near future?

Specifically, the author analysed some of the more representative judicial decisions in Aragon. Essentially, these can be divided into two categories: in the first place, there were the judicial decisions in cases which had begun before the state reform in 2021. In general terms, these decisions follow the old model. Consequently, in many of these cases, some disabled people were declared 'incapable' and a 'tutor' or full guardian was appointed, with partial or total representation. In the second place, there are cases dating from 2022 which were decided after the coming into force of the 2021 state law. These do not contain rulings of judicial incapacity. They provide for an assessment of the degree of capacity in order to know what the disabled person in question could do for himself or herself and to what extent he or she needed help and support. In these cases, full guardianships (tutelas) were not appointed. When necessary, partial guardianship was representative but only for specific actions.

Until the coming into effect of the new regional law, the so-called de facto guardianship was a much-used measure of support in Aragon. It was applied in 60 per cent of the cases of judicial support measures. Usually, family members of the disabled person were responsible for their daily care. However, when family care was lacking, the court appointed someone to assist the disabled person. Alternatively, the court appointed the Public Foundation for Support of the Autonomy and Capacities of Persons in Aragon[5] as a de facto guardian. Specifically, the Foundation can participate in the taking of decisions for people with disabilities.[6] It also works with adults whose families are not able to take care or responsibility for them. This situation will probably continue to be applied under the new Aragonese Law 3/2024. In addition to this, the Public Foundation supports and supervises the partial guardianship of intellectually and psychologically disabled people. Also, where there has been a conflict of interest between the disabled person and the family member or guardian who assists, in Aragon the court provided a support measure known as 'judicial defence'. This can be an individual person or the Public Foundation.

Regarding the specific judicial support measures previously implemented in Aragon, the so-called 'restoration or extension' of family authority was applied with respect to sons and daughters legally of age with disabilities (a characteristic figure of Aragonese law which is broader than parental authority of common or state civil law). In the new Aragonese law 3/2024, described in the next section, this measure has been discarded on the grounds that it is inconsistent with the New York Convention and has been replaced by a special curatorship of the parents over their sons or daughters with disabilities.

In the course of exploratory research, the author conducted an interview with a public notary in Zaragoza who explained that some notaries in Aragon are very much in favour of empowering the disabled while others advocate the former more protective and controlling model.

The author also interviewed a judge who explained that in the case of elderly people with cognitive impairment, Alzheimer's or senile dementia, guardianship

[5] The author also interviewed informally (by telephone) the President of the Public Foundation (Fundación para el apoyo y la autonomía y capacidad de las personas en Aragón) about their function in relation to people with disabilities in Aragon.

[6] Orden PRI/117/2023, of 3 February, por el que se dispone la publicación del Convenio de asistencia jurídica entre la Dirección General de Servicios Jurídicos del Departamento de Presidencia y Relaciones Institucionales del Gobierno de Aragón y la Fundación para el apoyo a la autonomía y las capacidades de las personas en Aragón: https://www.boa.aragon.es/cgi-bin/RECO/BRSCGI?CMD=VEROBJ&MLKOB=1261805202222.

was often not necessary, but rather a 'de facto guardianship', which is, as noted above, one of the most widely used support measures in Aragon. There are many cases in which the daily care management or even the management of the dependency benefits of the disabled person are already being handled because there is a family member taking care of these matters. If the families of these disabled people need to go to the court, it is verified whether the day-to-day needs of the disabled person are covered and, this being the case, it is established that there is a 'de facto guardianship'. As the de facto guardian in most cases is not appointed by the court but acts on their own initiative providing support for the disabled person, in practice this can lead to problems, for example in dealing with banks or other institutions. Consequently, the new Aragonese law 3/2024 states that a notarised affidavit is sufficient to accredit a de facto guardian without having to go to the courts.

The judge also explained that curatorships or partial guardianships have been applied in Aragon for cases of mental illness, for example, when a person stops taking the medication that keeps them stable, or does not attend medical appointments. They also operate in cases of bipolar disorders or schizophrenia and other pathologies that lead the person, at the time of an outbreak or manic phase, to make compulsive purchases. In these cases, the courts have adopted a measure of curatorship or care guardianship, which consists of supporting the person and accompanying them when needed. During periods of stability, the person is asked for their agreement in writing that if an outbreak or acute phase of their pathology occurs, they accept the actions of the curator or carer.

Representative guardianships are exceptional, being appointed only for those serious cases in which a judicial examination shows that the disabled person does not speak or communicate and that the person requires constant support in the exercise of his/her legal capacity and in day-to-day activities such as eating or taking medication.

Before the new law, as a preventive measure any person was able to design his or her own support system in advance, in view of a possible future need for support. As one notary explained (Interview 24 May 2024), the involvement of a notary has been important in these cases, as they can assess the capacity of the interested party, provide support and even adopt possible supervisory measures at the time of being granted the power to do so. The new law 3/2024 has not changed this, but it has reinforced the role of notaries, for example with measures such as 'el mandato de apoyos' (a new term which can be translated as 'support mandate') and the new provision for a notarised affidavit to accredit de facto guardians.

The 'support mandate', like de facto guardianship, is a voluntary support measure that does not require judicial intervention. However, unlike de facto guardianship (which is based on day-to-day circumstances and is unofficial), the support mandate is a formal official measure.

Aragonese Law 3/2024 empowers the de facto guardianship measure[7] for day-to-day decisions in relation to third parties (banks, electricity companies, etc). In the event that this de facto guardianship, designed for specific day-to-day situations and decisions, is not sufficient, the judge can grant a guardianship that can cover communication and accompaniment, assistance or, ultimately, with representative powers. This guardianship measure, if necessary, could coexist with other support measures (such as de facto guardianship, support mandate, etc).

Regarding the support mandate,[8] a person (by contract) undertakes to provide the necessary support to the person with disabilities to manage their personal or property interests in the exercise of their legal capacity (art 168.1 Código Derecho Foral Aragonés). The support mandate can coexist with other support measures such as guardianship; in cases in which the support mandate is inadequate or is not being carried out effectively in practice, the court may establish a guardianship measure.

This section has described in general terms the judicial and institutional practice in Aragon in relation to disabled people up to the coming into force of Aragonese law 3/2024 on 15 July 2024. The following section briefly addresses the principles and essential features of this new regional law and some of the most significant changes introduced in order to adapt Aragonese legislation to the New York Convention and within the framework of Spanish state law 8/2021.

THE NEW ARAGONESE LAW 3/2024, AMENDING THE REGIONAL CIVIL CODE OF ARAGON IN RELATION TO THE LEGAL CAPACITY OF PERSONS[9]

As stated in the Explanatory Memorandum of Law 3/2024, the inspiring principle of this law is the recognition of the full legal capacity of all persons without exception, which is a consequence of the dignity they possess. Therefore, from now on it will no longer be possible for the courts to deprive any person of his or her legal capacity in Aragon, as had occurred until the coming into force of this law.

Specifically, the general principles that should govern the actions and the provision of support measures are: to respect the autonomy and independence

[7] See C Bayod López, 'La guarda de hecho de las personas con discapacidad', in C Bayod López (coord), *Reforma del Código Civil de Derecho Foral de Aragón en materia de discapacidad* (A Coruña, Colex, 2024), 137–59.

[8] See A Calatayud Sierra, 'Mandatos de apoyo y poderes preventivos sin mandato', in C Bayod López (coord), *Reforma del Código Civil de Derecho Foral de Aragón en materia de discapacidad* (A Coruña, Colex, 2024), 111–36.

[9] A detailed review of the Aragonese Law 3/2024 undertaken by the members of the Aragon Commission on Civil Law can be seen in C Bayod López (coord), *Reforma del Código Civil de Derecho Foral de Aragón en materia de discapacidad* (A Coruña, Colex, 2024).

of persons with disabilities, taking into account their will and preferences, including the freedom to make their own decisions whenever possible. When this is not possible, or when doing so would pose a significant danger to the person or his or her dependents, or cause serious harm to third parties, action shall be taken in accordance with what is objectively the best for the dignity, rights and interests of the person concerned (art 37).

Law 3/2024 provides that a person with a mental disability will be able to organise his or her own support system in the presence of a notary and will be able to designate the helper and request the type or types of support he or she wants. This law gives a major boost to the already existing measure of 'de facto guardianship', which consists of a person providing, on their own initiative, support to a person with a disability, something very common in Spanish society (between parents and children, between couples, etc). As the de facto guardian is not officially appointed and acts on his or her own initiative to support the person with a disability, in practice there have been many problems, for example with banks, so this new law provides for a notarised affidavit as a mechanism for the guardian to prove that he or she is in fact the de facto guardian. The judicial measure of guardianship is maintained, which can be varied according to the specific needs and circumstances of the disabled person. Depending on the circumstances, the functions of the support may consist of help in communication, consideration of options and understanding of legal acts, assistance and, ultimately, representation in decision making.

This new Aragonese law responds to the basic principle that each person is different, so the support measures provided are varied and must be carefully chosen for each specific case. Under this law, these support measures must be compatible with the will of the disabled person, from the most minimal to the most extensive support measures, and from de facto guardianship to representative guardianship.

To recap, there are currently three ways to exercise support for disabled people in Aragon. The first is in those cases in which the person with a disability (but with mental capacity) voluntarily and before a notary organises his or her support system. This is the so-called 'support mandate'. The second is the de facto guardian, that is, any person who on their own initiative informally provides support to a person with a disability. Thirdly, the courts can order the support. This can only occur if there are no voluntary measures or de facto guardianship in place. In the most severe cases of disability, the court will not be able to deprive the disabled person of his or her legal capacity but will establish the appropriate support and appoint a guardian.

Finally, the coming into force of Law 3/2024 has automatically meant that persons who had been judicially declared 'incapacitated' under the previous legislation are no longer incapacitated. That is, this law has had the effect of 'reinstating' the legal capacity of all those persons who had previously been declared incapacitated by a court ruling. While the support measures to which these persons with disabilities were subject remain in force (Transitory Provision

5ª Law 3/2024), such support measures must be adjusted to the current law, so that at any time the judicial authorities may be asked to review such support measures.

SOME CONCLUSIONS

Before concluding, it is important to take into account the plurality of civil laws existing within Spain (ie 'foral' or regional laws) relating to people with disabilities. Each autonomous region has its own jurisdiction over laws and regulations concerning social assistance under the Spanish constitution of 1978 and there is considerable diversity in the various regional laws on disability. Some of these regional laws regulate accessibility measures for people with disabilities in various environments, services, urban spaces, companies, etc so that they can have access under equal conditions (Asturias, Canary Islands, Catalonia, La Rioja, Madrid, Basque Country, Balearic Islands, among others). However, other laws, such as the Andalusian Law 4/2017 of September 25, the Navarre Regional Law 31/2022 of November 28 or the Aragonese Regional Law 3/2024, are more advanced and comprehensive on the rights of people with disabilities.

Furthermore, there are regions in Spain which not only have their own civil laws, but also different institutions and different terminologies to describe what are basically the same or similar support figures. For this reason, the situation can be very complex, especially for people with disabilities who may move from one part of the country to another, for example for retirement or to be with relatives.

In closing, the following observations can be made:

First, given that Aragon has its own civil law, some of the innovations contained in state Law 8/2021 have not been followed by the legal operators in this region. This continues to generate controversy and debate between legal operators and experts. Until the beginning of 2022, the courts continued to declare legal incapacity following the Aragonese law 5/2019. However, since then the courts have not done this. In this respect, following the coming into effect of the 2024 regional law, the courts in Aragon have been complying with the state law and the New York Convention.

Secondly, it is important to mention that legal operators in general have a very positive opinion of the work carried out by private entities with disabled people in Aragon.

From a critical perspective, in the debates about the state law, many legal operators in Aragon have pointed out that there are many cases in which it is not possible to know the will of persons with a disability, so that it cannot be interpreted or construed in any way. There are cases of people who from birth have an intellectual limitation that prevents them from making conscious or autonomous decisions, or cases where a severe disability prevents the person from expressing their will and the person helping them is unable to know what their will would have been. A question then arises in the minds of many experts: in these cases, given their special vulnerability and lack of protection, does the best interest criterion not better guarantee the rights of the person with a disability?

This seems to be the main criticism raised by the state law that has provoked unease among many professionals who do not agree with the law enabling the exercise of the autonomy of disabled people to such a degree that that it has completely displaced the legal criterion of their 'best interests', turning its back on the reality of some of the real situations faced on a daily basis by judges and notaries, and other legal operators, in their work with disabled people.

From a socio-legal perspective in Aragon, with the coming into force of the new Aragonese Law 3/2024, the judicial guardianships of disabled persons which had been granted under the previous law to persons declared 'incapable' have been replaced by guardianship with representation. Furthermore, the support measures and mandates which had been granted under the previous law are maintained as long as they do not conflict with the new Aragonese Law 3/2024.

The author considers that the recent legal change from the medical model to the social model in the exercise of the rights of intellectual and psycho-social persons in Spain and, very recently in Aragon, can only be put into practice if it is accompanied by a change in social mentality, especially of legal and social professionals and operators who have competences and functions in disability matters, among others judges and magistrates, notaries, lawyers, social workers, etc.

Specifically, this legal model imposes significant changes in the social and ethical model such as: (a) considering people with disabilities in general and in particular those who need support as subjects of rights who must be able to choose and pursue their life projects; (b) understanding that actions in the field of disability must be aimed at protecting and promoting the satisfaction and exercise of the rights of these people; (c) understanding the vulnerability of these people as a social issue and overcoming the barriers they encounter in the exercise of their rights; (d) supporting a community approach recognising the role of the community (family, society and the State) in the development of rights of people with disabilities; (e) emphasising the importance of self-determination and respect for the choices of people with disabilities in their own ways of life and in the support they receive.

Following these important legal reforms, people with disabilities have the right to choose where, with whom and how they want to live their lives (articles19 and 12 CRDP). According to the Committee on the Rights of Persons with Disabilities, independent living does not necessarily imply living alone or carrying out activities on one's own, but relates to personal autonomy, freedom of choice and control over one's way of life and daily activities. Choice and control over one's own way of life is a fundamental component of the exercise of autonomy in support systems for people with disabilities. Therefore, people with disabilities have the right to have support systems and networks involving family, friends, neighbours, or trusted people who are essential for the development of independent living.

All of the above undoubtedly constitute a great challenge, from all points of view, when it comes to bringing these principles of action and rights into the day-to-day lives of people with disabilities.

7

Moment for Change in Bulgaria? The Bill on Persons and Support Measures

VELINA TODOROVA

THE RATIFICATION OF the Convention on the Rights of Persons with Disabilities (CRPD) by Bulgaria in 2012 was widely and warmly accepted by civil society as an opportunity to bring the attention of the public and the state to human rights issues and particularly the rights of persons with disabilities as the most excluded members of society. The Ministry of Justice took the lead for legal reform regarding the legal capacity of persons with disabilities, inspired by the Convention and the General Comment No 1 on Article 12 of the Committee on the Rights of Persons with Disabilities. The movement was strongly supported by civil society organisations including those representing persons with disabilities which supported expertise, advocacy and mobilisation of supporters.[1] The joint efforts resulted in a Draft Persons and Support Measures Act that went through three public consultation processes and was submitted to the National Assembly in 2016. The Bill introduces a shift in the protectionist approach to persons with disabilities and elaborates measures for supported decision making to replace substitute decision making. Since then, however, the Bill has not progressed.

This chapter discusses the current legislation and the stalled reforms in the context of the policy and academic debates around the concepts of protection and empowerment of persons with disabilities. Some key concepts of the Bill will then be presented and the reasons for the failure of the Bulgarian reform will be outlined.

[1] This active position could be explained by the human rights related profile of the Minister at that time who is now the Bulgarian Judge in Strasbourg Court as well as of the author of this chapter who was a deputy minister over the same time period.

THE LAW: A LOT OF 'PROTECTION' VS CAUTIOUS AUTONOMY

The current legal framework in Bulgaria considers persons with disabilities as vulnerable and in need of protection. It consists of the Constitution (1991), The Persons and the Family Act (1949), which provides the substantive grounds for the limitation of legal capacity; the Civil Procedure Code (2008) which regulates the incapacitation procedure; and the Family Code (2009) governing guardianship.

The Constitution does not regulate legal capacity per se, but denies voting rights for persons with limited capacity.[2] The Constitution also stipulates that persons with disabilities are under the special protection of the state and society.[3] The 'special protection' is further enshrined in the legislation in two ways. First, there is a range of economic and social rights of people with disabilities such as social benefits, health and rehabilitation care and social services. Some of these forms of protection could also be interpreted as measures for the empowerment of adults, for example through home-based services and personal assistance.[4] On the other hand, there is a regime of legal protection that enables intervention in the capacity to act of a person with disability followed by the appointment of a guardian.

Deprivation of Legal Capacity

The Persons and the Family Act (PFA) establishes the grounds for and the effects of the limitation of the legal capacity of adults. It contains the concepts and terminology that have been transplanted into Bulgarian legislation since the establishment of the current independent state in 1878. The Guardianship Act (1889) then regulated the guardianship of children, and the Persons Act (1907) sets out the limitation of legal capacity of adults. In 1949 both regulations were merged into The Persons and the Family Act, including the appointment of a guardian for incapacitated adults. These regulations were transplanted into the Family Code later on and remain to a large extend unchanged to this day.

The PFA sets out the grounds for the full and partial incapacitation (capacity to act) of a mentally sick person who is unable to take care of their own affairs. There must be a medical condition (dementia or mental illness) that results in the adult being unable to take care of their interests and actions (ie an inability to act).[5]

[2] Article 42 para 1 of the Constitution.

[3] Article 51, para 3 of the Constitution.

[4] See more as well as recent statistical data in: Todorova, V Empowerment and Protection of Vulnerable Adults. Bulgaria Report. FL-EUR Academic Network: https://assets-us-01.kc-usercontent.com/7099fcf9-715f-0061-5726-009a48410fee/de2d4691-135e-4e03-a964-7f1c7ce3d251/Bulgaria.pdf

[5] This is the interpretation of the legal grounds for incapacitation of the former Supreme Court, acting after 1947 until the adoption of the current Constitution of 1991. See Resolution No 5/79 of 13.II.1980, Plenum of the Supreme Court, para 1. The same reading by the Supreme Court of Cassation in Order No 1301/12.11.2008, case No 5560/2007, Judgment No 1301/12.11.2008, case No 5560/07 and Judgment No 379/07.05.2009, case No 1320/08.

The deprivation/limitation of capacity should be ordered by the District (second instance) court following a special action procedure. The claim may be submitted by the spouse, by a relative, by the public prosecutor or by any interested third party. The court must examine in person the adult whose legal capacity's limitation is being sought. This must take place either in the court room or in a medical facility, if necessary.[6] The Supreme Court of Cassation holds the view that the personal impression of the judge may make other evidence unnecessary – 'where the court . . . finds that the defendant is neither mentally ill nor feeble-minded but is of normal mental capacity' – meaning that medical/psychiatric assessment should not be amount to decisive evidence.[7] In spite of this, however, the value of psychiatric expertise is very high, which illustrates the medical approach to legal capacity. What is also problematic is the usual approach of psychiatrists to refrain from answering questions that should be essential for the court (eg how does the person act in relation to various situations or under various conditions), but rather to ground their expert reports on the medical records of the person and on what is theoretically known about the diagnosis.[8] This reaffirms the person's helplessness and sums up the absence of capacity as a result of the disability.

The degree of incapacity is determined by the severity of the diagnosed mental condition and by the functional assessment of the abilities of the person concerned compared to the cognitive, evaluative and behavioural abilities of a person with full capacity. The court may decide on full or partial limitation of legal capacity, but can take neither a tailored nor a time-bound decision. The deprivation and limitation of legal capacity results in lowering of the legal status of the adult concerned. In the case of full deprivation, the adult is reduced to the status of a minor child (0–14 years of age) and is thus excluded from all decision making which has legal implications.[9] Partial deprivation (limitation) leads to a status equivalent to an adolescent child (14–18 years of age).[10] This allows the given person to take legal actions, but these must be confirmed by their partial guardian. Although the limitation of legal capacity automatically affects all aspects of the legal agency of the person, it is considered as a protective measure because it prevents them from undertaking actions which are presumably harmful to their interests.

To sum up, the PFA has been at the core of the system of guardianship in Bulgaria up to the present. This bears the following features: incapacitation covers all legal areas of a person's activity for an indefinite period of time; it

[6] Article 337 of the Civil Procedure Code.

[7] Resolution No 5/79 of 13.II.1980, Plenum of the Supreme Court, paras 3, 4, 6; the same in Order No 235 of 31.03.2022 of the Supreme Court of Cassation, case No 3203/2021, IV.

[8] Voices for Justice. Victims of crime with disabilities in Bulgaria. Information and Communication: Cornerstones of justice for victims of crime with disability (878604 – InfoComPWDs) JUST-AG-2019 / JUST-JACC-AG-2019-878604. In: <validity.ngo/projects-2/voices-for-justice/ > last visited 21.11.2024.

[9] More about the consequences of deprivation of legal capacity on contractual capacity and on personal rights, in Todorova, V Empowerment and Protection of Vulnerable Adults. Bulgaria Report.

[10] Article 5, para 3 and article 4, para 2 PFA.

is not subject to periodic review which hinders the opportunity to reflect the dynamics of the individual's state;[11] persons under guardianship are deprived of any access to the court and redress for violations of their human rights; it is difficult for it to be revoked[12] and the legal consequences of partial guardianship are very similar to those of full guardianship.[13] Neither of the individuals who have won cases relating to guardianship against Bulgaria before the European Court of Human Rights (ECtHR) – Mr Stanev[14] and Mr Stankov[15] – have had access to court proceedings despite their legal capacity having been partially limited. Mr Stanev has made numerous attempts to have his legal capacity restored, but the courts have consistently refused his attempts solely on the basis of his medical diagnosis. Mr Stankov has not filed an application for restoration of his legal capacity, due to a fear that by doing so he may lose his place in the supported home in which he has lived since being released from the institution. He has also been fearful that the legal system will not be able to meet his need for support or formally recognise the support network he has now established as a legitimate form of support in decision making.[16]

[11] Nedev, D Proceedings to change or revoke the incapacitation, 2022, in: <https://www.challengingthelaw.com/grajdanski-proces/zamiana-i-vdigane-na-zapreshtenie/> last visited December, 2024.

[12] In 1980 the Supreme Court referred to 'change in the circumstances' as a ground for revocation of legal capacity. Resolution No 5/79 of 13.02.1980 г. of the Plenary of the Supreme Court. Although to challenge guardianship is still as difficult as it was before ratification of the CRPD, the case law is getting richer due to increased activity of persons with disability themselves legally supported by NGOs. The courts would rather consider as a ground the improvement of the health situation of the person (Judgment No 232/21.02.2020 District Court Burgas, case No 826/2019) or the factual ability to care for their affairs irrespective of the medical assessment (Judgment No 260614 of 12.10.2020 of the District Court – Varna in case No 1148/2020).

[13] Findings of ECtHR judgment in the case *Stanev v Bulgaria*. While in accordance with Decree No 5/79 of 13.02.1980 of the Plenary of the Supreme Court, a person under partial guardianship can, on their own or with the consent of their custodian, including the one under Art 108 of PFA, request the revocation of their guardianship, M. Stanev who had been placed under partial guardianship had not been able to access the court.

[14] *Stanev v Bulgaria*, ECtHR, no 36760/06; GC Judgment, 17 January 2012. Briefly the facts are: in 2000, Mr Rusi Stanev was placed under partial guardianship by a Bulgarian court and a municipal employee was appointed as his guardian. In 2002, without ever having met Mr Stanev, she had him placed in a social care institution in a remote mountainous area 400km from his home. Once there, the director of the institution became his guardian and controlled all his affairs. The conditions in the institution, as documented by the Council of Europe Committee for the Prevention of Torture (CPT), were unlivable. Food portions were inadequate, the residents had to sleep in their coats in the winter due to a lack of heat, and the sanitary facilities were nothing more than holes in the ground in wooded areas outside the buildings of the institution. Mr Stanev had no ability to challenge this situation as he could not initiate any type of legal proceedings, including a proceeding to have his guardianship lifted, without his guardian's consent.

[15] *Stankov v Bulgaria*, ECtHR, no 25820/07; GC Judgment, 17 March 2015. The case concerned Mr Stankov's partial legal incapacitation and his subsequent placement by his mother, as his guardian, in a care facility for people with mental disabilities. In June 2006 Mr Stankov, through his lawyer, requested the public prosecutor's office to grant restoration of his legal capacity on the grounds that his condition allowed him to manage his own interests. The prosecutor refused to institute proceedings for restoration of his legal capacity.

[16] See more in NGO information to the United Nations Committee on the Rights of Persons with Disabilities to the initial report of the Republic of Bulgaria, 2017, INT_CRPD_ICO_BGR_28482_E.

Many of the above features of the legal incapacitation of adults were confirmed by the Constitutional Court.[17] The Court reviewed a request of the Ombudsman claiming that article 5 of the PFL is in breach of the Constitution since it poses a restriction of their legal capacity, which is not proportionate to their condition and thus is discriminatory. The Court states that 'the lack of detailed legislative regulation leads to *unjust limitation* of . . . *rights, the exercise of which carries a risk to the interests of incapacitated person, third parties or the society, but also limits the exercising of unreasonably wide range of rights, including the constitutional ones*'. Having said that, the Court also considers that 'the current legislation does not take into account the CRPD requirements – the restrictions of the rights of such persons to be proportionate to their condition, to apply for the shortest possible time and to be subject to regular review by an independent body'. Despite these comments, the Court did not state that the legal regulation of deprivation and limitation of capacity was unconstitutional. It did, however, hold to its decision that urgent measures must be taken to amend the legislation in the area of the independent enjoyment of rights by persons with disabilities in the spirit of Article 12 of CRPD: '. . . The protection of the rights of persons with mental disabilities is within the remit of the National Assembly which should pass the relevant legislation regarding legal incapacity'.

It is worth mentioning, however, that following the ratification of CRPD, the Bulgarian legislation – not just the PFA but also a number of other laws restricting the rights of people with mental problems – is contrary to international standards, which, under the Constitution have a status overriding national law which is contrary to them.[18] How do the courts resolve this conflict? First, there was an attempt by the Sofia Court to apply CRPD directly in one of its decisions where the court refused to limit legal capacity and instead ordered measures for protected decision making.[19] The Supreme Court of Cassation took another position, following the reasoning of the Constitutional Court. The court stated that in a situation, where the CRPD standards are not domesticated, the PFA rules should be interpreted narrowly and in a way that fulfils the constitutional requirement to give enhanced protection to the rights of the mentally disabled people.[20]

[17] Constitutional Court, Decision No 12/17.07.2014, case No 10/2014 in: < https://www.constcourt.bg/bg/case-479 > last visited December, 2024.

[18] Article 5, para 4 of the Constitution. This situation is also ascertained in the judgment delivered by the Grand Chamber of the ECtHR in the *Stanev v Bulgaria* where the Strasbourg Court explicitly emphasises 'the growing importance which the international instruments for the protection of people with mental disorders are now attaching to granting them with as much legal autonomy as possible'.

[19] Decision of Sofia District Court of 4.11.2013 on case No 16532/2012.

[20] Decision No 226 of 31.10.2016 on case No 4922/2015 of the Supreme Court of Cassation.

Guardianship

The Family Code sets out two types of legal support for incapacitated adults: guardianship and partial guardianship.[21] The Guardianship authority is the mayor of the given municipality,[22] who, following a court decision, appoints respectively a guardian/representative or partial guardian. The job of the guardian is voluntary. The guardian should live with and take care of the well-being of the person, of their rights and obligations, administer property and report annually to the guardianship authority. The person under guardianship is fully subordinated to their guardian, and does not have any mechanism available to ensure respect for their wishes or preferences. The guardian should act in the best interests of the person and may be dismissed if it is established that there is a conflict of interests.[23] In a case of partial incapacitation, will and preferences do matter since the adult can act alone but the consent of the partial guardian is also necessary.

As a rule, the guardian should be either a family member of a close friend of the person. Where these are not available or refuse, officials from the municipality must be assigned. In a case where the adult has a parent or a spouse, these will become *ex lege* guardian/partial guardian.[24] It should be noted that in practice, due to a lack of effective support services, guardianship presumably remains a desirable outcome for the family of the person who suffers any incapacity. It relieves them of the burden to take a close look at the decisions related to everyday life and property and financial matters of the person. On the other hand, it is not rare to instrumentalise the incapacity of an adult for preserving their property in the interests of the family and heirs.[25]

As for society, guardianship is also an easy and cheap solution because it reduces the need for investment in reasonable accommodation and also because it used to provide for an easy means of entry to institutional care for persons with disabilities since their consent was not required until 2017.[26] The degrading conditions in institutional care for incapacitated adults were considered by the ECtHR as a violation of Article 3 ECHR in the judgments of *Stanev v Bulgaria* and *Stankov v Bulgaria*. The degrading material conditions in care institutions, their inadequate staffing and other resources, including deprivation of liberty of adults were also a focus of the monitoring reports of the Council

[21] Articles 153–73a of the Family Code.

[22] Article 154 of the Family Code.

[23] Articles 156 and 160 of the Family Code.

[24] Article 173 of the Family Code.

[25] For example, the Supreme Court of Cassation admitted that the ex-spouse has a legal interest and therefore a legal standing to claim termination of the legal capacity of her ex-spouse. The reasoning was that the property of the ex-spouse should be preserved as an inheritance of their minor daughter. Judgment No 711/30.12.2010, Case No 1915/2009/ III).

[26] See more in Mental Disability Advocacy Center, Guardianship and Human Rights in Bulgaria. Analysis of Law, Policy and Practice, 2007, p 29. Incapacitation as a direct entry point of adults to institutionalisation was analysed in the two ECHR judgments against Bulgaria.

of Europe Committee for the Prevention of Torture but also of the National Ombudsman.[27, 28]

THE MOMENT OF CHANGE

Various stakeholders were involved in the reform process, as discussed below.

The Civil Society and the Government

Civil society happened to be divided on the issue of legal capacity. The debate on social inclusion/empowerment of vulnerable adults began some 25 years ago and was led by organisations of persons with disabilities and by human rights organisations.[29] It was the activism of human rights organisations that triggered the debate on Article 12 CRPD immediately after its ratification in 2012.[30] On their initiative the relevant national legislation was reviewed[31] and the Ministry of Justice was pressured to draft Persons and Support Measures

[27] Report to the Bulgarian government on the visit to Bulgaria carried out by the Committee for the Prevention of Torture from 25 September to 6 October 2017, published on 4 May 2018, p 57, available at: https://www.coe.int/en/web/cpt/bulgaria, and the 2017 Annual report of the Ombudsman acting as National Preventive Mechanism (p 27, p 28 and 34), available at: http://www.ombudsman.bg/pictures/file/5751_Annual_Report_NPM_2017_EN.pdf . The main observation of the 2017 CPT's visit to Bulgaria was that a number of patients in the psychiatric hospitals are de facto deprived of their liberty due to reasons such as a lack of adequate care and accommodation in the community resulting in much longer hospitalisation than is practically needed. A significant proportion of patients, formally regarded as voluntary, are locked up in hospital wards and subjected to paternalistic control by the staff, including illegal detention.

[28] NGO information to the United Nations Committee on Economic, Social and Cultural Rights, For consideration when compiling the List of Issues to Bulgaria Prior to Reporting during the 57th Session of the Committee, 2016: <http://www.mdac.org/en/resources/cescr-submission-bulgaria-10216> last visited, December, 2024.

[29] This discussion is led by NGO 'Centre for Independent Living'. See the archive and current issues at: <https://cil.bg/en/news-en/> last visited, December, 2024.

[30] The leading NGO was the Bulgarian Centre for Non-for-profit Law that was joined by some organisations of persons with intellectual disabilities: https://bcnl.org/en/projects/capability-and-responsibility-true-prospects-for-people-with-disabilities-2010-2012, last visited, December, 2024. Some international NGOs were also very actively supporting the debate on Article 12: See for example MDAC Report on Disability and Human Rights in Bulgaria, 2007, available in: <English_Guardianship_and_Human_Rights_in_Bulgaria.pdf > last visited, December, 2024.

[31] That review resulted in *Concept paper for legislative changes in relation to implementing the standards laid down in Art 12 of CRPD,* which proposed the incapacitation to be replaced by supported decision making. It was adopted by the Council of Ministers on 14 November 2012. Available in Bulgarian in: <https://bcnl.org/uploadfiles/documents/news_docs/2012/proekt_koncepcia.pdf> last visited, December, 2024. See the summary in: Bulgarian Helsinki Committee, Alternative report about the rights of persons with disabilities in Bulgaria under the CRPD, Sofia, 2017, p 30: <https://www.bghelsinki.org/en/news/delayed-reform-and-implementation-rights-persons-disabilities-bulgaria> last visited, December, 2024.

Act.[32] Some NGOs of persons with disabilities started systematic projects to demonstrate the opportunities for supported decision making,[33] to support the capacity building of the state administration[34] and judiciary.[35] The contribution of civil society was recognised by the Government in its Initial report to the Committee on the Rights of Persons with Disabilities.[36] In 2018, the Draft on Persons and Support Measures was submitted again to Parliament but did not reach the voting stage. As a response to the inaction of the deputies, a significant mobilisation took place within civil society. This included a huge advocacy movement, comprising a media campaign, exhibitions, public marches and assemblies.[37]

Other organisations of persons with disabilities, particularly those in receipt of state funding, have not been associated with this debate. For example, organisations of parents/others of children with disabilities pushed for the extension of social support measures but did not engage with the issue of guardianship.[38] This resulted in the adoption in 2018–20 of a package of legislation, including the Persons with Disabilities Act (PDA), the Personal Assistance Act (PAA) and the Social Services Act (SSA). The new legislation aims to implement the principles and major norms of CRPD, such as inclusive services to persons with disabilities based on their individual needs assessment

[32] It was eventually submitted to the Parliament by the Council of Ministers on 4 August 2016 but was stayed. Bill on Persons and Support Measures, available in Bulgarian in: <https://www.parliament.bg/bg/bills/ID/44032> last visited December, 2024.

[33] The plan was to provide evidence from the ground to support the legal reform. The projects involved persons with disabilities living in institutions but also independently, which received professional assistance to establish circles of trustworthy persons that could support them in taking decisions with legal implications: https://bcnl.org/en/projects/advancing-art-12-the-next-step-in-bulgaria-2012-2014 and https://bcnl.org/uploadfiles/documents/osi%20researches/guidelinespolicyresearchscontenteng.pdf last visited December, 2024.

[34] In https://bcnl.org/en/projects/advancing-crpd-article-12-next-step-program-in-bulgaria-2014-2016 Events and materials available in: <http://www.equalrights.bcnl.org/bg/nav/48-%D1%81%D1%8A%D0%B1%D0%B8%D1%82%D0%B8%D1%8F.html> last visited, December, 2024.

[35] Judges were offered study visits to German courts and training to apply individual assessment regarding the social functioning of the person rather than their medical status. The aim was to help judges to move away from the medical assessment and to use available social and family support networks to protect and empower vulnerable adults. A new type of expert emerged in the process – the interpreter for the purpose of supported decision making (SDM). Their task is to assist the court in the interpretation/expression of the individual's will and preferences. Guide for interpreters in: https://bcnl.org/en/analyses/supported-decision-making-theoretical-and-practical-guide-for-interpreters, last visited, January, 2024.

[36] See: CRPD/C/BGR/1, 2014, para 67.

[37] The '7000' initiative was established on 27 March 2018 by a Committee of parents of children with disabilities and took place in 15 cities in Bulgaria where over 20 civil organisations and many advocates, self-advocates and volunteers gathered nearly 12,000 signatures for the abolition of incapacitation and the introduction of supported decision making: https://bcnl.org/trainings/blizo-12-000-choveka-pod krepiha-naczionalna last visited, December, 2024. The '7000' initiative, supported by the Bulgarian Centre for Non-for-Profit Law received the 'Valor of the Year' by the Bulgarian Helsinki Committee:, https://bcnl.org/trainings/priz-doblest-na-godinata-za-naczion, December, 2024.

[38] It was adopted following massive year-long street protests of mothers of children with disabilities: https://www.investor.bg/a/332-ikonomika-i-politika/268644-maykite-na-detsa-s-uvrezhdaniya-gotvyat-novi-efektivni-protesti; https://webcafe.bg/bulgaria/247204238-mayki-na-detsa-s-uvrezhdaniya-otnovo-izlyazoha-na-protest.html last visited December, 2024.

(although with a high value attached to the medical approach), increased public investments in rehabilitation programmes, inclusive education and vocational training, access to the labour market and public spaces, reasonable accommodation and improved mobility as well as targeted financial support.[39] Although these were signs of a break with the purely paternalistic paradigm, the impact of this legislation on paradigm shifting to empowerment of persons with disabilities is difficult to predict since it will be applied together with the regulation on legal incapacitation.[40] The state declared its intention to make policy changes such as deinstitutionalisation of care for the elderly, the development of community-based services, investing in personal assistance and quality of services and care.[41] Although the intention to move from substitute decision making to the personal exercise of rights was mentioned in the strategies, the revision of the legal framework of legal capacity, has been sidelined within this debate along with policies promoting social inclusion and support for persons with disabilities as decisive factors for their independent living.

European Court on Human Rights

The two ECtHR judgments discussed above, *Stanev v Bulgaria* (2012) and *Stankov v Bulgaria* (2015) contributed to some extent to the legal reform. These cases concerned limitation of legal capacity and the subsequent placement of both men in care facilities for adults with mental disabilities without their consent. The ECtHR found that placement in institutional care, against their will and for an unspecified period of time, amounted to deprivation of their liberty in breach of Article 5(1) of the European Convention on Human Rights (ECHR). The Court stated that Mr Stanev's mental health condition that had led directly to the decision to place him in the institution had not been a sufficient justification for deprivation of liberty. Then, the limitation of legal capacity deprived Mr Stanev of legal standing to challenge the lawfulness of his detention, which was a violation of Article 5(4) of the ECHR. The Court also found violations of Articles 3 and 6 of the ECHR.[42] The same violations were found by the ECtHR in the second case.

[39] For the critique of this legislation, see the report of the Bulgarian Centre for Independent Living: Disability and the Social inclusion of Persons with Disabilities, 2021, at: https://cil.bg/wp-content/uploads/2022/07/Analysis-Disability-Act-2020.pdf, last visited, December, 2024.

[40] N Watson and S Vehmas, *Routledge Handbook of Disability Studies* 2nd edn (NY, 2020); Series, L. Chapter 6 Disability and Human Rights.

[41] See National Disability Strategy 2016–2020; National Disability Strategy 2021–2030; National Strategy for Active Ageing (2019–2030), in: Microsoft Word – STRATEGY_03_10_ 2016_FINAL-GM-corrections_04_11_06_11_KK Last.docx and National Strategy on Long-Term Care (2012–2020), available in Bulgarian in: < https://www.mlsp.government.bg/strategicheski-dokumenti> last visited, January, 2024.

[42] The Court further criticised Bulgaria for continuing to maintain a legal framework which denies people with mental disabilities the opportunity to achieve redress for human rights violations by denying them access to court.
Unfortunately, Mr Stanev died on 9 March 2017, without his guardianship being lifted, after 12 years of judicial proceedings and five years after he won his ECHR case.

Following the two judgments, the Social Assistance Act was amended in 2016 to address the arbitrariness and unlawfulness of the deprivation of liberty of incapacitated persons. A court procedure for placement of incapacitated adults in care institutions was instigated, with a duty being placed on the court to respect the will and preferences of the adult.[43] This amendment, however, was assessed as being ineffective in preventing the institutionalisation of incapacitated adults. It is mainly the lack of alternatives for independent living that pushes the courts to decide on placement rather than respecting the right of persons to choose where and with whom they would like to live. This regulation was moved to the new Social Services Act.[44] The court should hear the adult and have their consent for the placement. In 2017, five years after the ECtHR judgments, the Civil Procedure Code was amended also to provide standing to a person with limited legal capacity with a view to seeking its restoration.[45]

CRPD and the Committee on the Rights of Persons with Disabilities

In October 2018, the UN Committee on the Rights of Persons with Disabilities, issued its Concluding observations on the initial report of Bulgaria under the Convention. The Committee explicitly stated that it is concerned that Bulgarian legislation still restricts the legal capacity of persons with disabilities and provides for the guardianship of persons with psychosocial or intellectual disabilities. It is also concerned about the delay in the adoption of the Persons and Support Measures Act, the main purpose of which is to harmonise national legislation with Article 12 of the Convention. The Committee recommended that Bulgaria amend its legislation and adopt the Persons and Support Measures Act, and uphold and recognise the full legal capacity of all persons, regardless of their impairment, in accordance with the guidelines given in general comment No 1 (2014) on equal recognition before the law. It also recommended that, in consultation with organisations of persons with disabilities, Bulgaria should establish support for decision-making procedures and provide continuous training on Article 12 of the Convention to the stakeholders concerned, including members of the judiciary and health-care and social protection professionals.[46] So far no actions have been taken to address these recommendations.

[43] See NGO and DPO Joint Submission, For Consideration at the 20th Session of the UN Committee on the Rights of Persons with Disabilities, to the First Periodic of Bulgaria, Additional Information to the List of Issues.

[44] Articles 95–99.

[45] Article 340, para 2.

[46] Concluding observations on the initial report of Bulgaria, CRPD/C/BGR/CO/1, paras 29–30.

The Academic Debate

Academic circles reacted slowly and cautiously to the challenges posed by CRPD and the General Comment on Article 12. The first ever publication related to the paradigm shift with regard to the legal capacity of persons with disabilities was authored by both NGO activists and academics.[47] The Constitutional Court decision (2014) gave another impetus for academic discussion. The positions were divided between the strong supporters of reforms,[48] vigilant researchers proposing abolition of the full incapacitation only,[49] and the supporters of the status quo.[50] In general the opponent's view reads as 'while dating back to the early 20th century (1907), this Act (Persons and Family Act) is still effective, the case law is not contradictory, and an explicit public need to revise it has not been expressed'.[51] In a recent article Professor Ivan Ruschev, a full member of the Bulgarian Academy of Sciences took the position that no reform is necessary because the so-called new paradigm of Article 12 is mere propaganda for a new approach from protection to empowerment of persons with disabilities.[52] The author considers empowerment as problematic in a case where the person is not able to form a will to act. Another strong view of his is that the call for equality before the law is a meaningless and non-natural call because people are by nature unequal, and the exercise of rights always pre supposes will and its sensible expression. Legal incapacitation, according to the author, is in line with international human rights standards and therefore proportional and acceptable under the law. The exercise of the rights through a competent person is a guarantee for the rights of persons with disabilities.

THE PERSONS AND SUPPORT MEASURES BILL

The Bill on Persons and Support Measures proposed very radical legislative reform: to completely abolish any restriction of the legal capacity of persons

[47] N Shabani, P Alexieva, M Dimitrova, A Genova, V Todorova 'New Formula for Legal Capacity: Article 12 of UN CRPD' (2014) *Pravna Missal*, No 1, 91.

[48] V Todorova, 'The Bulgarian Discussion on Incapacitation between the Constitutional Court Judgment and the Draft on Persons and Support Measures' (2015) *Pravna Missal*, No 2. R Yankulova, 'Rights to Vote and Persons with Intellectual Disabilities and Mental Health Problems' (2016) *Pravna Missal*, No 3 and R Yankulova, 'The Guardianship in the Jurisprudence of the European Constitutional Courts' (2017) *Pravna Missal*, No 3.

[49] S Stavru, Incapacity to Act of Physical Persons. Contemporary Challenges, Sofia, 2016, in: https://bcnl.org/en/analyses/incapacity-to-act-of-natural-persons-contemporary-challenges-sofia-2016-2 and S Stavru, 'Does the Guardianship have an Alternative as Legislative Approach for the Incapacity of Physical Persons' (2018) *Pravna Missal*, No 2.

[50] Tz Tzankova, 'Issues of the Capacity to Act', in *Jubilee Collection Dedicated to the 80th Anniversary of Prof Vasil Mrachkov* (Sofia, 2014), p 205.

[51] Ibid.

[52] I Ruschev, 'The Deprivation of Legal Capacity: Compulsion or Sanction? Scientific Readings on "Law and Coercion"', Sofia University 'St Kl. Ohridski', Sofia, 2023, 91–118.

with psychosocial or intellectual disabilities and uphold and recognise the full legal capacity of all persons, regardless of their impairment.[53] Instead of guardianship and substitute decision making, the Bill introduces a combination of measures for protection and empowerment. Supported decision making is anticipated for all actions implying legal consequences according to personal wishes and preferences. This refers to all personal and life-care decisions, social and health care consent, management of property and financial issues, property transactions, and participation in legal proceedings. Support measures shall not be determined for: contracting a marriage or requesting the dissolution thereof; making a will; or exercising reproductive rights. Those rights shall be exercised independently after providing the person with appropriate consultation. The Bill also introduces a lasting power of attorney and advance medical directives – neither of which have yet been legalised in Bulgaria.

The Bill stipulates for a right to supported decision making to any adult who, as a result of intellectual impairment, mental disorder or dementia, has serious difficulties exercising their rights independently in carrying out specific legal actions. The key concept here is not the disability per se, but the serious problem in exercising rights where there could be a difficulty in understanding the information on which the decision to carry out a specific legal action is based, or a difficulty in assessing the nature and the consequences of the potential decision on the specific legal action or inability to relate the information to the assessment in the process of making a specific decision.

The Bill explicitly excludes from the concept of 'serious difficulties' the inability of the person to independently express their will and preferences through the generally accepted means of communication, if that person uses ways and means appropriate to their state, including non-verbal communication forms, visual presentation, etc. Therefore the Bill explicitly prescribes that such communication difficulties shall not serve as grounds for determining support measures but rather as grounds for providing the person with such reasonable assistance as will allow them to understand others and be adequately understood, without the disability hindering the independent enjoyment of their rights.

The Bill defines the supported decision making as a support measure whereby the supporting person, approved by the court shall, under the conditions of a trusted relationship, assist the supported person in carrying out specific legal actions. A trusted relationship excludes relations of undue influence, violence, or abuse by the supporting person. The quality of the trusted relationship is assessed by the court which also rules on the support measures with various degrees of intensity. The supporting person is obliged to perform their obligations in person, which may include: (1) providing assistance by explaining in an accessible way the information needed to make the decision, and providing

[53] More about the Bill, in N Shabani, M and Dimitrova, 'Changing the Paradigm of Substitut ed Decision-making in Bulgaria: The Tipping Point', in M Bach and N Espejo-Yaksic (eds), *Legal Capacity, Disability and Human Rights* (Intersentia, 2023).

assistance with consultations with specialists, meetings and communication with persons affected by the decision, and other persons; (2) providing assistance with receiving in an accessible format any information, consultations and documents needed to make the decision; (3) providing help with clarifying the supported person's wishes and preferences, and with formulating and expressing the decision; (4) taking care of the correct and precise implementation of the supported person's decision; (5) informing the persons affected by the legal action that it is carried out via supported decision making. The leading principle in applying the measures is exhaustiveness: the first step is to provide support measures, and, if they do not produce any effect and there is a specific risk, the next step may be protection measures.

A specific feature of the Bulgarian understanding of supported decision making is the use of the concept of 'wishes and preferences', instead of the concept of 'will'. According to the legal preferences doctrine, will is mainly inherent to a rational person. A cognitive deficit results, respectively, also in deficiencies of will. In order to break out of this paradigm, the Bill refers to 'wishes and preferences' in the decision-making process. The purpose of the support in each individual case will be to reveal the wishes and preferences of the supported person, or to create conditions for these wishes and preferences to be manifested or interpreted to the fullest possible extent.

Supported decision making shall always be based on the personal choice of the supported person and shall be applied only within the time limit and for the legal actions determined in the court judgment. The support measures are: (1) a contract on supported decision making approved by the court; (2) co-decision making; (3) self prohibitions for disposition with certain amounts and specific property; and (4) approval of an advance directive. Another key concept of the Bill is the fiduciary relationship. This is defined as a relationship between a supporting person and a supported person which is recognised by each of them and has a lasting nature. A common feature of all forms of supported decision making is the new value focus – they must always be based on, and take into consideration, the person's wishes and preferences. Empowering the person and ensuring their independence contributes to substituting the now existing legal concept of the best interest of people with disabilities with the concept of the best interpretation of the will of the person.

The Bill pays particular attention to safeguarding the rights of persons with disabilities. An important safeguard is the key role assigned to the court in the approval and monitoring of the protection measures. The court will always examine the request in the presence of the adult who is in need of support, and should apply a functional test. It aims to establish the stage in the decision-making process at which the deficit occurs, and the external conditions needed to make up for this deficit in such a way as to allow the person to independently enjoy their rights. Applying the test does not result in restricting rights, but in providing grounds for the determination of a support measure. When the request is granted, the court should: designate the supported person and the supporting person; determine the support measure and the content of the supporting person's obligations; specify the legal actions in need of support; as well as the property and the persons entrusted therewith when the legal actions pertain to the disposition and management of the property; and determine the time limit of the measure, which shall not exceed two years. The court has also the power to determine protection measures in case the support measure cannot meet the need of the supported person, for example if there is a risk of serious damage to health, or of a direct and considerable loss of property. The protection measure is a temporary prohibition on carrying out a disposition or action, or is the choice of an option for action affecting the person's health or his/her property.

The Bill provides for other safeguards such as a wide range of people entitled to request[54] a measure and its review; regulated duties of supporters; third-party attestation to support relationships; additional safeguards for some measures (eg co-decision making and self-restriction can be initiated only by the person concerned).

Safeguards are also provided for the interests of third parties, including a regime of registration of the supported decision-making arrangements. The mayor of the municipality is designated as the supported decision-making body with registration and oversight responsibilities. The mayor should register the court decision and the persons in respect of whom support and protection measures have been determined in the population register, draw up reports on the implementation of the support and protection measures when requested by the court, and may request determination of new measures when existing measures are terminated due to incompatibility.

POSSIBLE REASONS FOR THE STALLED REFORM

When analysing the factors that have contributed to the stagnation of the reform on guardianship, it is necessary to start with the overall deterioration of the political and democratic context in Bulgaria after 2017. The enormous wave of nationalistic and populist discourse has watered down the weak liberal and democratic thinking and practices in the country. Academic debate stayed with the old paradigm that favoured the protection aspect. In turn, this weakened the ability of the state to lead any positive change in public opinion. There then followed the COVID-19 lockdowns, followed by political instability which has continued up to the present.

Despite significant social mobilisation, the legal reform related to incapacitation and guardianship was opposed by the conservative attitudes of decision

[54] Determination of any support measure could be requested by the person in need of support or by a parent, spouse, siblings, a close trustworthy person, by the supported decision-making body or by the prosecutor.

makers and academia. The lack of research on human rights issues should also be mentioned as a reason for the vague debate and denial of support from academia. Human rights activism was not sufficient to overcome the high levels of stigma towards persons with mental disabilities shared even by intellectuals, MPs, judges and academics. The Bill was very progressive for such an environment and provoked fear, uncertainty and the usual reflex as something imposed from the outside that threatens the established order.

Another significant reason is the lack of adequate care and support systems for vulnerable adults. Such systems started to develop only along with attempts at legal reform, ECtHR judgments and on the model of the child protection system. Poverty, difficulty in accessing common services such as healthcare and education, as well as the lack of a supportive environment did not encourage persons with disabilities or their families to trust the concept of empowerment. The attitudinal research of 2016 aids an understanding of this position. The research suggested the existence in Bulgaria:

> . . . of hidden and overt, power and economic interests, pushed in the form of policies to maintain the status quo – ie passive and disempowered people with disabilities, deprived of freedom and dignity. This leads to measures based on control and dependency formation; activities aimed more at primary care and less at support to overcome the limitations associated with disability. Unfortunately, similar attitudes exist among relatives of people with disabilities, whose expectations of them and their standards of freedom and dignity are far lower than those of their non-disabled relatives. Thus the social attitudes and those in the immediate environment logically lead to people with disabilities accepting life without freedom and dignity as the natural state of the world in which they live.[55]

In such a context the efforts of civil society to focus on empowering close communities of persons with disabilities to seek reforms failed, with a complete lack of state support.[56]

The several years of strong civic and political activism have not resulted in reform of legal capacity but still managed to create some understanding within society about the issues around persons with disabilities. The top three priorities that public opinion considers for civil society organisations arising from a sociological survey focus on achieving greater independence and social inclusion of people with disabilities in terms of: (1) supporting people with disabilities to better integrate into society (ie employment, social contacts, participation in cultural and social events, etc); (2) fighting for more rights for people with

[55] K Panayotova and R Petrov, Living at will or by someone else's will! Advocacy for the human rights of people with disabilities, Sofia, 2016 available in Bulgarian in: <https://cil.bg/wp-content/uploads/2020/03/Report-General-Final.pdf> last visited, December, 2024.

[56] More about the empowerment of parents' groups of children with intellectual disabilities in: N Shabani and M Dimitrova, 'Changing the Paradigm of Substituted Decision-making in Bulgaria: The Tipping Point', in M Bach, and N Espejo-Yaksic (eds), *Legal Capacity, Disability and Human Rights* (Intersentia, 2023).

disabilities (ie job opportunities, education, travel benefits, etc); and (3) developing social services to support people with disabilities.[57] In spite of this, there is still a significant difference in understanding of the provision of care for children on the one hand, and for adults on the other. The support for family care for people with mental disabilities as adults is 30 points lower than for family care in relation to children. At the same time, thanks to the evolution of public attitudes, supporters and opponents of family care are almost equal (34.9% : 36.6%), whereas three years previously there was 10 per cent more opposition (41% : 31.6%).[58]

The same research also reveals slight changes in people's values. Although traditional values (health, family, children) continue to be an absolute priority for the majority (between 67 and 80 per cent) there is also a growth in modern values (ie right to privacy, freedom, personal dignity, the right to property, work, profession, freedom of movement). In all of these, the increase in four years is about 5 percentage points. The passage of time may well lead to the formation of empowered peoples and communities who will demand reforms.

[57] Sociological survey on public attitudes to civil society organisations, held in 2018 and 2022 by Alpha research, available in: https://bcnl.org/uploadfiles/documents/0922_GO_Report(2).pdf last visited January, 2025, 15–17.

[58] Ibid.

8

Adolescents and their Right to Access to Justice: The Case of Adolescents in Care Homes in Buenos Aires, Argentina

JULIETA MAROTTA AND LAURA LORA[1]

INTRODUCTION

THE INTERNATIONAL COMMUNITY, by means of the adoption of the Convention on the Rights of the Child (hereinafter, CRC), recognised in 1989 that adolescents are agents capable of holding rights (Committee on the Rights of the Children, 2012, 2009; UN General Assembly, 1989). Since then, national systems have adjusted to materialise this recognition in law and practice. Adolescents are holders of rights, and as such, the state must guarantee their access to justice by implementing specialised legal frameworks, providing trained professionals, and ensuring adolescent-friendly procedures that prioritise their evolving capacities and best interests. International and domestic law recognises that the form in which adolescents can obtain access to justice is defined by the chance that they are given to participate in the process and to be heard and have their opinions taken into consideration given their evolving capacity, according to age and degree of maturity. The best interest of the child, applicable to adolescents, is a principle that defines access to justice for that group as it considers that any decision taken when there is an adolescent

[1] The authors thank the Children's Rights research grant, which made their fieldwork activities possible (https://childrensrightsresearch.com/fund/grants), and Carla Virginia Gutierrez for her research assistance during fieldwork. The authors also thank members of the Proyecto UBACyT Derecho y Sociedad. Teoria y prácticas para el abordaje de los conflictos transversales a la niñez, Instituto de Investigaciones Jurídicas y Sociales Ambrosio L Gioja, Facultad de Derecho, UBA for their feedback on the research design. The authors are grateful to our gatekeepers who gave us access to the care homes, to the directors of the care homes who gave us access to the adolescents, and to all the adolescents who participated in this study.

involved needs to consider their best interest. In addition, to secure the right to access to justice during the legal process, adolescents need to have access to a specialised lawyer who can represent their rights (a procedural guarantee), and specialised judges who know how to secure their rights to be heard and participate given their evolving capacity and best interest.

This chapter is based on a study that explores how adolescents in care homes understand access to justice. It uses the family justice system in both the city and province of Buenos Aires, Argentina (hereinafter, Buenos Aires) as a case study. First, this chapter presents the legal framework for access to justice for adolescents in Buenos Aires. Secondly, it uses an inductive approach to explore how adolescents position the law and the justice system as factors that influence their reality. Participatory methods were used to allow adolescents to express their relation to the justice system. Three care homes in which adolescents were placed because of abuse or abandonment were each visited three times: in September 2023, in December 2023, and in January 2024. Finally, the chapter presents the main findings and concluding remarks.

Access to justice is viewed comprehensively by legal provisions, not limited to access to courts, which strengthens the possibilities and freedoms of individuals. This broadens the traditional notion of merely accessing courts and due process and acknowledges various mechanisms for delivering justice, highlighting the importance of all actors involved in the pursuit of justice (Marotta, 2017). The rights of vulnerable groups to access justice are explicitly recognised in tailor-made provisions, with strategies introduced to ease their access. Improvements in accessibility are largely seen in terms of location and cost, and the way vulnerable groups are included in legal processes. Working with a comprehensive understanding of access to justice means that people need to be able to understand the law, to have an effective system of administration of justice, and to be assisted by trained justice providers. People's awareness or understanding of the law is directly related to their possibility to participate in the legal process (Van De Meene and Van Rooij, 2008; Marotta, 2017).

Judicial cases that involve adolescents demand a particular response to ensure that access to justice is properly adjusted to the characteristics of the population (Bruce et al, 2007, 12, 14–16, 19, 35; Commission on Legal Empowerment of the Poor, 2008, 43; Gramatikov and Porter, 2010, 26–27; Van De Meene and Van Rooij, 2008, 6–8). The concept of access to justice for adolescents gained international attention (Liefaard, 2019), which was later reflected in some domestic laws, such as those in Buenos Aires, that recognise the need to have specific considerations for adolescents and enact tailor-made legal provisions. Access to justice for adolescents implies recognising them as subjects of rights and as procedural subjects, with a right to be heard. The exercise of the right to be heard by adolescents is by definition a guarantee of their access to justice, for the respect and realisation of all their human rights (Lora and Medina, 2025). Access to justice is a 'fundamental right to an effective remedy and revolves around the right of children [and adolescents] to seek remedies in case of (alleged) rights violations' (Liefaard, 2019, 196). Access to justice is directly linked to the possibility of adolescents obtaining a judicial or administrative remedy, providing a response that considers the adolescent in a holistic way (Liefaard, 2019). The possibility of adolescents understanding their rights is essential to overcome a barrier to access to justice (Liefaard, 2019). As with any other group, rights awareness is usually a prerequisite to access to justice, and hence, the importance of being aware of the law as a tool to empower groups to exercise their rights and overcome conflicts (Marotta, 2017). As stated by Lieffard referring to the UN High Commissioner and the CRC Committee, 'the significance of child-sensitive procedures and the legal empowerment of "all" children, . . . encompasses access to "legal and other services, child rights education, counselling or advice, and support from knowledgeable adults"' (2019, 204). Parents and other legal representatives are essential actors in allowing access to justice for adolescents, given their best interest and evolving capacity.

In Buenos Aires, the narrow approach of the Argentinian Constitution to the right to access to justice is broadened by the international duties that require the delivery of tangible ways for adolescents to seek justice. The influence of human rights treaties can be perceived by looking at how federal legal provisions address the right to access to justice for adolescents, which broadens the approach by following international standards (Marotta and Parise, 2014). The Civil and Commercial Code of Argentina upholds the principle of equality by recognising human diversity and incorporates general guidelines for family law procedures. Article 706, the key provision in this section, states:

> The process in family matters should respect the principles of effective judicial protection, immediacy, good faith and procedural fairness, officiousness, oral proceeding, and limited access [only for parties] to the file. The rules governing the procedure must be applied to facilitate access to justice, especially for vulnerable groups, and to achieve peaceful resolution of conflicts. Judges before whom these cases must be filed away should be specialized and obtain multidisciplinary support.

Access to justice is the right to seek and be granted justice (Macdonald, Roderick A, 2010). It is a fundamental right, since it is the vehicle through which other rights are conveyed (Lorenzetti, 2008). Access to justice can be secured when adolescents are informed of their rights; are heard and participate in the legal process, given their evolving capacity; are represented by a specialised lawyer and are heard by a specialised judge; and are able to secure that their best interest prevails in all instances.

The right to be heard and participate in the legal process is a fundamental aspect of sustainable conflict resolution, every time active participation in a conflict derives from an active relationship and reflection on what caused the conflict and how it might be overcome. This right is recognised in Article 12 of the CRC, which influenced family justice systems around the world, including that in Buenos Aires. In addition, family justice systems benefitted from the presence of psychologists, who provided scientific and expert tools and explanations on attitudes and behaviours of adolescents within decision making (Taylor and Gollop, 2015). As such, several systems introduced instances to foster communication and participation, such as mediation techniques and interdisciplinary groups (Marotta, 2023, 2022; Taylor and Gollop, 2015). The capacity of adolescents to express themselves has been underestimated, however, since they are still the people who know most about their own lives (Peleg, 2013). Moreover, the views of adolescents on their own lives cannot 'simply be guessed by adults', since they do have the capacity to identify problems and think of solutions (Lansdown, 2006). The environments and practices that enable adolescents to express and participate are essential and require the expertise of the adult (Taliercio, 2022). For example, it is the responsibility of a family judge to help make the adolescent visible during the legal process. Consequently, and as mentioned by Peleg, 'children's [and adolescents'] ability to express their views and preferences is not necessarily a matter of age, but of space and willingness of adults to listen to them as well' (Peleg, 2013, 528). The direction that adults give to adolescents needs to be in line with the ability of adolescents to participate, depending on capabilities at a given time and context. This concept understands that adolescents' exercise of the right to participate in the family legal process is progressive and it is linked to their capacities (Esteban, 2022). Hence, evolving capacity is a dynamic concept that needs to be assessed several times during the family legal process in which the adolescent is involved.

The best interest of the child prevails over that of adults and guides all other rights. The best interest of the child is recognised in Article 3 of the CRC, which states that 'in all actions concerning children, whether undertaken by public or private social welfare institutions, courts of law, administrative authorities or legislative bodies, the best interest of the child shall be a primary consideration'. General Comment 14 of 2013 of the CRC Committee addresses this principle. The best interest of the child is a principle, a guarantee, and a substantive right, which needs to be assessed on a case-by-case basis, considering the adolescent holistically. That holistic approach is linked to the psychological, educational, social, legal, environmental and economic resources of the adolescent (Lora, 2006). Medina points out that life still takes place in a culture that does not prioritise the best interest of the child and that the state does not have a genuine understanding of what it entails, which results in a lack of training of justice providers and appropriate monitoring mechanisms (2024). Moreover, lawyers, public defenders, and family judges need to support adolescents in their evolving capacity whenever they have the right to legal representation to secure their access to justice as a subject of rights.

Protecting the best interest of the child, the CRC mentions that adolescents can be temporarily or permanently removed from their families to protect them from being subject to abuse and/or neglect (Article 20). UNICEF reported that 59 per cent of children in Argentina (aged 1–14 years) experienced physical punishment and/or psychological aggression by caregivers (UNICEF DATA, 2022). In 2021, 5 per cent of adolescents in the city of Buenos Aires lived in care homes

(Consejo de los Derechos de Niñas, Niños y Adolescentes, 2021). These adolescents are displaced from their families because their rights have been violated, in most cases as victims of abuse and neglect. The lives of such adolescents are left to the capacity of the state to support them and their families to re-establish a healthy family environment, or to find a healthy alternative for the adolescents where they can enjoy their lives free of violence. Crespo highlights a concern regarding the number of cases of adolescents who, having experienced abuse and neglect, turned out to be automatically medicalised, resulting in an abuse of medication (2024). He argues that, in many cases, medication could be replaced with a proper interdisciplinary approach to the problem.

METHODOLOGY

The research question guiding the study on which this chapter is based is: *How do adolescents in care homes understand access to justice?* To address this question, the researchers employed a two-part approach. First, the study analysed the legal framework to consider the law as a tool determining social conduct. Second, it adopted participatory methods to explore how adolescents experienced their access to justice.

Legal Framework Analysis

The legal framework analysis focused on key documents applicable in Buenos Aires to assess how legislation addresses the fundamental pillars of the right of adolescents to access to justice. These pillars include their rights to be heard and participate in the legal process, given their evolving capacity; their right to be represented by a specialised lawyer and heard by a specialised judge; and their right to have their best interest secured in all instances. The selected legal documents were:

- Convention on the Rights of the Child;
- General Comments 4, 7, 8, 12, 14, 20 of the CRC;
- Federal Law 26061 of 2005: Law for the Integral Protection of the Rights of Children and Adolescents;
- Civil and Commercial Code of Argentina of 2015.

Participatory Methods

A sociolegal approach incorporating participatory methods was used to understand adolescents' life experiences and perceptions of access to justice (Sevón et al, 2023, 1–7). Participatory methods allowed for the use of the artwork technique, which provided insights into aspects of the experiences and perceptions of adolescents that might not be readily expressed in words (Mulcahy, 2020, 204). Data collection involved visual and linguistic methods, including artistic expressions, in-depth interviews, performance and workshops. These methods provided a space for adolescents to express their experiences and feelings within the care homes.

Data analysis was conducted using Atlas.ti. The coding was based on the core elements of access to justice for adolescents: the right to be heard and participate in the legal process, given their evolving capacity; the right to be represented by a specialised lawyer and to be heard by a specialised judge; and the right to have their best interest secured.

Fieldwork Activities

Fieldwork was conducted in three care homes for adolescents displaced due to abuse or abandonment. The visits occurred in September 2023, December 2023, and January 2024.

Visit 1: Introduction and Artistic Expression

During the first visits, the research team explained the project to adolescents and obtained their consent to participate.[2] Participants completed a socio-demographic questionnaire and were asked to create an artistic expression reflecting their experiences since entering the care home. Adolescents chose their preferred medium – painting, writing, or performance – and were provided with materials to complete their chosen form of expression. These creations offered insights into how adolescents perceive the law, moving beyond traditional legal symbols to more personalised representations (Mulcahy, 2020, 209). They allowed a space for adolescents to express their feelings, emotions and experiences.

Following the creative exercise, semi-structured interviews explored their artistic expressions, personal journeys to justice, recommendations for others in similar situations, and conceptual understandings of key terms such as 'access to justice', 'right to be heard', and 'best interest of the child'.[3]

Visit 2: Playwriting and Performance

The second visit began with interviews with care home directors to contextualise the adolescents' situations and gain insight into their experiences with justice.

[2] The design of the study was revised and approved by the Ethics Committee at Maastricht University.

[3] This part of the interview took place by the end, and we asked them: 'If I say to you "access to justice" you tell me . . .' We explained that we were not looking for right answers, just to know what came to their minds when they listened to these words.

Adolescents then participated in a collaborative playwriting exercise. Groups of up to five adolescents wrote and performed a play titled '*Who Hears Me?*' The play comprised four scenes: (1) who heard them before entering the care home; (2) who heard them upon arrival; (3) who hears them now; and (4) who they would like to be heard by.

Performances took place in a theatre setting, except for one group that performed on an improvised outdoor stage at the care home. The activity was well-received, since it enabled them to foster creativity and joy, and to engage through music and costumes.[4]

Visit 3: Workshops and Capacity Building

The third visit involved workshops at the Faculty of Law, University of Buenos Aires. Participants attended sessions led by a painter and a creative writer to expand on their initial artistic expressions with professional guidance. Additionally, a workshop on the CRC, with a focus on the best interest of the child was offered to address gaps identified during earlier visits regarding adolescents' understanding of their rights. A visual summary of the fieldwork activities is available on YouTube.

Validation Process

As part of the validation process, several participants were invited to join the research team voluntarily during different events, in different parts of the globe, where findings were presented. For example, participants joined the research team during an international conference where preliminary findings were presented in Buenos Aires, and participants shared their reflections on the exercises done as part of the methodology in the panel[5] (III Congreso Federal, Internacional e Interdisciplinario. DD.HH. para la niñez y la adolescencia, 2024; Lora and Marotta, Forthcoming). In addition, a care home director and a family judge participated in an online conference on the right to be heard in Maastricht, the Netherlands, where preliminary results were discussed.

Sample Composition

The sample is composed of 38 female adolescents, mostly aged 13 to 18 with the exception of two participants who were 12 and 21. These two participants were included in the sample even when they would not be categorised as adolescents

[4] Some of the music selected was: *Si no estas* by Inigo Quintero, *Ojitos verdes* by Pauline Reese, *Yo te extrañaré* by Tercer Cielo.

[5] The panel where the adolescents participated is available on YouTube.

by Argentinian law, and the insights were useful for this study. The adolescents were living in one of the three care homes that were visited by the research team. Two care homes were in the Province (50 per cent and 24 per cent) and the third in the City (26 per cent). Most of the participants were born in Argentina (52 per cent), while 2.6 per cent were born either in Bolivia or Paraguay, and 18 per cent reported not knowing in which country they were born. Most participants reported going to school (81 per cent) and most of them were between second and fourth grade in secondary school (out of six grades). Almost 20 per cent reported being employed, and 60 per cent mentioned a career or profession they wanted to pursue after finishing school (eg medical doctor, photographer, lawyer, psychologist, cook, singer).

THE LEGAL FRAMEWORK

The Argentinian legal framework for protecting adolescents' right to access justice is influenced by the CRC. This convention changed the way adolescents are viewed within the justice system and recognised them as individuals capable of holding rights, shifting the paradigm from passive subjects to active holders of rights. In essence, the CRC changed how states interact with people under 18 years of age and included further stakeholders in the legal processes that involve adolescents. The Civil and Commercial Code of Argentina also introduces the category of adolescents and establishes that those who are below 18 years of age are minors, and those from 13 to 18 are adolescents. The notion of adolescent replaces the previous classification of pubertal minors and adult minors. Article 26 refers to the exercise of rights by minors (Medina, 2021).

The CRC ensures the right of the child to be heard and participate in decisions that affect their lives given their evolving capacity and best interests (articles 3, 5, 12). Moreover, the Third Optional Protocol to the CRC allows adolescents directly to submit complaints to the CRC Committee, thus reinforcing their access to justice on an international level. General Comment 12 of the CRC stipulates that the expression 'who is in a position to form his or her judgment' (article 12) should not be seen as a limitation but as an obligation for states to evaluate the ability of adolescents to form an autonomous opinion to the greatest extent possible. The CRC Committee highlighted the need to incorporate non-verbal ways of communication, like games, drawings, and pictures (Taliercio, 2022). In this sense, the right of adolescents to express their opinions requires that those responsible for listening and the parents or guardians inform adolescents of the issues, options, and possible decisions to be adopted, along with their consequences. Listening to adolescents means discovering the authenticity of their opinions (Taliercio, 2022). There are different opinions about the fact that adolescents need to be heard at court, or that judges or court staff need to go to the location where the adolescents are. Adolescents need to have the capacity to be aware of conflict and be supported to express their desires and needs (Taliercio, 2022). The interdisciplinary approach to secure the right to be heard is indeed essential.

Federal Law 26061 consolidates the rights of adolescents in Argentina by explicitly recognising adolescents as subjects of rights (Congreso de la Nación Argentina, 2005). The Civil and Commercial Code of Argentina defines the best interest of the child as a primary consideration, in line with Article 3 of the CRC, and adopts an evolving capacity approach to the right to be heard and to participate. It also notes that while the legal age of majority is 18, there is a need for flexibility in the light of the evolving capacity of the person. The comprehensive approach to the protection of this age group, introduced by Federal Law 26061, involves public and private actors working together to guarantee the rights of adolescents (article 32).

Administrative bodies, such as the regional ombudsmen or local services, may determine the need to adopt an exceptional measure once the comprehensive protection measures of the law have been exhausted because the adolescents are temporarily or permanently deprived of their family environment or because their best interest requires that they cannot remain in such an environment (article 39) (Lora and Medina, 2025). In addition, Federal Law 26061 guarantees adolescents the right to a lawyer to defend their rights in court (article 27). The law mentions that adolescents have the right to a pro bono attorney if they cannot afford one. It is argued that legal representation for adolescents must always be pro bono, as they do not have access to financial resources (Taliercio, 2022). Hence, adolescents have a right to a specialist lawyer, paid by the state and who does not fall within the sphere of influence of any of the parents of the adolescents, regardless of age.

The local authority where the application is made decides and establishes the procedure to be followed once the exceptional measure is declared admissible. The procedure to follow must be legally founded, and the measure adopted must be notified within 24 hours to the competent judicial authority in family matters. That competent authority, within 72 hours of notification, with the summons and hearing of the legal representatives, must resolve the legality of the measure. Once resolved, the competent judicial authority refers the case to the competent local enforcement authority to implement the pertinent measure (Lora and Medina, 2025).

The measures shall be applied by considering the opinion of the adolescents, the continuity of education, and their ethnic, religious, cultural, and linguistic origin. One measure is a temporary stay with someone from their family environment (someone related to the relevant adolescents, through blood or affinity lines of kinship, or other members of the extended family or the community, according to local custom). Another measure – only granted exceptionally, and for the shortest possible period – is an alternative form of cohabitation (such as a care home) to that of their family group. The return of the adolescents to their family and community group or environment should be promoted through rapid and flexible mechanisms. These measures shall be implemented under forms of intervention that do not replace the family group of origin, and that preserve the family identity of adolescents. Moreover, measures must consider groups of siblings who must retain their cohabitation. These measures shall be supervised by the competent local administrative and judicial body involved.

The Civil and Commercial Code of Argentina incorporates international principles to which the Argentinian state adhered in 1994 when several international human rights treaties were given constitutional standing (Medina, 2021). As such, the code reinforces adolescents' rights to participate in legal processes, particularly in family matters, and establishes that the best interest of the child must be of primary consideration (Congreso de la Nación Argentina, 2014). Several articles of the Civil and Commercial Code of Argentina provide for the participation of adolescents (eg articles 26 and 595).

This code also introduces the concept of evolving capacity (progressive autonomy), acknowledging that adolescents' capacity to exercise their rights increases with age and maturity, and 'those who count with age and sufficient maturity can exercise by themselves certain acts allowed by law'. With the inclusion of the figure of the adolescent and evolving capacity, the code allows for other laws to rule on the evolving capacity of the child. For example, the law on the rights of the patient allows children aged 13 to 16 to make non-invasive decisions over their bodies (Lorenzetti et al, 2012). The code establishes that every human being has the capacity to be holders of rights and duties (article 22) and adds that the law may deprive or limit this capacity with respect to simple acts or determined juridical acts (article 23). Article 24 explicitly limits that capacity to three groups, (a) the unborn person, (b) the person who is not of sufficient age and degree of maturity, and (c) the person declared incapable by a judicial sentence.

The code also addresses the right of the adolescent to be heard and participate in the decisions that affect their person during the entire family legal process. Article 706 of the code emphasises that procedural rules should facilitate access to justice for vulnerable groups and promote peaceful conflict resolution. Hence, 'the rules governing the procedure must be applied to facilitate access to justice, especially for vulnerable people, and to achieve peaceful resolution of conflicts. Judges should be specialised and have multidisciplinary support' (Marotta & Parise, 2014).

When an adolescent is placed in a care home, the family court must control the legality of the placement, make decisions on the alternatives available for the adolescent, and work with the local service (an office that assists in the implementation of measures). These decisions must be made within 90 days of the time that the adolescent is placed in a care home, or renewed for another 90 days (Executive Order 3415/06). The public defender presents the plan to leave the care home, which might be due to a request for adoption, an exit strategy when they find a family member who can take care of the adolescents, or adolescents reach the legal age of majority. The judge signs the final judgment. The public prosecutor intervenes in cases when there is a complaint about whereabouts or sexual abuse.

In cases of adoption, the code stipulates that adolescents must give their consent from the age of 10 and, if the adopter has descendants, they must be heard by the judge and their opinion must be valued according to their age and degree of maturity. Article 617 lays down the rules of procedure in adoption proceedings, according to which (i) the prospective adopter is a party to the proceedings and, if of sufficient age and maturity, must appear with legal assistance; and (ii) the judge must personally hear the prospective adopter and take his or her opinion into account according to his or her age and maturity. In addition, article 655 establishes that the parents must ensure the adolescents' participation in the education plan and its modifications; while article 707 establishes as a rule of family proceedings that adolescents have the right to be heard in all proceedings that directly concern them. The opinion of adolescents must be considered and valued according to their level of understanding and the subject matter of the proceedings. Article 707 must be applied in harmony with the provisions of article 26, which states that adolescents have the right to be heard in all legal proceedings and to participate in decisions concerning them.

THE PERCEPTIONS OF ADOLESCENTS

Despite the advances in the legal framework, the practical application of adolescents' rights to access to justice remains challenging. A family judge was interviewed in 2023 and stated that 'the [CRC] Convention is amazing, but in the application, it is very difficult. Understanding the child as a subject of rights is not easy; traditionally, children were always seen from above.'

Path to Justice

Hospitals and schools were the main referral points to the justice system, followed by non-family members such as extended family, friends, community members, or individuals from church communities. In some cases, adolescents themselves reached out for help and were referred to care homes. In other cases, they were sent to care homes without explanation, creating further stress. As recounted by a participant:

> We were in the local service and my mother went upstairs. When . . . they gave us a check-up, you saw that the doctor checked us, I don't know, they gave us a check-up, and they bought us a little ice cream, which was a joke, that little ice cream, I remember, and it was really bad. And when we were going towards the door because they told us we had to leave, I asked him for my mother, and he didn't answer. Then we were about to get into the van, and they told us 'no, she's going somewhere else', and they put my two little brothers in another van and me in another one . . . and that was the part that hurt me (A030).

Family members, school personnel, or sometimes nobody at all were mentioned as having listened to the adolescents before entering care homes. Listening often involved asking about their well-being or offering acts of care, such as hugs or reassuring advice ('things will be better'). While at care homes, adolescents felt heard by directors, 'aunts', and some family members. However, many adolescents expressed the view that those who listened were not always the people they would have chosen to be heard by, such as biological family or the care home director.

Modes of Expression

Adolescents preferred to express themselves through drawings, performance, or writing.[6] These were the means they selected when asked to share their experiences during their initial stay at the care home. These means of expression suggest potential ways to involve adolescents in exercising their right to be heard and participating in legal processes.

Six drawings included hearts – either whole or broken – accompanied by text. Another six depicted people, with half of these representing groups (family or care home peers). These expressions reflected a range of emotions, including:

- shame
- contradictory feelings (eg sadness and liberation)
- desire to be loved
- anxiety, stress, and depression.

Contradictory feelings were often expressed by participants. For example, participants manifested feelings of being sad and liberated; having good and bad moments with parents; and being enthusiastic about freedom and fearing bad experiences happening again.

Some adolescents expressed assimilation to being a 'bad person', but being able to learn how to improve. Activities like practising sports or going on trips provided positive feelings. Adolescents' expressions demonstrated ongoing struggles with their past, fears for the future, and a longing for stable, loving relationships.

Institutions and Individuals Listening

Adolescents mentioned schools, hospitals, and police stations as places where they were heard regarding abuse and/or neglect. Specific participants included

[6] A total of 23 adolescents (out of a sample of 38) participated in this exercise, of which 13 drew; 5 wrote either a story about their experience, lyrics of a song, a diary of their week; 5 performed and expressed their experience, either with a custom or through an activity such as cooking, doing the hair of a mannequin.

teachers, 'aunts', or community members who helped them on the streets. Means of expression included sessions in a Gesell dome or writing about their future aspirations. However, no adolescents mentioned being heard by anyone from the justice system or care homes, apart from during adoption processes for justice representatives, and one care home director who was particularly praised for being present and listening to adolescents. Contact with justice system representatives, such as judges, public defenders, or specialised lawyers, was minimal and often limited to one or two interactions.

Care homes elicited mixed feelings. For some participants, care homes became 'home' or 'family', while for others they were seen as disruptive environments due to the prevalence of psychological crises. Adolescents appreciated expressions of care through clear rules, active listening, and shared activities. However, they disliked being forced into undesired activities or denied preferred ones without explanation.

Rights Awareness

Adolescents demonstrated limited understanding of their rights. In addition, through the coding of word frequency, it could be observed that words related to rights and the justice system are peripheral and hence, mentioned less frequently (see Figure 8.1 below, in Spanish).

When asked about terms like 'access to justice', 'right to be heard', 'right to participate', and 'best interest of the child', the responses of adolescents were superficial. Adolescents often viewed themselves as passive holders of rights, rather than active participants. For many participants, access to justice was perceived as the involvement of an authority figure (eg a judge or lawyer) doing something on their behalf.

The right to be heard was more familiar for adolescents, being associated with:

- doing what adolescents want;
- getting help;
- trusting someone to listen empathetically and act.

The right to participate was linked to inclusion, sharing moments with peers, and expressing opinions. The concept of 'best interest of the child' was least understood, though some adolescents associated it with being protected, cared for, or free from harm. Adolescents who mentioned anything relating to the right to be heard, related it to being cared for, being protected, to not be harmed, to be guided, to not be subjected to violence, to be able to overcome, and to be free. After this experience, the research team offered a one-hour workshop on the meaning of the best interest of the child. After this workshop, adolescents were asked to express in writing what they now knew, and they did indeed show a basic understanding. Other rights mentioned by adolescents were the right to

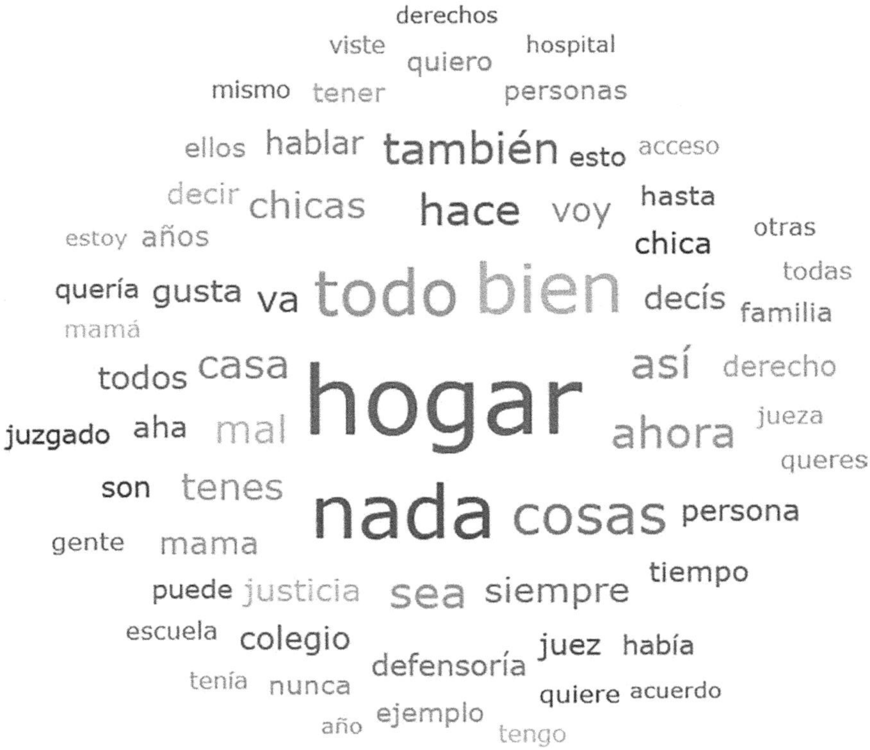

Figure 8.1 Word frequency

go to school, the right to die, the right to be loved, the right to a family, and the right to employment.

Relation with the Justice System

Artistic expressions rarely reflected a relationship with the justice system. In follow-up interviews, few adolescents recalled meeting judges or lawyers, and those who did often could not remember details. Adolescents struggled to understand the purpose of the justice system and their role within it (eg 'I met the judge a couple of times via Zoom' (A002)). Two adolescents mentioned specific techniques proposed by the justice system that were meant to allow them to express themselves: Gesell dome and expressing in writing all their hopes for the future.

As explained by the director of one of the care homes: '[adolescents] have a hard time understanding the justice system: who is the child's lawyer, the judge . . . Some children have contact with the justice system, others do not. Some have an idea of what it is.'

Adolescents emphasised the need for justice system representatives to listen empathetically, explain processes clearly, and be reliable. Awareness campaigns could help bridge this gap.

Relation with the Care Home

The violations of rights of those who arrive at care homes differ between adolescents. In all cases, however, adolescents had experienced abuse and neglect, and in some cases, they had been displaced from different family environments several times, this being a displacement from their biological family, adoptive parents, or changing care homes. Adolescents who are placed in care homes need to be resilient. Their environment changes, the people they regularly engage with change, rules change, and they often have to change schools, and to adjust to being labelled as a person in a care home. Some adolescents noted that they did not tell their peers at school that they lived in a care home and others said that they were bullied because of this (A024). Therefore, being able to preserve any stable emotional support is important, while providing a stable environment and clear rules provides adolescents with a possibility to feel at ease. Some adolescents wanted to maintain contact with their biological family, even when this implied having contact with their abuser. They did not want the abuse but they still wanted to be in contact with the abuser, and they disagreed when the directors of the care homes or judges did not grant them the chance to reconnect with the abuser. Other adolescents mentioned that they did not want to see their abuser again, but they wanted to maintain communication with their extended family.

Adolescents' experiences at care homes varied widely. Many entered care homes feeling uncertain, stressed, or nervous. Most lacked clarity about the purpose of the care home, the duration of their stay, or of decision-making processes. Building trust with adults at the care home took time.

Adolescents appreciated:

- clear rules;
- adults who cared;
- obligations, such as attending school.

These three aspects gave adolescents hope for a different future and helped them learn social norms. With support from psychologists, adolescents also learned that 'they have themselves' (A014), and of their power to overcome traumatic experiences. They valued the presence of those who provided consistent care and emotional support. However, adolescents disliked restrictions on desired activities or mandatory participation in others. Attempted suicide and psychological crises among peers triggered additional stress.

Some adolescents rejected adoption due to fear of rejection and frustration arising from previous failed attempts. Adolescents in care homes receive financial subsidies from the state to support them to complete school and to gain independence. Examples of these subsidies include, the 'Progresar' and 'Beca Sosten' programmes (CEPAL; Congreso de la Provincia de Buenos Aires, 1996; 'Progresar', 2018). Care home directors often teach financial literacy to prepare adolescents for adulthood.

Theatrical performances created by adolescents showed that they felt that society expected them to show negative feelings about their experience at the care homes. In addition, the plays showed reinforcing labels that summarised their experiences.

Recommendations for Others with Similar Experiences

Adolescents recommended others to:

- speak up;
- take care of themselves;
- focus on the future while also accepting the past.

Speaking up was indeed a recurrent recommendation. A participant stated that, 'for example, for me it was very heavy because I had nightmares all the time . . . But when I let go of that [by speaking up] . . . it did me good, I stopped having the nightmares' (A015).

Adolescents also recommended the inclusion of further means of expression for themselves including meditation, playing games, being silent, and reading books like *Psicoanálisis Para Todxs*. Adolescents recommended reaching out to schools, psychologists, trusted adults, or the police. They emphasised the importance of being treated as people rather than as case numbers.

The school, psychologists, family members/friends, trusted adults, and the police (in this order of relevance) were mentioned as people who adolescents would recommend to others in similar situations to reach out to for help.

The voice of a participant addressing why the school is the place to go when in need of help states:

> Because if you talk to the school [teacher, director, or the psychologist], the school will do something, because otherwise who are you going to talk to, if you do not know what a public defender's office is. Because I did not know what a public defender's office was either, and those things (A023).

When asked about what adolescents would advise a judge or someone from the justice system to do, they mentioned listening, not judging, being empathetic, and being reliable. Being reliable was assimilated to an act of love. In addition, informing adolescents about the process·and what to expect, and explaining to them the process is not easy, was mentioned as valuable.

Adolescents, furthermore, stressed the need to focus on the future, acknowledging that the past will always hurt and that there is a need to be strong, and to 'dream high' (A025). As explained by a participant:

> She should not do stupid things, like cutting her arms or running away, someone will come into her life and adopt her, or she will have a new family, or maybe leave home quickly, and she will get something she likes to do, and those things, there is always a life, do not hurt yourself, because what is going to happen? The same thing is going to happen, they are going to take you to the hospital, they are going to put you in the hospital. And those things. And nothing, I would tell him, that life should not always hurt you all the time because you have people who love you (A033).

The Future

The idea of thinking about the future triggered instability for some adolescents. 'We are now present, but the future is tough' (A003). A care home director summarised this situation by stating that 'fear of nothingness itself, here is where she was taken care of [referring to the care home], accompanied by . . .'

Seven adolescents mentioned future professions, mostly in caregiving fields (eg nursing, psychology, law). These choices reflected their desire to help others based on personal experiences. However, the future often brings uncertainty and fear, for example of homelessness or lack of support.

Adolescents exiting care homes receive financial support from the state for two years which is meant to support them until they can find stable employment and gain financial independence. However, they lose their health insurance. It was mentioned by directors of care homes, that some adolescents study and secure employment, but others return to previous abusive environments and discontinue psychological support.

CLOSING REMARKS

The reality is that adolescents in care homes experience cannot be tackled solely by means of a law that addresses the right to access to justice. These realities are immersed in complexity. They are realities that adolescents do not choose to experience. Realities choose them (Marotta et al, 2024). Within this complexity, those who assist adolescents in their access to justice must be specialised and ready to guide and support them in a process that involves understanding why they were displaced from their families, understanding what rights were violated, and how they can participate in decisions that affect their lives, and by doing so, support them in gaining autonomy and decision-making power. All of the above are needed, without ignoring the fact that adolescents have a right to a mentally and physically healthy life.

Previous studies and legal frameworks acknowledge the importance of the right of adolescents to access to justice. Moreover, participatory methods remain vital for capturing adolescents' perspectives, and programmes for raising rights awareness among families, schools and professionals are essential. Art expressions are shown to be a tool that allows adolescents to express their feelings and experiences in a non-revictimising way. The findings of this study reveal that adolescents in care homes perceive access to justice through a lens that is shaped by their life experiences, often characterised by limited agency and understanding. Their understanding of justice centres on the presence of empathetic listeners, clear communication, and actionable support from trusted adults. These factors were highlighted by adolescents to a greater extent than formal interactions with the legal system. Many adolescents associate justice with emotional support, guidance and inclusion, rather than institutional processes. These perceptions underscore the importance of fostering environments where adolescents can actively participate, express themselves in meaningful ways, and be educated about their rights to transform their roles from passive recipients to active holders of rights within the justice system.

Fostering collaboration between care homes, schools, tribunals and health professionals is key to create supportive environments. Moreover, justice systems can benefit from sharing good practices, and can help to develop further innovative techniques to explain rights and legal processes to adolescents. Only then, would adolescents be empowered to participate and exercise their rights.

The physical spaces of care homes should be designed to inspire trust and motivation, incorporating private and welcoming areas to address psychological crises effectively. Empowering adolescents to understand their relationship with the justice system, including when and how it supports them, is critical for enabling them to act as active holders of rights rather than passive recipients. Before adolescents are placed in care homes, it is of pivotal importance to explain to them why they are displaced from their families, where they are going to go, what the space looks like, what is expected of them in this new community, who are the actors available to support them, and what the next steps are given their possibilities to leave the care home.

This study on which this chapter is based provides further understanding of how adolescents in care homes perceive their right of access to justice. Further empirical research is necessary to assess practical and effective methods to foster the participation of adolescents in care homes at the different stages of the legal process.

REFERENCES

Bruce, JW, Garcia-Bolivar, O, Hanstad, T, Roth, M, Nielsen, R, Knox, A, Schmidt, J, 2007. Legal Empowerment of the Poor: From Concepts to Assessment.

CEPAL, n.d. CEPAL Innovación Social [WWW Document]. Exp. Innovacion Soc. URL https://dds.cepal.org/innovacionsocial/e/proyectos/ar/sistemasosten/ (accessed 12.23.24).

Commission on Legal Empowerment of the Poor, Making the law work for everyone. Vol I (Report of the Commission on Legal Empowerment of the Poor) (Commission on Legal Empowerment of the Poor and United Nations Development Programme, New York, 2008).

Committee on the Rights of the Children, 2012. General comment No 14 (2013) on the right of the child to have his or her best interests taken as a primary consideration (art 3, para 1).

Committee on the Rights of the Children, 2009. General comment No 12 (2009): The right of the child to be heard.
Congreso de la Nación Argentina, 2014. Código civil y comercial de la nación.
Congreso de la Provincia de Buenos Aires, 1996. Beca Sosten.
Consejo de los Derechos de Niñas, Niños y Adolescentes, 2021. Situación de las Infancias y Adolescencias en la Ciudad Autónoma de Buenos Aires. Consejo de los Derechos de Niñas, Niños y Adolescentes, Ciudad Autónoma de Buenos Aires.
Crespo, H, 2024. Medicalización de NNyA. Internados por salud mental.
Esteban, MB, 2022. Children's Participation, Progressive Autonomy, and Agency for Inclusive Education in Schools. Soc Incl 10, 43–53. https://doi.org/10.17645/si.v10i2.4936.
Gramatikov, M, Porter, RB, 2010. Yes, I can: subjective legal empowerment. Tilburg Univ., TISCO Working Paper Series on Civil Law and Conflict Resolution Systems No 010/2010 46.
III Congreso Federal, Internacional e Interdisciplinario. DD.HH. para la niñez y la adolescencia, 2024.
Lansdown, G, 'International Developments in Children's Participation: Lessons and Challenges', in *Children, Young People and Social Inclusion: Participation for What?* Kay Tisdall (ed) et al (Bristol: Bristol University Press, 2006), 138–156.
Liefaard, T, 2019. Access to Justice for Children: Towards a Specific Research and Implementation Agenda. https://doi.org/10.1163/15718182-02702002.
Lora, L, 'Discurso jurídico sobre el interés superior del niño', in *Avances de Investigación En Derecho y Ciencias Sociales*, Slavin Pablo (Dir) (Mar del Plata, Ediciones Suárez Argentina, 2006), 479–488.
Lora, L, Marotta, J, Forthcoming. 'Voces de la adolescencia: Sociología jurídica y metodologías participativas', in Derec*ho, Arte, Literatura y Hábitat Universitario* (Facultad de Derecho de la Universidad de Costa Rica, Costa Rica).
Lora, L, Medina, LV. Sistema de protección integral para la niñez y la adolescencia. Problemas actuales y desafíos en su aplicación, in *Teoría y prácticas para el abordaje de los conflictos transversales a la niñez y la adolescencia* (Departamento de Publicaciones de la Facultad de Derecho y Ciencias Sociales de la Universidad de Buenos Aires. Facultad de Derecho y Ciencias Sociales, 2025).
Lorenzetti, R, 'Acceso a la justicia de los sectores vulnerables', in *Defensa pública: garantía de acceso a la justicia* (La Ley, Buenos Aires, República Argentina, 2008), 61–74.
Lorenzetti, RL, Highton de Nolasco, E, Kemelmajer de Carlucci, A, 2012, Comisión Redactora. *Fundamentos del Anteproyecto de Código Civil y Comercial de la Nación*, available at https://perma.cc/2TG8-TK7W.
Macdonald, Roderick A, 'Access to Civil Justice', in *The Oxford Handbook of Empirical Legal Research* (Oxford: Oxford University Press, 2010), 492–521.
Marotta, J, 'The Inclusion of Mediation in the Family Justice System of Argentina: An Empirical Study of Law, Courts and Actors', in Resear*ch Handbook on Family Justice Systems* (Cheltenham: Edward Elgar, 2023).
Marotta, J, 'Developing Holistic and Inclusive Family Justice in Argentina', in *What Is a Family Justice System For?* (Oñati International Series in Law and Society, Spain, 2022), 191–217.
Marotta, J, *Access to Justice and Legal Empowerment of Victims of Domestic Violence through Legal Organisations in the City of Buenos Aires: A Qualitative Empirical Legal Study* (Maastricht University / United Nations University, the Netherlands, 2017).
Marotta, J, Lora, L, Gutierrez, CV, 2024. Participatory Research Methods: A Win-Win Approach to Understand Children's Rights [WWW Document]. URL https://childrensrightsresearchnew.mannenvan80.nl/index.php/stories/83-childhood-legal-capacity/514-participatory-research-methods-a-win-win-approach-to-understand-childrens-rights (accessed 12.26.24).
Marotta, J, Parise, A 'On Codes, Marriage, and Access to Justice: Recent Developments in the Law of Argentina' (2014) *J Civ Law Stud* 7, 237–269.
Medina, LV, *Sociología de la Infancia y acceso a la justicia. Alcances en el Código Civil y Comercial de la Nación en Lora Laura* (comp) (Sociología Jurídica e infancia Buenos Aires, Argentina, 2021) 99–138.

Medina, G (2024). Interés superior del niño [Video]. En Tercer Congreso Federal Internacional e Interdisciplinario. YouTube. https://www.youtube.com/watch?v=qpxkBcexe3s.

Mulcahy, L, 'Sociology of Legal Images', in *Research Handbook on the Sociology of Law*, (ed) Jiří Přibáň (Cheltenham: Edward Elgar Publishing, 2020), 2003–2014.

Peleg, N, 'Reconceptualising the Child's Right to Development: Children and the Capability Approach' (2013) *Int. J. Child. Rights* 21, 523–42. https://doi.org/10.1163/15718182-02103003.

Progresar [WWW Document], 2018. Argentina.gob.ar. URL https://www.argentina.gob.ar/educacion/progresar (accessed 12.23.24).

Sevón, E, Mustola, M, Siippainen, A, Vlasov, J, 'Participatory Research Methods with Young Children: A Systematic Literature Review' (2023) *Educ Rev* 0, 1–19. https://doi.org/10.1080/00131911.2023.2215465.

Taliercio, AE, *Grupos vulnerables y acceso a la justicia. Niñas, niños, y adolescentes* (Ediciones Juridicas, Argentina, 2022).

Taylor, N, Gollop, M, 'Children's Views and Participation in Family Dispute Resolution in New Zealand', in Smith, AB (ed), *Enhancing Children's Rights: Connecting Research, Policy and Practice* (London: Palgrave Macmillan, 2025) 242–255. https://doi.org/10.1057/9781137386106_17.

UN General Assembly, 1989. Convention on the Rights of the Child.

UNICEF DATA, 2022. Argentina (ARG) – Demographics, Health & Infant Mortality [WWW Document]. UNICEF DATA. URL https://data.unicef.org/country/arg/ (accessed 10.30.24).

Van De Meene, I, Van Rooij, B, *Access to Justice and Legal Empowerment. Making the Poor Central in Legal Development Co-operation* (Leiden: Leiden University Press, 2008).

Part III

Underlying Policies

9

Legal Incapacities in France: Who is in Charge?

BENOIT BASTARD

IN FRANCE, MORE than 800,000 adults[1] are subject to a legal measure – guardianship, curatorship or other measures.[2] The question of how these measures are taken and especially how they are applied has remained little studied in recent decades. Indeed, while the law and methods of care have evolved considerably as a result of various factors, there are no empirical studies available to describe the evolution of the methods of action with vulnerable people and the way in which these people experience the action taken for their protection.

The transformations of law and public policies have been analysed, particularly with regard to the field of disability, which partly covers that of vulnerable people (Revillard, 2020). In this area, all sorts of questions have been addressed: law and recognition of disability, urban planning and accessibility, etc. As for the more specific policies for caring for vulnerable people, they have been the subjects of work, which has shown in particular how this domain has transformed itself by becoming institutionalised in the first decade of the twenty-first century (Eyraud, 2009, 2010). However, the question of how the sector is organised in practice today and how the measures, guardianship, curatorship and others, are felt and experienced by the people concerned remains little studied from a perspective of sociology of law and justice. We can only mention a set of works carried out 20 years ago under the aegis of the National Union of Family Associations, a powerful institution that is the main operator in the

[1] This chapter only concerns the protection of adults. The issue of the protection of minors has been excluded, and is the subject of a specific law and specialised bodies. The protection of minors in danger is the administrative responsibility of Child Welfare Services at the departmental level. At the judicial level, it is the responsibility of the public prosecutor's office and the juvenile judge, who has civil and criminal jurisdictions.

[2] Cf Ministère de la Justice, *Infostat*, 2024, n°197. At the end of 2023, 712,000 adults benefitted from a protection measure (guardianship or curatorship), to which must be added the people who benefit from 'family habilitation', who are estimated at more than 100,000. These measures will also experience a remarkable increase in the years to come, given the ageing French population.

field of guardianships.[3] This work, including in particular empirical elements on the action of social workers, can serve as a point of reference, particularly with regard to questions relating to taking into account the wishes of people concerned (Family Research, 2004). However, to our knowledge, such work has no equivalent today. Apart from the issue of physical disability, particularly highlighted in France on the occasion of the 2024 Paralympic Games in Paris, the issue of implementing the protection of vulnerable people remains under invested from an empirical sociology perspective compared to other fields of social intervention.

Without claiming to fill this gap, we propose here, with an exploratory study, to initiate a reflection on this subject. We would like in particular to raise the question of the directions taken in the care of vulnerable people, in particular through the implementation of legal measures of protection in the private sphere.

Even though the European institutions wish to increase the responsibilities conferred on vulnerable people themselves, to give them more rights and for them to be able to at least indicate what they want for their care, and while this trend is operationalised in different countries – which can be seen in other parts of this work – we may wonder how the French system is oriented in this regard.

The search for greater autonomy for vulnerable people is clearly evident in France at the legal level – through a set of measures that we will detail later. As for its operationalisation, it is questionable, because it seems to be constantly balanced against the other dominant vector of the system, the maintenance or even the increase of protection with regard to the same people.

Is there a risk that the legal changes introduced in favour of greater autonomy granted to those concerned will not be enough to change existing practices, given the continued strong preference for control over vulnerable people through the strengthening of a network of actors of all kinds? This is the hypothesis that can, in any case be drawn from the work of Benoit Eyraud: by evoking the introduction, in France, of the principles relating to the care of disability following the International Convention more than 15 years old, he calls into question the institutional system which acts as if it were difficult to think of a society 'without the existence of a coercive measure of protection' (Eyraud, 2023, p. 70). In this perspective, we must imagine that the French system, with judges at its centre, themselves supported by the logic of the medical world, has had to evolve

[3] UNAF was created after World War II, at the initiative of General de Gaulle, and was given a special and exclusive mission – that of representing French families before the institutions of the Republic. This association brings together as many departmental unions (UDAFs, departmental unions of family associations) which are themselves made up of associations in the field of family support and social intervention. The UDAFs have services bringing together legal representatives for the protection of adults and are one of the main providers in charge of guardianship and curatorship. They also provide support to private individuals who play this role with a member of their family. In 2004, UNAF created a research journal, *Recherches familiales*, the first issue of which was devoted to the protection of vulnerable people (*Recherches familiales*, 2004).

to take into account expectations of autonomy, but that in reality it evolves like a large tanker that takes a long time to turn, and it remains firmly anchored to its fundamentals. If this hypothesis is confirmed, we can ask ourselves the reasons for this slow evolution and this persistence of the protection paradigm. Is it due to the increase in the number of measures and actors concerned? Is it the effect of tax pressure, which reduces available budgets and pushes towards privatisation? Or is the observed force of inertia due to professional ideologies, whether it is a form of caution among professionals in the sector[4] or 'the central historical place of family and managing associations'?[5]

Without having all the elements necessary to go far in verifying such a hypothesis and answering these questions, we would like to develop it by resorting to limited empirical material, with exploratory research aimed at examining how the actors – legal professionals, social workers, families – describe their action and where they place the 'cursor' between the protection of the persons concerned and the search for their will. The use of this material will involve the writing of short case studies that aim to grasp how these situations present themselves to the actors and how they intervene in them – with their ideas both on the protection and on the capacities of the persons in their care.

Before coming to this analysis, we will take stock of recent laws to show how the project of making the search for the autonomy of persons more effective has materialised in recent years, at the same time as the concern for control has been maintained.

EVOLUTION OF LAW: FROM INCAPACITY TO VULNERABILITY

The law on the protection of vulnerable people has undergone successive changes over the last few decades, which have had different aims: increasing the security of their care, in particular by institutionalising and professionalising it, but also giving more weight to the family in the care of the people concerned and finally promoting the autonomy of people under protection and better recognising their rights. These developments have brought great complexity to this legal matter and we will only give a very brief overview here from the perspective that interests us.[6]

It should first be noted that the field of the protection of people has been regulated in France since 1968 by a law that specified the conditions for the

[4] 'It is up to the judge to adapt the measure while preserving, as much as possible, the person's usual lifestyle and respecting their desires and wishes. In any event, they must take into account their needs and habits, through a humanized and proportionate approach. The judge should not fear for the commitment of his responsibility when he favours the choice, the will, the preferences of the person, over the security of assets' (*Défenseurs des droits*, 2016, 55).

[5] Eyraud, 2023, 70.

[6] The law applicable to the situations discussed here is included in Articles 425 to 515 of the Civil Code and therefore constitutes a dense and rapidly evolving subject. For a complete legal statement, see Peterka, Carson-Déglise, 2021.

intervention of the judge and defined the measures that still form today, after various additions and modifications, the very framework of the system.[7] The law stipulates that when an adult is unable to look after his or her own interests due to a medically confirmed impairment of his or her mental or physical faculties such as to prevent the expression of his or her will, the judge may order a legal protection measure in order to protect his or her interest (Art 425 Civil Code).

The various measures then provided are as follows. Judicial protective supervision (*sauvegarde de justice*), Art 433 CC, is an emergency measure which is in principle temporary. In theory, the person concerned retains the exercise of his rights.[8] Guardianship (*tutelle*) and curatorship (*curatelle*), Art 440 CC: the first in which the person is 'represented' in a continuous manner in the acts of civil life – in other words, the guardian (*tuteur*) acts in place of the protected person; the second which concerns people who are in less difficulty and who only need to be accompanied and controlled in the important acts of life.[9] Without being necessary to go into detail here, the law establishes the modalities according to which guardians and curators are appointed – either members of the family of the person concerned or professional guardians (ie legal representative for the protection of adults). It also explains the course of the measure, the tasks assigned to the guardians and the manner in which they refer to the judge if necessary. Furthermore, it establishes the conditions under which the measure ends. It should be noted here that all of these provisions take place within the framework of civil justice, within the precincts of the district court (*tribunal d'instance*). In this context, the judicial procedure is in principle in the hands of the parties. In other words, the appointment of a guardian can only take place at the request of persons, spouse, family members, relatives, who consider that the person concerned is unable to take charge of his or her interests. The action can also be brought at the request of public prosecutors acting within the framework of their civil powers. The judges respond to the proposal made to them and may, where appropriate, confirm or modify the measures proposed.

[7] Law No 68-5 of 3 January 1968 reforming the law of incapacitated adults (*réformant le droit des incapables majeurs*). The conditions under which the law in question was drafted are analysed by Benoit Eyraud, who shows how it resulted from a desire originating with hospital doctors in the psychiatry sector who wanted the issue of protecting property and that of protecting the person to be separated. The reform was developed from 1963 under the leadership of Jean Carbonnier – the author of much of the French civil legislation of that time (cf Eyraud, 2010, 3).

[8] 'The judge may place under the protective supervision of the court a person who, for one of the causes listed under Article 425, has need of temporary legal protection or to be represented in order to accomplish certain specified acts' (Art 433 CC). 'The person placed under judicial protective supervision continues to exercise his rights' (Art 433 CC).

[9] 'The person who, without being unable to act himself, is in need, for one of the causes mentioned in Article 425, to be assisted or supervised in a continual manner in the important acts of his civil life may be placed under curatorship. Curatorship is ordered only if it is shown that judicial protection cannot assure sufficient protection. The person who, for one of the causes mentioned in Article 425, must be represented in a continual manner in the acts of civil life, may be placed under tutorship' (Art 440 CC).

This law, based on the work of the jurist-sociologist Jean Carbonnier, was originally part of the perspective of 'legal pluralism': 'It was necessary to arrive at legislation where each patient could be prescribed their dose of capacity on prescription by the doctor. Because modern psychiatry insists on this hope: participation in legal acts can have psychotherapeutic virtues.'[10] This influence has not ceased to be felt since, even as new methods of care were developed.

In 2007, a new large-scale reform reorganised the sector of legal protection of adults.[11] Justified by the increase in the number of people concerned, it reaffirmed the existing principles by placing greater emphasis on preserving the autonomy of individuals:

> Adults receive the protection of their person and of their assets that their condition or situation renders necessary as laid down in the present title. This protection is established and ensured while respecting individual freedoms, fundamental rights and the dignity of the person. Its purpose is the interest of the protected person. It promotes, as far as possible, the autonomy of the latter. (Art 415 CC)

Guardianship or curatorship is no longer possible unless the person suffers from an alteration of his personal faculties noted by a precise and detailed medical certificate. Situations in which a person was placed under protection for reasons of 'prodigality, intemperance or idleness', which continued under the previous law, are excluded. In addition, while the measures taken for the protection of vulnerable persons were decided by the judge without a term being set for them, things change with this law and judges are now required to review their decisions to take into account any change in the situation, at least every five years. This is an important step forward for the rights of protected persons and has also had an impact on the functioning of the courts, as we will see later.[12]

In order to respect the wishes of individuals, the law also introduces an innovation, the 'mandate for future protection', a provision that allows individuals to designate in advance the third party they would like to see in charge of looking after their interests or their person at such time as age or illness makes such protection necessary.[13]

[10] Jean Carbonnier, in Jacques Massip, *Les incapacités*, Paris, Répertoire Defresnois, 2002, 23, quoted by Eyraud, 2010, 4.

[11] Law No 2007-308 of 5 March 2007 reforming the legal protection of adults (*portant réforme de la protection juridique des majeurs*).

[12] Following this law of 5 March 2007, the Charter of Rights and Freedoms of Protected Adults was adopted (Appendix 4-3 of the Code of Action and Families).

[13] 'Any adult person or emancipated minor who is not under any measure of tutorship may entrust one or more persons, by a single mandate, with the responsibility to represent him for one of the causes listed in Article 425, in the event he could no longer see to his own interests alone.' The mandate for future protection is included in Articles 477 to 494 of the Civil Code. However, some of the modalities of its implementation are still under discussion today, in particular the creation of the dematerialised register on which future protection mandates must be published (Decree No 2024-1032 of 16 November 2024 relating to the register of the mandate for future protection).

In a different sense, the law also specifies the conditions for monitoring the exercise of measures. But above all, it reorganises the conditions of activity of guardians and curators outside the family. This is a major change – the professionalisation of the activity of 'protectors': legal representatives for the protection of adults (*mandataires judiciaires à la protection des majeurs*), ie in particular guardians and curators, will obey common rules that will organise their training, their evaluation, their control, their responsibility and their remuneration. The financing of their activity is unified and defined according to new criteria, with participation of the protected persons in the financing of the measures, to the extent of their means.

In 2015, while the issue of the country's adaptation to ageing was receiving increased attention in parliament,[14] a new measure was created, family habilitation (*habilitation familiale*), which reflects both the desire to better recognise the participation of relatives in caring for vulnerable people and the State's inability to cope by itself with the increase in costs of an ageing population.[15] Aiming at simplifying and modernising family law, family habilitation is another mechanism designed to protect adults whose mental or physical faculties are impaired. A doctor chosen from a list drawn up by the public prosecutor must certify this impairment. Family habilitation allows a relative of an adult who is unable to express their wishes to represent them in carrying out acts relating to their property or person. The mechanism requires an agreement within the family and a decision by the judge of protection disputes (*juge des contentieux de la protection*). He or she may designate the person's spouse, civil union partner, common-law partner, ascendant or descendant, brothers and sisters, following a request from them. Family members must agree on the choice of the relative responsible for exercising the measure. This person exercises his or her mission free of charge. Depending on the situation, the judge may also designate several relatives to represent the person. In this case, he or she determines the conditions of exercise for each of them. The family habilitation may be 'special' (ie limited to one or more specific acts), or 'general' and cover all acts relating to the protected person. The acts in question may concern the day-to-day management of the person's accounts and expenses, but also the choice of their place of residence or procedures related to the health of the protected adult.

What is remarkable is that the judge intervenes when the measure is issued – and then only in a very limited number of situations, such as selling the home or in the event of a conflict of interest. The relatives of the protected adult or the public prosecutor may refer the matter to the judge only in the event

[14] Law No 2015-1776 of 28 December 2015 relating to the adaptation of society to ageing (*relative à l'adaptation de la société au vieillissement*).

[15] Order No 2015-1288 of 15 October 2015 on the simplification and modernisation of family law (*portant simplification et modernisation du droit de la famille*). Decree No 2016-185 of 23 February 2016 issued for the application of Order No 2015-1288 of 15 October 2015.

of difficulties. Otherwise, the designated person is not required to submit a management account.

All the provisions relating to protected adults were again put back on the table after the 2007 law was subject to a great deal of criticism. Among the reports produced, we can cite a 'white paper' issued by a group of federations and services, including UNAF, in 2012 (White Paper on the Protection of Adults, 2012) and a report from the Court of Auditors (*Cour des comptes*) whose title is suggestive with regard to the criticisms of the 2007 reform: 'An ambitious reform, a deficient implementation' (Court of Auditors, 2016). Finally, another report, that of the Defender of Rights (*le Défenseur des Droits*), an independent institution develops with great force the argument that France does not respect the international commitments it has made, in particular with regard to the Convention on the Rights of Persons with Disabilities (CRPD), adopted in 2006 and entered into force in 2010 (*Défenseur des Droits*, 2016). In fact, this report highlights that even though the legislative changes introduced in 2007 and 2015 have profoundly modified the system of protection of adults by proposing in particular the inclusion of the autonomy and rights of individuals at the heart of the systems that concern them, it remains the case that 'the legal framework and current practices do not allow us to fully meet the requirements of the convention'. In particular, the existing provisions and current practices do not provide a guarantee to protected persons that they will not be deprived of their legal capacity (with the guardianship system and also 'reinforced curatorship') and that the decisions taken by the person responsible for representing them will, in all cases, respect their autonomy, will and preferences.[16] This report advocates the transition from a system of substitute decision making – embodied by guardianship – to a system of supported decision making –which is found in particular in simple curatorship. This involves placing greater value on support measures for the persons concerned, without giving the desire to respond 'objectively' to their best interests.[17]

As a response to the criticisms and expectations expressed, the 2019 law includes a variety of measures, some of which are specifically aimed at restoring certain rights of the protected person while recognising new rights.[18] One example is the right to vote: it is no longer possible to deprive people of this right as was previously the case. A provision also concerns the right to marry or enter into a civil partnership – which no longer requires prior authorisation by the judge. Another example is that, whereas previously the judge systematically intervened

[16] In particular, the guardianship measure as a substitute decision-making mechanism appears to be contrary to the CIDPH in that it undermines the legal capacity of the protected adult. This is why the Defender of Rights indicates that it should be considered as an exceptional measure reserved only for situations in which the person concerned is completely unable to express his or her choices and preferences (*Défenseur des Droits*, 2016, 54).

[17] *Défenseur des droits*, 2016, 15.

[18] Law No 2019-222 of 23 March 2019 on programming 2018–2022 and reform for justice (*de programmation 2018-2022 et de réforme pour la justice*).

in the event of a serious medical act, this judicial intervention is now limited to cases of disagreement between an adult and the person responsible for their protection. Similarly, the law removes the prior authorisation of the judge for certain acts of a patrimonial nature (opening or closing a bank account, making investments, etc). However, judicial control is maintained in situations where the interest of the protected adult must be assessed. Other changes are introduced in the control of management of accounts which was previously the responsibility of the chief clerk of the court – a heavy undertaking for the jurisdiction – and which now relies more on the protection bodies or on professionals designated to do so. Furthermore, as will be discussed later, this reform modifies judicial organisation and establishes the judge of protection disputes (*juge des contentieux de la protection*) in place of the guardianship judge (*juge des tutelles*).

Here, we should add a final legislative development, which is included in the law of 8 April 2024 aimed at creating a 'society of ageing well and autonomy'.[19] This text provides for a whole set of social intervention measures aimed at supporting the elderly and combating their mistreatment. It does not develop specific provisions in relation to the people taken care of within the framework of protection measures, but specifies the texts relating to legal representatives for the protection of adults and creates a national dematerialised register in which all legal measures taken for vulnerable people, guardianship, curatorship, etc will be recorded. This register must be operational by 2026 at the latest and will undoubtedly provide a better understanding of the state of the field of judicial protection of adults.

Ultimately, the successive reforms undertaken over the last few decades have aimed to free the care of the people concerned from a vision of social control that is alienating and stigmatising. Very clearly, we have moved from a system of recording and monitoring 'disabilities' to a system of supporting 'vulnerable' people. However, the development of this vision, which increasingly gives space to the will of individuals, has not prevented the legislator from maintaining or even strengthening the control dimension, particularly on issues of assets.

We therefore find ourselves today with a wide range of measures as if it were a question, as we have said, of offering a diversity of solutions to adapt to each situation. These measures include:

- Curatorship (*curatelle*) represents the largest number of decisions with different levels of protection. The most common is reinforced curatorship (*curatelle renforcée*), in which the persons concerned face increased limitations on the exercise of their rights – and in particular from the point of view of the use of funds, since the guardian (*curateur*) is then the only one to receive the income of the protected person and to settle their main expenses. The judges of protection disputes made 32,686 curatorship decisions in

[19] Law No 2024-217 of 8 April 2024 containing measures to build a society of healthy ageing and autonomy (*portant mesures pour bâtir la société du bien vieillir et de l'autonomie*).

2023, including 29,153 reinforced curatorships (source: Ministère de la Justice, 2024).

- Guardianship (*tutelle*) also covers a very large number of situations. – 28,306 new tutorships were decided in 2023. It must be revised within five years following its establishment (and can then be renewed for 10 years, if there is no idea of improving the person's state of health).
- Family habilitation is growing rapidly. It is decided for 10 years (and can be renewed for 10 or 20 years depending on the situation; family habilitation between spouses may not be limited in time). In 2023, 39,257 decisions were taken on this measure.
- Judicial protective supervision, a provisional measure decided for one year and renewable once, is reserved for emergency situations. Judges make many such decisions as a provisional measure, before tutorship or curatorship. Still, only 446 were formally recorded in 2023.
- Finally, one last solution remains marginal, the judicial support measure, decided at the request of the prosecutor and which concerns people who are supported only in the management of their budget. In 2023, 237 were decided.

THE SEARCH FOR A BALANCE BETWEEN PROTECTION AND AUTONOMY OF THE PERSON

This second part, discusses the practices of the protection of vulnerable people and outlines, based on different cases, how the question arises as to how to respect people's wishes and how to ensure their protection. To do this, we will consider the example of a judge in the court environment, that of a legal representative, the case of a family member in charge of the guardianship of his mother and finally the example of a lawyer who has managed different situations. In each case presented, we will discuss the elements that suggest that the interests involved are sometimes in tension, between 'care' and protection.

Judges on the Front Line

Different dimensions of the judicial organisation were reformed in 2019, which had an impact on the management of situations encountered by protected adults. Different bodies were brought together, with the aim of further streamlining the functioning of justice: the district courts (*tribunal d'instance*) where guardianship judges sat, and the high courts (*tribunal de grande instance*), and the ordinary jurisdiction where the majority of trials began.[20] This resulted in

[20] Law No 2019-222 of 23 March 2019 on programming 2018–2022 and reform for justice (*de programmation 2018-2022 et de réforme pour la justice*). Article L 211-1, Code of Judicial Organisation (*Code de l'organisation judiciaire*).

the creation of the judicial courts (*tribunal judiciaire*), which came into force on 1 January 2020. Within the framework of these courts, a new institution was established on the same date – the judge of protection disputes (*juge des contentieux de la protection*). There are one or more in each of the 164 judicial courts (Article L213-4-1 of the Code of Judicial Organisation). These judges, whose responsibilities are distinct from those of family court judges, take over, among other functions, those previously belonging to the guardianship judge (Article L213-4-2 of the Code of Judicial Organisation). They also have many other responsibilities, which make for a versatile magistrate, including disputes over residential leases, over-indebtedness or consumer credit. However, they are mainly in charge of all the cases that interest us here – guardianship, curatorship, judicial protective supervision, questions relating to family habilitation, etc.[21] Again, it should also be noted here that they are civil judges, which means that, unlike other magistrates who intervene in the social field, such as the juvenile court judge, they cannot take action on their own initiative. They can only respond to requests made by family members or relatives of a person in difficulty or, where appropriate, by the public prosecutor within the framework of his civil responsibilities. The revision and renewal of the measures taken are decided at the request of guardians, either professional or family members.

To illustrate how the law is being implemented and how these judges see their role in caring for protected persons, we will mention here the figure of one of these judges of protection disputes, a woman of about 40 years old, who belongs to a medium-sized jurisdiction in a city in the south of France – a judicial court located in the heart of a population of 400,000 inhabitants.

The department to which she belongs, within the civil part of the court, is composed of three judges of protection disputes. This department, she explains, works well, even if it is overloaded with work. Together, the judges manage some 7,500 ongoing cases (not counting designations in matters of family habilitation). Our judge does not seem to complain about it and on the contrary emphasises solidarity within the department and the interest of her work.

Typically, the judge has hearings (*auditions*) two or three mornings per week. The summonses are spread over each of these half-days. They are scheduled as follows. If it is the renewal of a measure (which accounts for the majority of cases), the hearing is scheduled for a quarter of an hour. And if it is a new file or a problematic file, half an hour. Every two weeks, at a more formal hearing (*audience*) at which the parties are not present, the judge delivers her decisions.

To understand how this judge positions herself in relation to the question discussed in this chapter, we can note that she indicates:

[21] It is difficult to say exactly how many judges of protection disputes there are, as these magistrates are chosen from among judges in the judicial court without being the subject of a special appointment. There is at least one in each of the 164 judicial courts – there is a single court in 53 French departments and several in the others, with considerable variations in size.

> Putting the emphasis entirely on the will of the person is not the spirit of the law. In France we have a good balance: we must seek this will, but we put it into perspective in relation to the cognitive disorder.

The question then is how this 'balance' is created and managed. In practice, the judge of protection disputes is at the centre of the system. In any case, she sees herself at the centre, and the dimension of the control of situations is ever-present in her speech.

She explains that she relies on a small number of social services bringing together legal representatives for the protection of adults that she knows well. She describes her work environment as follows:

> We work with a lot of services, with their specificities. The trend is to group together and we regret it. So, we have five large services. What I find interesting is to have slightly specialised associations to be able to adapt our action: disability, ageing people, and psychiatric illness. The needs are not the same. We work also with agents attached to a hospital establishment; they are employees of the establishment with prefecture agreement. Then we have 'liberal' legal representatives – who act on a private basis as guardians or curators. They have different availability. They have fewer measures, they choose the time they spend on it. There are excellent on complex files. Still, for certain files, it is good to have a service – typically, harassing profiles. A single person will quickly give up the file. Whereas with a service, it is the structure that is designated and different people can intervene. There are strategies depending on the profiles.

What the judge wants is to be able to get a clear idea of the situations submitted to her and, in principle, she wants to really know the people and meet them:

> As much as possible, I want to meet them. The hearing of the protected adult is mandatory, unless the medical certificate says that the person is unable to express their wishes. We try not to make too many exemptions, to see the people as much as possible. We have also asked the doctors to objectivise their opinion, to explain why the person cannot express their wishes.

She explains that she has a 'broad vision' of the will, even when people are suffering from significant disorders:

> Someone who tells me that they do not want to go to a nursing home, that is the expression of a will.

The judge travels with her clerk for the day and visits the nursing homes (Ehpad, *Etablissement d'hébergement pour personnes âgées*):

> If we are told that the person can say their name, and say how many children they have, we go for it.

She notes that the COVID-19 epidemic period was difficult in this regard:

> It was complicated for us. No access to nursing homes. Difficult to go to homes. We were less careful, we accepted exemptions more easily.

She does not like to conduct hearings by videoconference, something she experienced during the epidemic. How can we think that people, who already have some difficulty understanding what the judge represents when he or she meets them in person, can get an idea of the situation remotely?

> Doing it by videoconference and by telephone is very complicated. I have done a few. Doing them in person is already difficult. So, if you have a voice coming out of a telephone: it is very unsatisfactory.

This is why the legislator's wish to see this type of hearing expanded, for obvious reasons of cost, seems to her to be entirely inappropriate for this type of measure:

> I am worried: a new civil procedure text wants to expand the use of videoconferencing, 'except for legitimate reasons', when, in these situations, we deprive people of their rights, we take away all their freedom. These are violent measures: no more access to their rights, to their bank accounts, no longer signing anything. The minimum is to talk with them, to check that we are on the right measure, to explain a little, to check that they agree that it is their loved ones. That is the minimum.

Beyond the observations made during these visits, the magistrate relies on the expertise of the doctor, as it appears in his or her opinion:

> I am not a doctor, I cannot assess the extent of the cognitive disorder, I need someone knowledgeable who assesses its place. I draw the consequences in relation to taking a risk. We refer to the medical certificate. If the certificate says that the person is unable to measure the risk they are taking, we draw the consequences.

Based on these elements, the judge sometimes ends up modifying the decisions proposed to her and not doing what is expected of her:

> Most often, in this type of interview, I confirm the decisions. But there can be surprises. For example, it happens that a person recovers since the assessment took place. After a stroke, for example, there can be a recovery that was not expected. In this case, we change the measure. We say: it is not going to be possible. Or, it happens that I decide to put in place a reinforced curatorship when what was planned was a family habilitation. This is a measure that is very detrimental to personal freedom. If the person is relatively independent, they do their shopping, they have their bank card. With the family habilitation, it is over, they no longer have a bank card, it is frustrating.

Through medical expertise and hearings, the judge therefore seeks a fair balance that allows the autonomous activity of the persons concerned to be maintained to the fullest extent possible.

More generally, she does not cease to take steps to ensure that the service operates efficiently and regularly.

This is how she describes the – marginal – phenomenon of fraud observed in the context of her activity. These are rare and generally come from the indiscretion not of professional guardians, but rather of family members, who 'confuse their pocket and that of the protected person'. For example, she cites a situation in which a person in charge of a family member changed the recipient of a life insurance policy.

Similarly, with the entire service, she was led to strengthen the control of accounts, the verification of measures, an activity that is carried out in particular towards guardians and curators belonging to the family of vulnerable persons:

> Here, there was no control until 2017 – because the registry director had decided that it was like that and he did not have the staff to do it. A colleague who arrived decided that it was necessary to change and from 2017, there was an inventory control at the start of the measure, that is the basis. Then, we carry out controls, but not all the files. The management controls concern a good part of the families and all the files that concern us. We transmit to the registry director, he is the one who has the competence. A part-time person takes care of it. We have set up reminders, it is fundamental, for guardianships and curatorships. It is especially important for family guardians and curators. Since there have been reminders, 100% of the accounts have been filed. The control over family guardians and curators is important, perhaps not every year, but at least every two years. We see things. We see if people take care of the loved ones entrusted to them. And in some cases, we see problems – more often in curatorship. All it takes is for the protected adult to agree for the curator to have access to all the assets, whereas in guardianship, you have to go through me, that limits the risks.

Another phenomenon, the periodic review of measures, has a considerable impact on the department's activity. Until 2007, no limit was set to the measures decided by the guardianship judges. Once taken, the measure continued as long as no event occurred, and often until the person's death. In 2007, a maximum period of five years was set for the review of measures, so that in 2012, for example, then in 2017 and in 2022, considerable flows of situations to be reviewed give the judge more work, without sufficient resources being provided.

The judge's entire statement aims, as a whole, to reassure on the objective of her mission and on its achievement: to ensure the security of the care of the people for whom justice is required.

However, the judge notes at the same time that a whole element of some cases is beyond her jurisdiction, in particular since the introduction of family habilitation. Once it has been decided, this measure allows wide freedom of action in the private sphere. Even if a majority of the court's cases consist of reinforced curatorship, the measure whose use is increasing most quickly is family habilitation. This measure is 'interesting', says the judge, because it gives weight to the family, but the fact remains that the judge 'controls nothing' in these situations. Everything happens outside of justice:

> It puts the family at the centre of the system. But families are not always loving. Some can give the impression of a façade: we have a good relationship with them, in thirty minutes, at the hearing, even though they are not on good terms with the protected adult. The adult will not be protected, but I cannot realise it.

The judge does not see everything and is not supposed to see everything:

> This means that society accepts that not everything is seen and that some protected adults are not.

In short, these reflections on family habilitation push us to question the position of judges in relation to their dealings with vulnerable people. Are they still 'at the centre' of the system, as our judge likes to see herself? Or are judges not partly marginalised by the increased role given to the private sector, to habilitated persons?

The Legal Representative for the Protection of Adults: A Relationship of Assistance between Support and Control

The mission of the legal representative for the protection of adults (*mandataire judicaire à la protection des majeurs*) is to support and protect adults who encounter difficulties in exercising their rights on a daily basis – due to a state of health that is impaired due to age, disability, or illness. This protection takes the form of one-off or more long-term support and can cover different aspects of daily life, administrative, social, legal or financial. The judge of protection disputes adopts measures, based on medical expertise. The judge designates the person who will be responsible for ensuring the protection. The priority in this designation goes to the family: since 1968 and the first reform mentioned above, it is first and foremost a member of the family of the person concerned, or failing that a close relative, who can fulfil the role of 'protector'. Where such person cannot be found among the family grouping, the judge appoints a legal representative for the protection of adults (see Bouttier, 2010, 94).

The professionalisation of the legal representative is a slow process and is still ongoing. In 2007, as mentioned above, the framework of the profession was clarified, including the formalisation of training and ethics (see Bouttier, 2010).[22]

The functions of the legal representatives are varied and obviously depend on the protection measure issued by the judge – judicial protective supervision, guardianship, curatorship – as much as on the situation of the protected person, their health and their needs. To varying degrees, they include administrative tasks – taking inventory, making budgets, collecting resources, paying expenses, doing accounts, and reporting these to the judge. Other tasks relate more to support, with still significant variations – managing, where appropriate, the question of the person's place of residence, supporting them in certain procedures or carrying out certain procedures on their behalf. Managing employment

[22] Law No 2024-217 of 8 April 2024 containing measures to build a society of healthy ageing and autonomy (*portant mesures pour bâtir la société du bien vieillir et de l'autonomie*). This law also intervened to supplement the provisions relating to the ethics of legal representatives for the protection of adults.

issues with them, allocation issues, etc. As will be discussed later, the range of these tasks is unlimited. It must be recalled that, in the field of civil justice and liberties, what is not explicitly forbidden by the law cannot be prevented, which in principle gives very broad scope for guardians' potential to act.[23] Indeed, the support relationship carries within it – or at least should carry within it – the hope of an evolution of the situation of the protected person. According to Robert Castel, the 'helping relationship' or the 'service relationship' is a type of professional technicality located at the heart of the practice of social work, due to the evolution of the social worker's activity over the course of his or her history.[24]

As noted earlier, legal representatives for the protection of adults work within different institutional frameworks. They can work individually, like a 'liberal' professional. Usually, however, they belong to a structure: either they belong to a hospital establishment or to an Ehpad (nursing home for elderly people); or, and this is the most common case, they are employees of a service (*association*) of legal representatives for the protection of adults. Among these services, some are specialised and others are not. Here, we must mention the role of the UDAF (*Union départementale des associations familiales*). These local structures are united within the national framework of the UNAF, the national association mentioned above. The UDAF have developed from their departmental headquarters a whole activity in the field of guardianships.[25] Alongside this reference body, there are many other services (*associations*) that bring together professionals in guardianship.

To discuss the work of guardians, and the way in which the question of how to promote the autonomy of people under protection is considered in their activities, we will discuss the example of a woman who undertook this role for a few years.

The woman is in her thirties and worked as a legal representative for the protection of adults after completing her studies as a social and family economics advisor (CESF, *conseillère en éducation sociale et familiale*).[26] She chose not to work in an institution – nursing home or hospital. Because, she says, such institutions, mainly deal with people who 'are no longer in their right mind' and with whom there is no interaction and few decisions to make. On the contrary, her work concerns people who live at home and who need to be supported – particularly in

[23] Pécaut-Rivolier, 2004, 66.

[24] R Castel, 'Du travail social à la gestion sociale du non-travail', *Esprit*, À quoi sert le travail social, mars-avril 1998, 28–47, quoted by Bachimont, Bungener, Huet, 2004, 75.

[25] In 2023, 90 departmental unions, the UDAFs, had services comprising legal representatives for the protection of adults, who operate in 93 departments. As a result, 160,000 people benefitted from a protection measure exercised by a service of legal representatives belonging to a UDAF, which makes this network the leading legal protection network for adults in France (Source: UNAF, Rapport d'activité, 2023, 73).

[26] This is a non-university diploma at Bac+3 level, which is prepared in one year after a BTS (Higher Technician Certificate) in social and family economics.

the case of reinforced curatorship, which constitutes the bulk of the measures for which this legal representative is responsible. She explains:

> When we work in institutions, each legal representative has 110 files in progress. There are fewer relationships and less contact. Outside of institutions, normally, each of us follows 60 measures. In practice, it is more like 63 or 65, a small excess that is quite a bit – 60 is already a lot.

In the context of curatorship, which constitutes the bulk of this agent's work, the law stipulates that the agent should 'work with' the relevant persons; it is they who sign. And so, this legal representative, trained in social work, adheres to this way of doing things (which is not the case, she explains, for all agents). She follows this principle while simultaneously ensuring that the obligations of control are respected – for example, carrying out inventories and rendering accounts which are part of her work.

> We, the legal representatives, are there and we are not there. In reality, the person sees us three times a year. We have an obligation of once a year, and if not, we can do it on the phone. These are structural choices. Where I work, they force us to go and see the person in person once a quarter. I think that is the minimum, it is not even enough. When we are asked for a reinforced guardianship, the idea is not to do things 'in place' of the person. If we see them once every three months, it is not enough. The goal then is to find partners who can take over, a social worker, a social life support service – in the disability sector, help to manage your budget, do the shopping, manage the maintenance of the house. We call a service to bring in a home help, help with the small steps of daily life. There are structures made for that, we make files for the 'departmental house for disabled persons' (MDPH, maison départementale des personnes handicapées). We ask them: Mr X needs someone to help him do his shopping. These people are important, we will rely on them, because we are not there much.

The social workers addressed by the legal representative often have difficulty identifying her intervention:

> Social workers do not know our job. Sometimes we have to put things back in place. A social worker tells me: 'You are their legal representative, it is up to you to prepare this file'. But if the protected person is in curatorship, they are supposed to do the steps themselves more or less. We have to re-explain what curatorship is and how the management is different from guardianship. The judge ruled that the person could do things, give them a certain amount of freedom. Finally, the social worker prepared the file. Protected adults, on the other hand, do not see the differences. They say 'I am under guardianship'.

The legal representative holds her mandate from the judge. Judges play a considerable role in the sense that they organise the activity of the representatives and, at the same time, they are distant figures. They only intervene at the outset of the measures, then, barring any incident, their role is limited to renewal which only occurs every five years. However, appearing before the judge is an intense moment, both for persons under guardianship and for their legal representative.

> The hearing is impressive. Three months before, we send a whole report to the judge: who are the partners around the person, how is it going, how is the budget management, the state of the accounts. What have we done with the person, if they can do more, if it has stagnated or if there have been difficulties and the measure needs to be 'worsened'. We give our opinion, a short conclusion: is this measure appropriate or should we consider a change . . . The adult is aware and we have to defend our point of view with the adult. It is impressive. It takes place in a small office, but I can feel that the protected adults are stressed by the situation. They don't always come. If they don't come, the judge postpones the hearing.

The work to be done by the judicial representatives with the protected adult is only very schematically defined by the judicial decision. 'Neither the law nor the case law have wished to give an explicit outline their mission' (Pécaut-Rivolier, 2010, 65). We find in the judgment the principle that implies a protection regime and sometimes some more precise directives, but certainly not the answers to the problems with which the legal agent is confronted in daily life (ibid, 66). The issue that then arises, and which is always difficult to resolve, is that of knowing how to deal with protected persons and how far to go in their support. Usually, the representative interviewed explains that she is unable to do what she would like – in the precise sense of being able to work with the protected person on a project that could make them more independent. In this regard, the question of money is omnipresent: protected people are always afraid of not having enough 'to go on holiday or buy clothes'. But the negotiations, says the agent, are 'expeditious'.

> In reinforced curatorship, we manage the bills but we do nothing in place of the person. It is a support, you have to negotiate your agreement, do it according to your project. If she wants to buy a car without a licence for 12,000 euros and she earns 1,000 euros per month, it is a project that needs to be worked on. We will have to wait. She will not have the car right away. It is a project that we can discuss with the teams of social workers. For example with disabled people who work in sheltered workshops, we discuss.

There is also the fact that relationships with protected persons can sometimes be strained, especially when they do not accept a measure, as in the following case:[27]

> With her, it was a complicated reinforced curatorship. She said that she did things and she didn't do them. She lied. It was not an honest and constructive relationship.

[27] Here we find more general observations on social work and the helping relationship, cf Bachimont, Bunger and Hauet, 2004, 75 et seq. The 'helping relationship', as these authors conceive it, 'is constructed on a daily basis in the interaction between the guardian and the protected person. However, the objectives of each may be different and come into opposition. It is then that the limits of the 'helping relationship' are visible and a conflictual relationship can set in.'

> She didn't understand why I wasn't sending money to a man in Cameroon, 'because they were getting married in a year'. She wanted me to send money to people she met on the Web, and she told me that she was married to a Parisian – it wasn't true, it was fantasies. It was difficult to make her understand that this man was perhaps malicious and that it was better to wait until he came to France to meet him. She did not accept that.

The legal representative regrets having to spend too much time with demanding people – those who constantly oppose measures. On the other hand, in her opinion, people who accept proposed measures and do not cause problems are not given enough attention. When the people she cares for are volunteers, she feels that she does not have time to engage more deeply with their projects and interests. The excessive number of files prevents her from doing so:

I think that for protected adults who are in acceptance and cooperation, we tend to take less care of them, when there are necessarily things to do. A budget is something that needs to be worked on in this work. It seems logical given my training as a social and family economy advisor, but we do not have time to do well. We do the minimum. We share the expenses with the person, 'roughly', explaining and negotiating barely, but we don't really work on gaining independence. We don't have time to do that and it's a shame. That's not the point of the protective measure. We have to do more, when possible given their pathology. If we do it, normally, we are led to a reduction in the measure.

Conversely, in some very exceptional examples, she explains that she does 'too much' for a given person. Is it her job to write a cover letter for a job search? She has done so, but she considers that it is beyond her mandate, which is rather to seek to mobilise support – social workers, around the person to be helped – a role of hub, of mediator.

Ultimately, when it comes to knowing how to maintain the balance between the question of protecting the person and that of respecting their rights, the judicial representative regrets not being able to do more to promote and encourage the autonomy of that person.

One last example, however: she is happy to have been able to resume, with an elderly lady who had been the victim of a botched surgical operation, a procedure that had been abandoned by her predecessor. She was able to support her in finding a lawyer. She explains that for this woman, it was a question of recognition and that she was then able to move forward with her to obtain the abandonment of the curatorship measure.

We can then underline a final point which explains the feeling of helplessness of this judicial representative in relation to situations where she would wish to be able to take more care of people, their projects and their budgets. In this woman's experience, the problem lies in the organisation of the structure to which she belongs. Strong pressure is exerted on agents; the organisation of their activities aims only to maximise the profitability of their work; and there is constant change. The professional environment has become uncertain. This makes working with protected people – which she enjoys and whose social usefulness she appreciates – difficult in practice. These challenging working conditions, which will not be described in detail here, are the lot of many services. They explain the very high turnover in a profession which remains little known today, poorly paid and lacks recognition.

The Family: In Charge, but Overwhelmed?

Families are increasingly involved, as guardians, curators or in the context of family habilitation measures. How do the family members concerned view the situation of their 'vulnerable' relatives and how do they think they can assist them? When they approach a court, how do family members assert the will and interests of the people targeted by the measures they recommend?

To discuss families faced with guardianship cases, we will take the example of a man we met in our survey, Dr H, a retired general practitioner, who had a dual experience of protective measures – he requested guardianship for his mother, for whom he became guardian, and then for his sister.

His mother was elderly, over 90, and had had a first heart attack. At that time, she lived in her own house with her daughter, the sister of Doctor H. However, certain psychiatric signs were evident in the sister, according to Doctor H who referred to 'paranoia' and a feeling of 'persecution', in a context marked by the occurrence of various personal traumatic events. As soon as they lived together, the mother found herself 'in the hands' of her daughter, who made all sorts of objections to the treatment, denigrated the medication prescribed to her mother and cooked with salt when this was prohibited. After various episodes, the mother was hospitalised, in particular to be given more regular treatment. However, Doctor H's sister went to the clinic, caused an uproar, and violently attacked a nurse. Dr H said that as these complications continued, he had a great deal of trouble stopping the problems caused by his sister. She was known to various authorities, the hospital and the police. They were aware of her extreme conduct and were reluctant to intervene.

Later, when the hospital professionals no longer wanted the mother – now incapacitated – to return home to where her daughter lived, Dr H thought it would be appropriate to request that his mother be placed under guardianship 'to protect her from her daughter's poor care' and 'because he no longer wants to decide alone' around her. At first, he hesitated to exercise this guardianship himself, then he decided to do so.

He sought the support of the institutions, while saying: 'I am the one who decided'. He requested that a lawyer draft the request – but considered that he could just as well have done everything himself. There was an expert assessment, then a hearing which he attended, but without his mother, who was exempted by the medical expert. He was appointed 'special representative' – an emergency, temporary solution – then his mother's guardian. He then had a subrogated guardian appointed to take care of the accounts.[28] He also said that he could have done this himself, but that he preferred this solution to avoid mistakes. From then on, he felt he had a little more control over the situation. He got his mother into a nursing home that he knew, and she lived there.

Later, the guardianship of this sister came into play. He requested this for a whole series of reasons: she needed psychiatric care but refused to get treatment, lived with completely limited resources and neglected to take care of her affairs. The guardianship came into play at his request. In order for the judge to rule, it was a requirement to obtain a medical expert report. This was difficult to obtain because she initially refused to accept this – she lived cloistered in their mother's house.[29]

> I filed a guardianship application for her, but I was told she needs to see the expert. I contacted a psychiatric expert. He sent my sister an appointment: 'In your interest, to assert your rights, please come forward.' She replied that she wouldn't go and she didn't go. I called back and the expert told me: 'I would be happy to go to her house, it's not very far from the hospital'.

Finally, guardianship was decided and set up, exercised by a local service. Everything continued to be difficult: the guardian was distant and the sister continued to live in her mother's house. She spent money extravagantly, which would then fall back on Doctor H.

From this complex situation, only summarised here, we recall the inextricable nature of the event. Doctor H became his mother's guardian because he saw the need to protect her from his sister's actions. When he then committed to requesting guardianship for his sister, things become even more complex, with a range of issues relating to housing, money, relationships with caregivers and with local institutions, at the same time as the question of this sister's health. In practice, Doctor H found himself involved in this stressful state of affairs for several years. He now says he has ambivalent feelings towards the relevant institutions: he relied on them and denigrated them at the same time. However, it is perhaps reasonable to assume that in his interactions with professionals – the judge, the subrogated guardian or the lawyer – he was aided by the fact that was himself a health professional.

[28] The question of how one becomes the guardian of a member of his or her family is raised by Le Borgne-Uguen and Penec. The authors describe the paths that lead family members to request intervention and, where appropriate, for a parent who has already shown support, to agree to take on the role of guardian or curator (Le Borgne-Uguen and Penec, 2004).

[29] If he or she considers it necessary, the judge may appoint a subrogated curator or a subrogated guardian to assist or represent, as the case may be, the protected person when the latter's interests are in opposition to those of the curator or guardian or when one or the other cannot provide assistance or act on his behalf due to the limitations of his mission (Art 454 CC). The judge may entrust a professional subrogated with the authority to verify the accounts.

The Lawyer, Representing Families, but what about the Wishes of the Protected Person?

Lawyers are rarely present in cases of protection of vulnerable adults. In fact, they intervene when difficulties arise and one may be of the view that they do so only at the request of a family member who considers that the situation requires judicial review. Although exceptional, the appearance of lawyers has a particular significance in relation to the question of access to justice in these situations. Indeed, while most protection measures are decided and implemented without giving rise to particular difficulties, those in which lawyers intervene are marked by the existence of friction and conflicts – opposing professional actors, family members or protected persons. These situations – which may or may not give rise to a request before the judge – provide an opportunity to understand the role of justice in the field of vulnerabilities and they illustrate particularly well the tensions that emerge on this subject in family relationships.

To illustrate these situations, we draw on the experiences of a lawyer practising in a large city in western France. The lawyer in question did not specialise in family matters, but practised for about 15 years in different fields, including real estate and construction law. She had occasionally been called upon to take on cases for clients who were experiencing difficulties regarding a parent in a vulnerable state. These situations were marked by certain complexities and by tensions and conflicts between the people involved.

The first situation highlights an opposition about what is 'good' for the protected person, in this case an elderly woman under guardianship whose only daughter was the guardian. Mrs W was 87 years old and she refused this guardianship. She had a 92-year-old neighbour, Mr M, who had in effect become her companion. Her daughter, as guardian, thought this man was 'taking advantage' of her mother. She thus called on the lawyer we interviewed. However, according to this lawyer, it appeared that if Mr M had indeed taken advantage of Mrs W's resources, it was not really a matter of assets. The mother, in fact, only owned a house, but her daughter had grievances against Mr M. She believed that the man was cutting her mother off from others, from her family and friends. The daughter felt he blocked her. She noted that it was becoming increasingly difficult to enter her mother's house because this man was always there. She viewed her mother as a child and considered that she was 'no longer able to think'.

For his part, Mr M appealed to the court, even though he had no authority to do so. He hired a lawyer himself and this lawyer also claimed to be Mrs W's lawyer. He claimed to have the consent of the protected person. This way of doing things seemed questionable and the situation was marked by a confusion of interests. What makes the situation complicated however, said the lawyer interviewed, was that these two people wanted to live together by osmosis. Furthermore, Mrs W appeared to be happy with that situation. Her daughter disputed this, while acknowledging that this was her mother's vision. The question raised, the lawyer emphasised, was then that of knowing what autonomy we wanted to preserve for the person under guardianship.

The second situation had a more institutional dimension, because the question of the good for the protected person was brought before the court and all the way to the Court of Appeal. This was a case that concerned a wealthy elderly woman, who lived in the north of France and who was under a guardianship exercised by a local organisation. Her daughter lived in the south and would have liked her mother to be able to come and live near her. However, the service that exercised the guardianship resisted this proposal and refused to communicate anything to her about her mother's accounts. The conflict was reported by the same lawyer, asked by the daughter to take charge of the file.

> Initially, the case was just so that the mother could live in Cannes next to her daughter – an only child. The guardianship service refused. It blocked the change of address. The daughter did not see the accounts. She was told: 'You do not have the right to see'. In fact, in the guardianship, you no longer see anything. The mother was at home and sometimes said: 'I no longer have enough to live on'. It was not entirely true. The family does not understand, it has no right of inspection, it only has the point of view of the protected adult.

The lawyer only took on this case at the appeal stage, which was initiated after the court in the northern city refused the mother's move to the south. The lawyer explained that this procedure before the Court of Appeal concerning cases of protected adults is very special, in particular because it gives an important role to the magistrates of the prosecution (*procureur*) who act as representatives of society:

> It is a special procedure, both written and oral. In the first instance, it is in the judge's office, it is a little informal. On appeal it is a hearing, with the prosecution. You give everything to the prosecution. There is a real hearing, which is not usual during an appeal. It is a bit like a criminal hearing, very unusual. And it is very parallel with judicial liquidation, where the civil prosecution is also present: a person is dispossessed of their rights, whether physical or moral. It is much more formal.

However, the hearing went badly:

> I had not anticipated that the prosecution would attack my client. I had not thought to prepare my client who considered that the guardianship body was not doing its job. The prosecution was very virulent; it considered that she wanted to get the inheritance before the inheritance. My client cried. The president of the chamber of the Court of Appeal was also surprised by the attitude of the prosecution – but there was a considerable estate. And then, we were suing a guardianship body and they did not like it. The hearing was chaotic. It was hard. I saw my client crying. Afterwards, I responded to the prosecution. I told them: you are making a case against us.

The prosecution's position appalled the lawyer – for whom the daughter's request was fully justified:

> She is an only child, she has always taken care of her mother, she came to see her, even though she lived in the south of France, she has always taken care of her mother. It was not an interested approach.

Following this hearing, the daughter and her lawyer obtained a right of inspection with the communication of the accounts, but were refused the change of guardian. Subsequently, by changing strategy, the lawyer was able to obtain the mother's travel to live near her daughter:

> I said: we are not going to ask to buy a house in the south – which is what she wanted to do. But we can offer a luxury nursing home in the south, near you. This was accepted. I asked at the same time to change guardian and I had the daughter appointed.

From there, the lawyer took over, on behalf of the daughter, the work of the guardian regarding the mother's assets:

> We took back control of all the assets. I have a bailiff with me. We assessed all the assets – with each change of guardianship, we have to make an inventory. We made an inventory of what the guardian had done before, a balance sheet. We did another audit, as we were moving the mother, hired an auctioneer . . . We spent money, but to earn some later. Every year I do the accounts. She is a good client and it is interesting to do.

She also explains that the work is not limited to the patrimonial question, but also includes attention to the protected person:

> Even when we present the accounts to the judge, we start by talking about the person. How they are, what care they have had, are they better or worse off. And we finish with the accounts.

In both of these situations, we can see how the question of what is 'good' and 'right' for the vulnerable person is subject to interpretations that can diverge greatly between the actors involved, family members, professional protectors and magistrates. Moreover, the lawyer who reports them does not work for the vulnerable people themselves, but for relatives who think they can ensure their safety and well-being. The observation is more generally clear that lawyers are rarely present in cases involving protected adults. In 2016, the Defender of Rights had already suggested that it could be provided for adults, as is the case for minors, that the judge requests the *ex officio* appointment of a lawyer when this seems necessary (*Défenseur des Droits*, 2016, 58).

CONCLUSION

This chapter outlines some of the questions that arise in the area of protecting vulnerable people. Through our illustrations, we have highlighted, the point of view of different actors concerned with the protection of adults. We have presented the point of view of the judge, a 'central' actor, without whom nothing is done – at least in the key moments of the life path of the persons concerned – but whose role is now being questioned, in particular due to the rise in family habilitation. We have also examined the activity of court-appointed tutors and curators. Their intervention at the request of the judge is an essential transmission belt for the protection of vulnerable people, but it is exercised, as we have seen, under pressure from protected adults and their families and under multiple constraints, starting with the weight of the number of measures they follow, with the additional difficulty of acting without substituting for the people concerned. All this with the feeling of an endemic lack of recognition. We then briefly illustrated the delicate situation of guardians within the family, and again mentioned the role of the lawyer in cases where the well-being of the protected person is the subject of friction and is brought before the courts for debate.

This analysis is only a sketch. Based on the practices described and the stories reported, we can easily imagine the extreme diversity of the elements of the system we are dealing with. To get a more precise idea, we would have to address the different ways in which judges proceed, the different practices of legal representatives in their work context and, of course, the infinite twists and turns of family stories with the multiple and sometimes contradictory interests that drive their members.

Other actors also intervene in this vast system – for example notaries, bailiffs, for the legal field, and of course doctors, particularly experts in the health field. The latter play an essential role as we have seen in some of our illustrations. In addition, other professionals can claim to play a role in the care of vulnerable people, for example family mediators who recently offered their intervention to deal with conflicts that may arise between protected persons, their family and the institutions that support them.

Without going further in this analysis, based on the elements presented, we would like to return to the question of how, in the current state of practice, the protection of people and respect for their autonomy and will are ensured concurrently. In France, in this area as in others, the law is adapting in successive waves, with jolts and reforms that pile up and reaffirm the same fundamentals, while also asserting new principles. For several decades, in fact, the law has attempted to destigmatise the situation of protected persons and, following the trend that is emerging internationally, to give them more autonomy and better recognise their identity. This objective is stated against a backdrop that goes in the direction of delegating its fulfilment to families – with reasons that relate to limited public resources in the context of an ageing population. At the same time, and in a way that is perhaps somewhat contradictory, the concern to prevent abuses of all kinds has led the legislator to strengthen the dimension of control over the measures taken.

This observation is confirmed by a recent opinion formulated by the Defender of Rights, regarding the bill on Ageing Well mentioned above:

> The Defender of Rights . . . regrets in particular that the policy dedicated to the legal protection of adults is lacking in coherence and does not benefit from any steering to effectively guarantee the fundamental rights of the most vulnerable (Défenseur des droits, 2024, 5).

As for the orientations that emerge from practices, they reflect the law, and go in different, sometimes contradictory directions. If the multiplicity of measures, all with specific names and conditions of application, retain their meaning today in light of the desire to have a range of solutions, the fact remains that the modes of action of the stakeholders do not all tend in the same direction. As noted above, the place of the courts is still central, but that of families continues to increase, in an area where the complexity of procedures is not easy to navigate for private individuals. In addition, the centrality of the role of the judge is partly called into question, as has been suggested in particular with the testimony of the judge of protection disputes, due to the increase in the number of family habilitations, which reflects the trend towards privatising the care for dependent persons.

This complexity and the question of privatisation are notably mentioned by the Defender of Rights in the 2024 opinion cited above.

> Family habilitation measures are enjoying increasing success. Nevertheless, the significant withdrawal of the office of the judge of protection disputes, guarantor of fundamental rights and freedoms, must be compensated by lasting mechanisms legitimately expected by adults themselves but also by families. Under no circumstances should the movement of dejudicialisation constitute a transfer of burden to them. In this regard, it is necessary to promote information and support for caregivers designated to ensure protection measures (Defender of Rights, 2024, 38).

Ultimately, it does not seem wrong to say that we in France find ourselves in a situation in which the question of what we want for vulnerable people is not really the subject of overall reflection and coherent policy. The law is made up of multiple accumulated elements and ends up forming a patchwork. Practices are fragmented and the meaning of the whole is difficult to grasp, so that there is no simple or unequivocal answer to the question of what significance is attached to the issue of taking into account the rights of vulnerable people. We seek to obtain more autonomy for them, in order to meet the expectations of the time, but we do not do this without at the same time maintaining a strong requirement for protection – represented in particular by the preservation of the figure of the judge. But this requirement itself is limited, in particular due to a lack of resources, whether in terms of judicial means or social service personnel – so that we come to favour an appeal to families, not without fearing the risks that this may present. The fact remains that our analysis suggests, through successive bills, the discussions that accompany them, as well as interviews with the actors, the extent to which the issue is present today in society, following the COVID-19 crisis and at a time when the ageing of the French population appears inevitable. This can be seen as an important result: the current situation is marked by a greater visibility of these situations, and a concern about the actors – professionals or family carers – who contribute to look after them.

REFERENCES

Bachimont J, Bungener M, Hauet E, 'Des gestions de tutelle qualifiées de difficiles: une négociation à construire entre tuteurs et majeurs souffrant de troubles psychiatriques' (2004) *Recherches familiales*, n° 1, 73–86.

Blanc A, *Sociologie du handicap* (Paris, Armand Colin, 2015).

Bouttier P, 'Le mandataire judiciaire à la protection des majeurs. De la professionnalisation à l'accompagnement' (2010) *Vie sociale*, n°3.

Défenseur des droits, Protection des majeurs vulnérables, 2016. /www.defenseurdesdroits.fr /rapport-protection-juridique-des-majeurs-vulnerables-357 (30.01.2025).

Défenseuse des droits, Avis du Défenseur des droits n°24-02 sur la proposition de loi n°193, adoptée par l'Assemblée nationale, portant mesures pour bâtir la société du bien-vieillir en France, 2024.

Eyraud B, 'D'une réforme à l'autre: le droit tutélaire à l'épreuve de son application' (2010) *Vie sociale*, Erès.

Eyraud B, 'La difficile institutionnalisation des services mandataires judiciaires à la prestation des majeurs', *Actes éducatifs de soins entre éthique et gouvernance* (Nice, France, 2009).

F Le Borgne-Uguen, S Pennes, 'Les solidarités familiales aux prises avec les mesures de protection juridique concernant des parents âgés' (2004) *Recherches familiales*, n°1, 45–63.

Livre blanc sur la protection juridique des majeurs, septembre 2012, www.atmp69.fr/wp-content /uploads/2012/11/120907-Livre-Blanc.pdf.pdf (26.12. 2024).

Ministère de la Justice, Infostat, 2024, n°197.

Pécaut-Rivolier, L, 'La protection des majeurs à l'épreuve de la pratique professionnelle' (2024) *Recherches familiales*, n° 1, 2004, 64–72.

Peterka, N, Caron-Déglise, A, Arbellot F, *Droit des tutelles; protection judiciaire des majeurs et des mineurs* (Dalloz, 2012).

Rapport sur la protection juridique des majeurs vulnérable (2016) Rapport du défenseur des droits, Paris.

Recherches familiales, n° 1, 2004, Les majeurs protégés.

Revillard A, *Des droits vulnérables. Handicap, action publique et changement social* (Paris, Presse de Science Po, 2020).

https://solidarites-sante.gouv.fr/affaires-sociales/personnes-vulnerables/ (26.12. 2024).

10

Considering People without Legal Capacity in Turkey

VERDA İRTIŞ

INTRODUCTION

WE KNOW THAT the literature on persons with 'disabilities' has developed considerably. At the crossroads of several disciplines and a variety of historical and political contexts, our times seem to be marked by a growing awareness not only of the place to be assigned to 'disabled' people, but also of the expressions used to name them. This does not mean that this movement of minds is at the same level in all societies. It differs even within the same society. The rights of the people with disabilities constitutes a constant multilayered struggle where – as the 'disability movement' illustrates in a particular way – 'disabled' people themselves play a significant role in getting societies to change the way they look at 'disability'.

As Laurence Parent in her article with the objective of analysing the differences between Francophone Quebec and Anglophone parts of Canada in their conceptualisation of disabled people expresses with reference to Fiona K Campbell (2008) and Gregor Wolbring (2008) 'ableism is an unattainable ideal, even for people identified as non-disabled. It is a fiction to which people must constantly try to conform.'[1] Thus, we can state recent years have been characterised by systematic criticism with regard to our 'conventional' ways of seeing and doing where the effects of 'abilisme' as a means of hierarchising and a source of violence are seriously considered. The same author who elaborates 'capacitisme' as reflecting both 'ableism' and 'disableism'[2] qualifies it 'as a discourse of power and domination'.[3]

The rights (to education, health, work . . .) of 'disabled' people have also brought back the question of 'access to justice'. This question, which already

[1] Laurence Parent, 'Ableism/disablism, on dit ça comment en français?', *Canadian Journal of Disability Studies*, 6(2), 2017, 188.

[2] Ibid, 200.

[3] Ibid, 203.

constitutes a quite complex subject, becomes more difficult when it concerns persons considered as 'disabled', and particularly thorny when it concerns 'mentally disabled' persons.

When we look at the available statistics, 'disability', as we still define it today, encompasses 'an estimated 1.3 billion people – about 16% of the global population – currently experience significant disability. This number is increasing due in part to population ageing and an increase in the prevalence of noncommunicable diseases.'[4] For Turkey, 'the proportion of the population with at least one disability (aged three and over) is 6.9% (4,876,000 people)'.[5] However, as this data dates back to 2011, it is likely, as various unofficial sources indicate, that this proportion is higher subject to updated figures.

Originating to a large extent in the UK and USA, there is a transformation of perspective operating with regard to disability rights. With regard to the law, as the literature on sociology of law and justice shows us, it is both an expression of changes in social structures and the source of these changes.[6] Accompanied by the international/supranational circulation of ideas and models,[7] these elements help us to grasp the shift from 'aid-based' to 'rights-based' approach. We see that the transformation in discourses and practices are transforming discourses and practices in Turkey as well.

The purpose of this chapter is to provide an account of the way people with legal incapacity are currently treated in Turkey. To do this, we will concentrate first on the local legal framework. Then, we will point out the importance of international dynamics in order to better understand the changes in Turkey. Before concluding we will report the observations from our investigation that we found through various sources. We hope that this chapter can draw attention to the question of the access to justice in the domain of legal incapacities.[8]

LAW AT THE LOCAL LEVEL

As the review of legislation by the Istanbul Bar Association shows, 'disability' is included in different laws and their related regulations (yönetmelikler) and decrees, such as the Constitution, the Social Services Law, the Law on

[4] See https://www.who.int/health-topics/disability#tab=tab_1 (12.1.2025).

[5] Ministry of Family and Social Services, Statistical Bulletin on Disabled and Elderly, April 2023, https://aile.gov.tr/media/135432/eyhgm_istatistik_bulteni_nisan_23.pdf, 6 (27.2.2024).

[6] For an exemple, cf Pierre Lascoumes, 'Changer le droit, changer la société: le moment d'un retournement', Genèses 77, déc 2009, 110–23.

[7] Benoît Eyraud, 'Adopter une approche du handicap par les droits humains? La domestication en spirale de la Convention internationale sur les droits des personnes handicapées en France', *Droit et Société,* 113, 2023.

[8] While there are studies on 'education, employment, health and rehabilitation, and financial assistance provided by the state', there are none focusing on access to justice (Taştan, 2018: 13). 'The lack of academic interest and work in the field of disability rights in Turkey' (Şimşek and Songur, 2018: 97) is also a known fact.

Combating Hereditary Diseases, the Turkish Penal Code, the Turkish Civil Code, the Law on Metropolitan Municipality, the Law on Social Security and the General Health Insurance, the Law on Encouraging Social Assistance and Solidarity, the Law on Basic Provisions of Elections and Voter Registers, the Law on the Organisation and Duties of the Supreme Electoral Council and the Notary Public Law[9] containing reflections and also rephrasing of expressions in relation to people with disabilities. The terms handicapped (özürlü) and crippled (sakat) have been replaced by the concept of disability (engelli). In 2005, a specific law on Persons with Disabilities (Law No 5378) was enacted. The draft mental health law, which is in progress, can also be mentioned as another potential legal reference. If it comes to fruition, it will be the first law specific to this domain and will allow involuntary treatment to be dealt with in a more adequate and inclusive manner.[10]

As regards the subject of our investigation, we will rely especially on the Turkish Civil Code (TCC) (Law No 4721), more precisely on articles 396 to 494 presented under the section on 'Guardianship' in the 'Family Book'.[11] Influenced by the Swiss Civil Code which was considered as 'the most modern' of its time, the first Turkish Civil Code (Law No 743) was accepted in 1926. The current version, entered into force in 2002, after a long period of preparation to adapt the previous one to contemporary conditions. It is also important to note that even though there is no independent field termed 'guardianship law', we do encounter expressions such as 'the institution of guardianship' or 'guardianship law', which can be a sign that it is gaining in importance. 'Guardianship law' is considered at the intersection of personal and family law.[12] It has both individual and collective dimensions explaining 'the existence of a debate on the legal character'[13] of guardianship. Taking all factors into account, there is a convergence of opinion on its 'public' character.[14] In other words, although guardianship law looks like private law, it is 'public' because it also concerns the protection of society.[15]

The current Turkish Civil Code designates that people with legal incapacity fall within two categories: 'fully incapacitated' (tam ehliyetsizler) and 'limited

[9] See https://www.istanbulbarosu.org.tr/files/komisyonlar/ehm/docs/ehm_mevzuat_1.pdf (28.2.2025).

[10] See https://www.tercuman.com/analiz/ruh-sagligi-yasasi-neden-onemli-413/ (21.2.2025).

[11] In the previous Code (Law No 743), articles between 346 and 437 were dealing with the people designated as legally incapacitated. In other words, while the initial Law contained 81 articles, the new one contains 94. As we see, articles on 'statutory advisorship' and 'restriction of freedom for protection' were absent.

[12] Aslı Açıkgöz, 'Dar Anlamda Vesayeti Gerektiren Hâller ve Vesayet Altına Almanın İşlem Ehliyeti Bakımından Sonuçları' (Cases for Legal Guardianship in the Narrow Sense and the Consequences of Legal Guardianship on the Capacity to Make Transactions), PhD Thesis, Istanbul University, Özel Hukuk Ana Bilim Dalı (Department of Private Law), Supervisor: Bilgehan Çetiner, 2016, 34.

[13] Ibid, 30.

[14] Ceyda Çınar, 'Türk Medeni Hukuku Kapsamında Vesayet İlişkisi ve Vesayet Makamının İzni ile Yapılabilen İşlemler' (Under Turkish Civil Law Guardian Relationship and With the Permission of the Guardian Authority Transactions that can be Taken), MA Thesis, Istanbul Aydin University, Özel Hukuk Ana Bilim Dalı (Department of Private Law), Supervisor: Ebru Ceylan, 2024, 4.

[15] Açıkgöz, op cit, 2106; Çınar, op cit, 2024.

incapacitated' (sınırlı ehliyetsizler) persons. This nomination is made with reference to capacity or power of discernment (ayırt etme gücü) which is 'the consciousness, understanding and will necessary for people to understand the causes and consequences, the importance and the scope of their actions and transactions'.[16] Consequently, 'the power to distinguish is a relative concept'.[17] And, 'what is to be understood from this relativity is that the presence or absence of the power of discernment is not determined in general, but according to a specific person or behaviour'.[18] Thus, it is important to note that 'the concept of the power of discernment is not determined in an absolute manner. Therefore, whether the person who committed the act has the power of discernment should be determined according to the characteristics of each concrete case.'[19]

Chapter three of the TCC organises guardianship in three major parts – the Guardianship System, Execution of Guardianship, and Termination of Guardianship – each having several sections. The *Guardianship System* contains the sections of guardianship bodies, circumstances requiring guardianship, authority, appointment of a guardian, curatorship and statutory advisorship, and restriction of freedom for protection. *Execution of Guardianship* is composed of the duties of the guardian, duties of the curator, duties of guardianship offices and the responsibility of guardianship bodies. As for *Termination of Guardianship*, this sets out circumstances where guardianship will cease, termination of guardianship and consequences of termination of guardianship.

These sections illustrate that[20] 'guardianship bodies are guardianship offices, guardians and curators' (article 396). Guardianship offices are composed of 'public guardianship' and 'special guardianship'. According to article 397 'Public guardianship shall be conducted by guardianship offices composed of guardianship board and supervisory authority'.[21] And the 'guardianship board is a civil court of peace', whereas the 'supervisory board is a civil court of first instance'. Special guardianship refers to situations where 'guardianship can be given to a family exceptionally when it is justified by the interests of the person under guardianship especially when it is necessary to maintain a community, an enterprise or similar work. In this case authority, duties and responsibilities of the guardianship board shall be handed over to a family council to be established'[22]

[16] Vehbi Umut Erkan and İpek Yücer, 'Ayırt Etme Gücü', *AUHFD*, 60(3), 2011, 488.

[17] Ibid, 494. Here and in the precedent quotation, the authors draw on several sources.

[18] Oğuzman et al, quoted by Erkan and Yücer, op cit, 2011, 494.

[19] Ibid, 495.

[20] For this chapter, it should be pointed out that for the articles of the Code, we have relied on two sources: one which has already been translated into English and is available at the following link https://rm.coe.int/turkish-civil-code-family-law-book/1680a3bcd4 and the other in Turkish. Where we have quoted from the English version, we have indicated these. In cases where they are translated from the Turkish source, in order to make the text easier to read, we have used inverted commas in the case of direct quotations accompanied by the number of the article concerned. In the case of reformulations we have only referred to the article number.

[21] See https://rm.coe.int/turkish-civil-code-family-law-book/1680a3bcd4, 8108.

[22] Ibid.

(article 398). The next article indicates that 'Special guardianship shall be established by the supervisory authority upon the request of two close relatives with capacity to act for the person under guardianship or one relative and his/her spouse'[23] (article 399). With respect to the family council, it is noted that it 'shall be composed of at least three relatives of the person under guardianship who are qualified to be guardian and they shall be appointed by the supervisory authority for a four-year term'[24] and the 'spouse of the person under guardianship can also be a member of the family council'[25] (article 400). 'Members of the family council shall guarantee that they are to fulfil their duties properly. Special guardianship shall not be established without ensuring guarantee'[26] (article 401). 'If the family council does not fulfil its duties or the interest of the person under guardianship necessitates, the supervisory authority can always change the family council or terminate special guardianship'[27] (article 402).

As for the guardian and curator, the Law underlines that 'the guardian shall be liable to protect all the interests of the minor or person under legal disability under guardianship regarding their personality and asset and to represent them in legal transactions' and 'curator shall be appointed to undertake certain work or to manage the asset . . .'[28] (article 403).

Therefore, situations requiring guardianship are grouped mainly in two categories. The first concerns the fact of being a child. In the case of minors, custody constituting a rule, guardianship is reserved to exceptional cases.[29] Nevertheless, as article 404 indicates 'every minor who is not under parental authority shall be placed under guardianship'. Juvenile courts can also act as a guardianship authority.[30] Moreover, if needed 'a decision can be made to restrict those who are not yet adults, but the decision to restrict will have consequences after they reach adulthood'.[31]

As for adults, constituting the second group which is the focus of this chapter, TCC stipulates four reasons leading to restriction. Firstly, for 'mental illness or mental weakness', article 405 says that 'Any adult who is incapable of functioning due to mental illness or mental weakness, or who requires constant assistance for his/her protection and care, or who endangers the safety of others, shall be restricted'. According to this article, 'Administrative authorities, notaries and courts who learn of the existence of a situation requiring guardianship

[23] Ibid.
[24] Ibid, 8109.
[25] Ibid.
[26] Ibid.
[27] Ibid.
[28] Ibid.
[29] Açıkgöz, op cit, 2016, 37.
[30] Ibid, 47.
[31] Songül Aldemir, 'Medeni Hukuk Çerçevesinde Vesayet İlişkisi ve Vesayeti Gerektiren Hâller' (Wardship Relationship Within the Framework of Civil Law and Situations Requiring Wardship), MA Thesis, Atatürk University, Hukuk Ana Bilim Dalı (Department of Law), Supervisor: Hatice Kübra Ercoşkun Şenol, 2020, 32.

while performing their duties are obliged immediately to notify the competent guardianship authority'. Secondly, for 'extravagance, alcohol or drug abuse, poor lifestyle, mismanagement of his/her assets', article 406 indicates that 'Any adult who, due to his/her extravagance, alcohol or drug addiction, bad lifestyle or mismanagement of his/her assets, causes a danger of plunging himself/herself or his/her family into hardship or poverty and is therefore in need of constant protection and care or threatens the safety of others, shall be restricted'. Thirdly, for 'deprivation of liberty', article 407 in its amended version in 2024 stipulates that 'An adult person who is in a penal institution for the execution of a sentence to imprisonment by a final court decision is restricted or a curator is appointed upon his/her request. An adult person who is in a penal institution for the execution of a finalised imprisonment sentence of five years or more in total may be restricted if it is deemed necessary for the protection of his personality or property, even if he does not request it. The authority in charge of executing the sentence shall immediately notify the guardianship board that the execution of the prison sentence has begun. The guardianship board shall hear the convicted person before making a decision.' Lastly, on request, article 408 specifies that 'Any adult who proves that he/she is unable to manage his/her affairs properly due to old age, disability, inexperience or severe illness may request his/her restriction'. It should be noted that article 1 of Law No 6462 dated 25/4/2013 substituted the term 'disability' for 'crippled' in this article.

In terms of procedure, the hearing of the person concerned and the expert report reveal the essentials: article 409 indicates that 'a person shall not be restrained without being heard due to extravagancy, alcohol, drug and substance abuse, poor lifestyle, poor management or upon request. Restriction due to mental disorder or weakness of mind shall only be decided based on an official medical board report. (Additional phrase:6/12/2019-7196/52 art.) The judge may hear the person to be restrained by taking into account the medical board report before making a decision.'[32]

As regards the appointment of a guardian, it is the guardianship board who 'appoints a person of age capable to fulfil this duty as guardian' (article 413). As the same article indicates, in some cases, more than one guardian can be designated.

Priority is given to spouses and close relatives on the condition that they meet the requirements (article 414). This article also stipulates that closeness of residence and personal relations are considered to be important factors in designating a guardian. Thus, people who are designated as guardians and residing in the domicile of the person for whom a guardianship is appointed, except for cases of attribution of family council, are obliged to accept this designation (article 416). Those who have reached the age of 60, those who can perform this duty only with difficulty due to physical disabilities (in 2013 with the same article of

[32] Ibid, 8110.

Law No 6462 2013, the expression of 'handicap' was replaced by 'disabilities') or permanent illnesses, persons having parental authority for more than four children, those who have a guardianship duty and the President of the Republic, members of Turkish Grand National Assembly, Vice Presidents of the Republic, ministers, judges and prosecutors (in 2018 article 139 of the Decree Law No 700 changed the wording 'and the Council of Ministers Members' to 'Vice Presidents of the Republic, ministers') may become guardians (article 417). Being a restricted person, being banned from public service or leading a dishonourable life, having interests that conflict with those of the person for whom they are to be appointed guardian or with whom there is conflict, or being a judge of the relevant guardianship offices are all obstacles to being a guardian (article 418).

The guardianship board has the responsibility to assign a guardian without waiting (article 419). 'The person appointed guardian can use their right to refrain from guardianship within ten days as of notification of guardianship decision to them. All people concerned can allege that appointment is unlawful within ten days as of the date they learnt about appointment of a guardian. If the guardianship board deems refrainment from guardianship or reason for objection is justified, they shall appoint a new guardian. If they do not deem it justified, they shall notify the supervisory authority of the case along with their opinion on the matter to make the necessary decision'[33] (article 420). And 'if the person appointed guardian is relieved of duty, the guardianship board shall immediately appoint a new guardian'[34] (article 424).

As regards curatorship, the guardianship board has the responsibility to nominate a 'representative' depending on the demand of the person concerned or *ex officio* (article 426). The same article mentions the following situations as requiring the attribution of a representative curator: '1 If a person of age is unable to do his/her own urgent work or appoint a representative due to a disease, being somewhere else or a similar reason, 2 If interests of the legal representative and those of the . . . person under legal disability are conflicting, 3 If there is an obstacle in the way of the legal representative fulfilling his/her duties'.[35]

The same board also has the responsibility to designate a management curator, '1 If a person has been absent for a long time and where they reside is not known, 2 If a person is unable to manage their property on their own or unable to appoint a representative for this although there is not a valid ground to place the said person under guardianship, 3 If heirdom rights to an inheritance are not yet clear or interests of a foetus necessitate, 4 If a legal person is devoid of the necessary organs and its management cannot be ensured by other means, 5 If a way to manage or spend money and other aids collected from the public for charity or other work with similar purposes cannot be ensured'[36] (article 427).

[33] Ibid, 8112.
[34] Ibid.
[35] Ibid.
[36] Ibid, 8112, 8113.

In addition, if there is any valid reason, the law makes provision for designating a curator on request of a person of age (article 428).

As for the statutory advisorship, he/she has appointed an adult person to limit his/her capacity to act in order to protect him/her in certain domains of life although there is no sufficient reason for his/her restriction (article 429). '1 Litigation and accordance, 2 Purchase, sale of and putting in pledge the immovables and establishing another in rem right on them, 3 Purchase, sale of and putting in pledge commercial papers, 4 Constructional work that is outside of ordinary management boundaries, 5 Lending and borrowing, 6 Withdrawing the principal amount, 7 Donation, 8 Making a commitment in foreign exchange, 9 Vouching for someone'[37] (article 429). As this article stipulates, 'authority to manage a person's assets can be revoked under the same conditions without prejudice to right of disposition on their revenues'.[38]

On the subject of restriction of freedom for protection, it is foreseen that 'any adult person who poses a danger to society due to mental illness, mental weakness, addiction to alcohol or narcotic substances, infectious disease posing a grave danger or vagrancy shall be placed in a suitable institution for his treatment, education or rehabilitation or may be detained if his personal protection cannot be provided in any other way. Public officials who learn of the existence of one of these reasons while performing their duties are obliged to immediately notify the competent guardianship authority. The burden on the person's environment is also taken into account. The person concerned is removed from the institution as soon as his or her condition permits' (article 432).

Article 435 states, 'The person placed in the institution or his/her relatives may appeal against the decision to the supervisory authority within ten days starting from the notification to them. This right may also be exercised in case the request for removal from the institution is rejected.'

Article 436 specifies that the 'restriction of liberty for protection purposes shall be governed by the Code of Civil Procedure, without prejudice to the following rules 1 When deciding, the person concerned shall be informed of the reasons for it and his/her attention shall be drawn in writing to the fact that he/she may appeal against the decision to the supervisory authority. 2 A person placed in an institution will be immediately informed in writing that he or she may appeal against the decision to detain him or her or against the refusal to remove him or her from the institution to the supervisory authority within ten days at the latest. 3 Any request requiring a court decision shall be submitted without delay to the competent judge. 4 The guardianship board or the judge issuing the placement order may postpone the consideration of this request depending on the circumstances of the case. 5 A decision may be taken on persons suffering from mental illness, mental weakness, alcohol or drug addiction, severe dangerous infectious diseases only after obtaining

[37] Ibid, 8113.
[38] Ibid.

an official medical board report. (Repealed sentence: 6/12/2019-7196/53 art) . . . 6. (Additional: 6/12/2019-7196/53 art.) (Amended: 2/3/2024-7499/7 art). In order to ensure that the official medical board report can be obtained, blood or similar biological samples and samples such as hair, saliva, nails may be taken from the person's body, necessary medical interventions may be made to the person and, if necessary, the person may be placed in a health institution for a maximum of twenty days upon the preliminary report of a doctor. The placement decision made upon a doctor's preliminary report shall be immediately notified to the person concerned and his/her relatives. The person concerned or his/her relatives may appeal against this decision to the supervisory authority within ten days of notification; the appeal shall not stay the execution of the decision. The objection shall be resolved immediately by the supervisory authority. 7 (Addition: 6/12/2019-7196/53md.) For the execution of the decisions taken under this article, force may be used against the person concerned and necessary medical assistance may be obtained from health officials.'

Article 437 sets out the procedure for the judge (this being modified in 2023). Instead of stating that that judge will listen to the person concerned and decide without delay, the amended wording states that the 'judge listens, completes the investigation and renders her/his decision within two days at the latest without delay'. The question of restriction of freedom for protection constitutes one of the most controversial areas concerning legal incapacities; this emphasis on completing the investigation appears to be a step in the right direction.

Significant duties of the guardian include, maintaining the books, preservation of valuable goods, selling movable properties, depositing money, providing the necessary instruction for commercial and industrial enterprises, and selling immovables (articles 438, 439, 440, 441, 442, 443 and 444).

Under the heading of care and representation, article 447 stipulates that the 'Guardian shall be obliged to protect the person under legal disability and help them with all their personal affairs. If delay is deemed to be inconvenient, the guardian can place the person under legal disability with an institution in line with provisions of restriction of freedom for protection or retain the said person in such an institution and immediately notify the guardianship board of the situation.'[39] 'Without prejudice to the provisions on the powers of the guardianship authorities [offices], guardian represents the person under guardianship for all legal transactions'[40] (article 448).

As regards limitations on guardianship, 'it is forbidden to act as a guarantor, to establish a foundation and to make substantial donations on behalf of the person under guardianship' (article 449). For cases where the person under guardianship has the capacity to express his/her opinion, the law provides that the guardian is bound to consider them as much as possible. And this does not

[39] Ibid, 8116.
[40] Ibid.

eliminate the guardian's responsibility with regard to decisions made (article 450). As a rule, the guardian is nominated for two years which can further be extended for a period of two years. Nevertheless, if he/she wishes to do so, the guardian can terminate his/her duty after four years (article 456). During these times, the guardian can ask to receive a salary which is determined by the guardianship board in the function of the guarded person's revenues. If the conditions of this latter do not permit, the fee can be requested from the Treasury (article 457).

When the person is given a curator, this will not affect his/her capacity to act while the statutory adviser provisions are reserved. The duration of duty of curator and his/her remuneration is determined by the guardianship board and the curator must act following the instructions of the guardianship board (articles 458 and 459).

With regard to the duties of guardianship offices, it should be stressed that the person with mental competence and every relevant person concerning the guardian's actions can object to the guardian's decisions (article 461).

We also note that permission from the guardianship board is necessary in the following cases: '1 Purchase, sale of and putting in pledge the immovables and establishing another *rem* right on them, 2 Purchase, sale of and putting in pledge movable properties that are outside of ordinary management and operation needs or other rights and assets, 3 Constructional work exceeding ordinary management boundaries, 4 Lending and borrowing, 5 Making a commitment in foreign exchange, 6 Drawing up immovable tenancy contract for three or more years or product contract for one year or longer, 7 The person under guardianship performing an art, 8 Without prejudice to power of the guardian to take interim measures in emergencies, litigation, accordance, arbitration and arrangement of bankruptcy, 9 Property regime contracts, apportioning of inheritance and making transfer of inheritance share agreements, 10 Declaration of insolvency, 11 Ensuring life insurance for the person under guardianship, 12 Drawing up an apprenticeship contract, 13 Placing the person under guardianship with a training, care or health institution, 14 Changing the residence of the person under guardianship'[41] (article 462).

In the following situations the permission of the supervisory authority should be sought in addition to permission of the guardianship board: '1 Adoption or adoption of the person under guardianship, 2 Naturalisation or renunciation of the person under guardianship, 3 Acquisition or liquidation of a business, entering into a partnership requiring personal liability or becoming a partner in a company with a significant capital, 4 Conclusion of lifelong pension or income binding or end-of-life care contracts, 5 Acceptance, rejection or conclusion of an inheritance contract, 6 Emancipation of the minor [by legal means], 7 Making a contract between the person under guardianship and the guardian' (article 463).

[41] Ibid, 8118, 8119.

It is the responsibility of the guardianship board to review the reports and accounts prepared by the guardian and to take necessary measures to ensure the interests of the person under guardianship (article 464). 'Actions taken by the guardian without receiving the permission of competent guardianship authorities although it is stipulated by law shall have the effect of actions taken by the person under guardianship without permission of the guardian'[42] (article 465).

In terms of the responsibilities of guardianship bodies, it is clearly stated that guardians, curators and statutory advisors are responsible for harm caused to the person concerned with these measures (articles 466 and 467). As indicated in article 468, the State has the responsibility for damages that cannot be compensated by the guardians, curators and statutory advisors. Compensation and other recourse cases are heard in the courts of first instance where the guardianship offices are located (article 469).

As for the termination of guardianship, when it concerns convicted persons, guardianship ends when imprisonment finishes (article 471). Moreover, 'During the continuation of imprisonment, guardianship may be terminated in the presence of the following conditions: 1 The person's request for restraining orders issued in connection with the execution of a total prison sentence of less than five years, 2 The disappearance of the reason for the protection of the person or assets upon the request of the person in respect of the restraining orders issued in connection with the execution of a finalised imprisonment sentence of five years or more in total' (article 471). When it concerns mental illness or weakness of mind, guardianship ends only if it is determined by an official medical board report that the reason for restriction has disappeared (article 474). A person 'who is restricted due to his/her extravagance, alcohol or drug addiction, bad lifestyle or mismanagement of his/her assets may request the removal of guardianship, provided that he/she has not filed a complaint for at least one year regarding the reason requiring him/her to be placed under guardianship' (article 475). Where persons are under guardianship at their own request, the causes that led to this restriction must have been removed (article 476).

Representative curatorship ends with the completion of the work that the curator is assigned to carry out, while for management curatorship it is necessary that the cause which led to the nomination has been removed so that the curatorship ends. As for statutory advisership, its removal will be decided by the guardianship board (article 477).

Additionally, if the guardian loses his/her capacity or dies (article 479), or if there is another reason to prevent the guardian from fulfilling his/her function, or if the guardian does not perform his/her duties as expected, these situations signify the end of his/her mandate.[43]

Lastly, in order to terminate the guardian's mandate, as article 491 stipulates, it is necessary to review the final report and final account, and to notify the

[42] Ibid, 8119.

[43] See articles 481, 482 and 483 for more detail.

person under guardianship, his/her heirs or the new guardian about the approval or rejection of the final report and account. In this notification, it is stated that they have the right to file a lawsuit for compensation and to end the guardian's duty (article 491).

GLOBAL LEVEL AND TRANSFORMATIONS

Even the local level had already been influenced by developments beyond Turkey's borders at different stages of the country's modernisation. Currently, the accelerated circulation of ideas, standards and debates taking place at supra-national levels, especially following the United Nations Convention on the Rights of Persons with Disabilities (CRPD) adopted in 2006, and the means of control developed in parallel, have caused Turkey to consider itself more systematically with regard to the rights of 'disabled persons'. As Eyraud demonstrates for the French case, this process of diffusion and appropriation of new values and practices requires action at several levels.[44] Moreover, it seems that the Convention has helped to mobilise different actors in terms of thought and devices in the field of 'disability'.[45]

As reported above, Law No 5378 on Persons with Disabilities was adopted in July 2005 just before the signing of the CRPD in Turkey, in 2007. The Convention was ratified in 2009. As for the Optional Protocol to the Convention recognising the right of individual application for persons with disabilities, this was accepted by Turkey in 2015.[46] According to the latest data (November 2024) we know that this Protocol has been signed by 107 states parties, whereas the Convention has been ratified by 190 States.[47]

As previously noted, from the late 1990s onwards, the rights of disabled persons have attracted increasing attention in Turkey. The Copenhagen criteria referring to the necessary conditions to become part of the European Union in particular had led to a review of policies in the process of democratisation. Issues relating to accessibility, right to life, access to justice, independent living, inclusion in society, and freedom of thought and expression[48] of disabled persons gained more importance, and either new bodies have been launched or existing ones have been reformed.

For example, the Directorate of Disability and Elderly Services was created by the unification of the Administration for Handicapped (Özürlü) People and the

[44] Eyraud, op cit, 69.

[45] The Convention has also been the subject of criticism, but that is beyond the scope of this chapter.

[46] Engelli Bireyler için Bilgilendirme Rehberi (Information Guide for Individuals with Disabilities), Engelli ve Yaşlı Hizmetleri Genel Müdürlüğü (General Directorate of Disabled and Elderly Services) https://aile.gov.tr/media/131394/engelli_bireyler_icin_bilgilendirme_rehberi.pdf, 34 (28.2.2025).

[47] See https://nda.ie/disability-policy/uncrpd (28.2.2025).

[48] See https://www.aile.gov.tr/media/42409/disability-policy-in-turkey.pdf, 1 (23.12.2024).

Directorate of Handicapped Care Services and the Directorate of Elderly Care Services under the General Directorate of Social Services and Child Protection Agency in 2011.[49] Designated as 'the focal point of Turkey for promoting the implementation and monitoring of CRPD at national level',[50] in 2013, its name became General Directorate of Services for Persons with Disabilities and the Elderly.[51] The Human Rights Equality Institution of Turkey was founded with the coming into force, in 2016, of the Law on Human Rights Equality Institution of Turkey (Türkiye İnsan Hakları Eşitlik Kurumu Kanunu).[52] It would appear that, compared to recent years, the Bars are becoming more actively involved in this area. They create units named 'centres', commissions, boards or committees to deal more specifically with issues relating to disability. For example, since 2023, the Istanbul Bar Association has published its 'Jurisprudence Bulletin' four times a year. While the İzmir Bar Association's Disability Rights Commission Working Report announced that 'The "Disability Rights Commission", established by the Izmir Bar Association member lawyers within the Bar Association and in which they participate on a voluntary basis, works to ensure that disabled citizens are not deprived of their fundamental rights and access to social resources, and that they can continue their existence in justice and social settings without being subject to discrimination and obstacles'.[53] Services are also increasing at municipality level. In the case of Istanbul, Branch Directorates for Disabled Persons (Engelliler Şube Müdürlükleri), under the Department of Social Services are located at several points in the city and they are growing in number.[54] Courthouses are making arrangements to make themselves more accessible, including sign language. The first deputy judge with vision impairment has taken office.[55] Debates around making the legal profession more accessible to people with disabilities continue. For example, services such as 'Barrier-Free Health Communication Centre' (ESİM) established by the Ministry of Health facilitate the access of persons with hearing impairment to health services in emergencies.[56]

This desire to do things differently is also reflected in various sources such as reports, strategy plans, newsletters and guides prepared by public and civil actors, as well as via digital sites of ministries, municipalities, bar associations and civil society organisations. This leads us to believe that a rights-based approach is increasingly coming into focus. Informing people with disabilities as well as their

[49] See https://www.aile.tr/eyhgm/genel-mudurluk/kurum-hakkinda/ (16.12.2024).

[50] See https://www.aile.gov.tr/media/42409/disability-policy-in-turkey.pdf, 2 (23.12.2024).

[51] See https://www.aile.tr/eyhgm/genel-mudurluk/kurum-hakkinda/ (16.12.2024).

[52] See https://www.tihek.gov.tr/kategori/pages/Kurulus (10.1.2025).

[53] İzmir Barosu Engelli Hakları Komisyonu Çalışma Raporu. Görüşmeler-Tespitler. Çözüm Önerileri (Izmir Bar Association Disability Rights Commission Working Report. Interviews-Findings. Solution Suggestions), Ocak 2024, https://www.izmirbarosu.org.tr/Upload/files/engelli_haklari_bulten.pdf, 4 (28.2.2025).

[54] See https://sosyalhizmetler.ibb.gov.tr/mudurlukdetay.aspx?ID=9 (22.12.2024).

[55] See https://www.youtube.com/watch?v=bgSoX6GhdqA (22.12.2024).

[56] See https://www.aile.gov.tr/media/94446/engelliler_icin_bilgilendirme_rehberi_2021.pdf, 17 (1.3.2025).

families (including in the virtual space) about their rights has become a recurring theme. An 'Information Guide for Individuals with Disabilities' (Engelli Bireyler için Bilgilendirme Rehberi)[57] prepared by the Ministry of Family and Social Services General Directorate of Disabled and Elderly Services is one illustration of this. Courses have been introduced in faculties of law.[58] Conferences have also been organised on the rights of people with disabilities. This includes the Association for Monitoring Equal Rights (EŞHİD) to deal with the question of access to justice by establishing platforms allowing people to discuss other countries' practices. Similarly, there have been meetings like that of the Izmir Bar Association 'with different disabled groups . . . to better understand the developments or deficiencies experienced in every field on a national scale and to act with the right perspective',[59] where the aim is 'to invite disabled individuals, caregivers and support mechanisms established in the field of disability to the meetings and to include them in the process'.[60] We are also witnessing heightened awareness of how the concept of being disabled should be expressed. Besides, the issue of 'intersectional spheres of discrimination'[61] attracts increasing attention, as do projects including (for example) 'Social Inclusion for Persons with Mental Disabilities' supported by the European Union and World Health Organisation.[62] Launched quite recently, '2030 Vision without Barriers' (2030 Engelsiz Vizyon) illustrates this will 'to build an inclusive society where people with disabilities can realise their potential as equal citizens'.[63] With regard to this, the first National Action Plan on Disabilities Rights (Engelli Hakları Ulusal Eylem Planı) has been prepared for the years 2023–25 through the participation of related public institutions and civil society organisations, especially those working in the field of disability.[64] This contains the following sections: 'Employment, Data and Statistics, Participation in Sporting, Touristic and Cultural Activities, Health and Well-being, Accessibility: Built Environment, Accessibility: Access to Information, Accessibility: Transport, Inclusive Education, Mainstreaming Rights-Based Approach, Independent

[57] See https://www.aile.gov.tr/media/94446/engelliler_icin_bilgilendirme_rehberi_2021.pdf (1.3.2025).

[58] A Aslı Şimşek and Damla Songur, 'Engellilik Çalışmalarında Adalete Erişim: Hak Temelli Farkındalık Üzerine Bir Değerlendirme', in Eşit Haklar İçin İzleme Derneği (ed), Uluslararası Engelli Haklarıte Erişimi, 2018, 109–10.

[59] İzmir Barosu, op cit, 4.

[60] Ibid.

[61] Nejat Taştan, Önsöz, in Eşit Haklar İçin İzleme Derneği (ed), Uluslararası Engelli Hakları Konferansı Engellilerin Adalete Erişimi, 2018, 13; A Aslı Şimşek Öner, 'Engelli Kadınlar İçin Engelsiz Bir Adalet Mümkün mü?: Adalete Erişim Hakkı Çerçevesinde Bir İnceleme' (Is Barrier-free Justice Possible for Women with Disabilities: A Review Within the Framework of the Right to Access to Justice), *Akdeniz Üniversitesi Hukuk Fakültesi Dergisi*, Haziran Cilt: 14 – Sayı: 1, 2024.

[62] See https://www.saglik.gov.tr/EN-55918/social-inclusion-for-persons-with-mental-disabilities.html (28.2.2025).

[63] See https://www.aile.gov.tr/media/94718/2030_engelsiz_vizyon_belgesi.pdf, 11 (2.3.2025).

[64] See https://aile.gov.tr/media/133056/engelli_haklari_ulusal_eylem_plani_23-25.pdf, 6 (2.3.2025).

Living, Participation in Political Life, Protection of Rights and Justice, [and] Participation in Decision-Making Mechanisms'.[65]

In addition to these, we observe a tendency to develop control and complaint mechanisms. 'Meeting the rights of disabled individuals arising from the Constitution, laws and international agreements that have become domestic law norms in accordance with Article 90 of the Constitution is a responsibility brought about by the state's status as a social state governed by the rule of law, the obligation to observe the equality of its citizens and ultimately a requirement of respect for human rights.'[66] For any violation of these rights, defence channels have been diversified and support channels have been strengthened. Accessibility Monitoring and Supervision Commissions (Erişilebilirlik İzleme ve Denetleme Komisyonları) have been established within governorships in 81 provinces[67] in accordance with the Accessibility Monitoring and Supervision Regulation (Erişilebilirlik İzleme ve Denetleme Yönetmeliği), which was accepted in 2013, as well as the ombudsman institution constitute another example.

It is also worth mentioning declarations concerning the need for both spreading awareness of the existence of these support channels and more specific data on different groups of people with disabilities and on their access to justice. These raise another dimension of monitoring, bearing in mind collaborative efforts between civil society organisations and universities such as 'Disability Rights Monitoring Group Project' (Engelli Hakları İzleme Grubu Projesi).[68]

Far from being an exhaustive range, these elements highlight how actors have become diversified/varied. It is important to reflect (among others things) on the (re)organisational dimensions, as well as political and social aspects. In addition, concepts are raised for thought and debate, and notions such as psychosocial support and judicial social work arise more frequently. Even so, we know that there are still many things to be done, including more field research at the level of practice. Disparities can also be observed within the country, 'In the Final Observation Report prepared by the United Nations Committee on the Rights of Persons with Disabilities upon the first report submitted in 2015 in accordance with Article 35 of the Convention on the Rights of Persons with Disabilities, to which Turkey is a party, important recommendations were made regarding the positive steps taken by Turkey in the field of disability rights, creating an agenda through social communication strategies with alarming issues, and implementing steps that will include stakeholders in the process'.[69]

[65] Ibid.
[66] İzmir Barosu, op cit, 3.
[67] See https://www.aile.gov.tr/sss/engelli-ve-yasli-hizmetleri-genel-mudurlugu/erisilebilirlik/ (5.1.2025).
[68] Cf https://www.engellihaklariizleme.org/tr/ (4.3.2025).
[69] İzmir Barosu, op cit, 4.

WHAT ARE THE IMPLICATIONS FOR THE LEGAL INCAPACITIES?

First, it is important to note that issues relating to the rights of persons with mental disabilities or weaknesses constitute an area that needs to be investigated through appropriate field studies in Turkey. This becomes even more important regarding people designated as legally incapacitated. From our observations, it seems that there is no direct reference to them in any of the sources. Thus, it is important to underline the fact that the legal and judicial handling of the family affairs of persons in a situation of legal incapacity is a field that is waiting to be explored.

Nevertheless, in the light of what we have noted above and what we have observed of current developments, we can make the following points.

Already, the modifications recently observed in the TCC can be considered to be results of these local and international dynamics concerning persons with legal incapacity.

Moreover, with the amendment made in the Swiss Civil Code in 2013, the Adult Protection Law[70] also gives rise to reflections in Turkey. By considering both the historical roots of the current TCC and the general sense of the debates and the restructuring in progress, it seems quite possible that this relatively new regulation will be a source of inspiration for the context of our study.

The need to listen more closely to those working in the field and to widen the sphere of civil society organisations are important priorities.

Moreover, training recently organised by two of the country's important bar associations relative to guardianship can be seen as a clear sign of the growing interest in this subject.

In order to achieve results on the question of access to justice 'it is not sufficient to rely solely on legal aid. More holistic changes in the system including all of the stakeholders appears necessary.'[71] Accordingly, 'the lack of development of means of expression in appropriate language for these persons (eg mentally ill persons with the power of discernment or persons with mental impairment) and/or the lack of supervision of the use of appropriate language by those who mediate'[72] can be considered in relation to this.

It is reported that the 'restriction should be to the extent required by the situation'[73] and the regulation mechanisms of guardianship should be reconsidered to better ensure 'the living conditions, physical and mental health of the restricted person . . . For example, a social worker may be acting as guardian for approximately 30 to 50 persons. In this situation, it is not possible for the guardian to

[70] See https://assets-us-01.kc-usercontent.com/7099fcf9-715f-0061-5726-009a48410fee/35a9984e-94ea-4c1d-9d93-08dd5bfca034/Switzerland.pdf (3.3.2025).

[71] Tolga Şirin and Ömer E Egeliği, 'Aradığınız Adalete Erişilemiyor'. Türkiye'de Dezavantajlı Grupların Adalete Erişim Sorunu, EŞHİD Yayınları 2024, 58.

[72] Ibid, 29.

[73] Ibid, 30.

develop an approach in line with the rights of persons with disabilities, and it is questionable whether they are complying with the main guarantees, including the provision of communication channels for other judicial proceedings.'[74]

The question of restriction of liberty for the purpose of protection emerges as one of the major concerns. When it should be decided, even if the objective is to avoid it, 'the institution must be specific and suitable for the person and the situation . . .'[75] And when restrictions are put in place, it is important that they are treated as a 'temporary measure'.[76] These make it essential to pay particular attention to psychiatric hospitals.[77]

As also expressed during exploratory conversations, we understand that it is more difficult for people with intellectual disabilities to describe abuse and mistreatment as well as physical or sexual violence that they may have suffered, or may suffer[78] in different life situations.

Moreover, in a recent study conducted in a forensic medical unit that investigated 482 cases brought between 2016 and 2020 requesting a restriction, among 461 new demands 'it was decided that there was no need to restrict the person in 210 (45.6%) cases, that it was appropriate to assign a guardian to the person in 179 (38.9%) cases, that it was appropriate to assign a legal advisor to the person in 37 (8%) cases, and in 35 (7.5%) cases the restriction status could not be decided, in the records'.[79] Besides, 'the increase in the proportion of these cases within the total cases over the years was found to be remarkable. The reason for this increase in the age group 65 years and older was the increase in their share in the general population, whereas in the younger age group, it was determined as the increase in the frequency of admissions due to the reasons such as alcohol

[74] Ibid.

[75] Emre Cumalıoğlu, *'Koruma Amacıyla Özgürlüğün Kısıtlanması: Özellikle Psikosoyal Engelli Bireyler Bakımından 'Elverişli Kurum' Sorunu'* (Deprivation of Liberty for the Purpose of Protection: A Focus on Suitable Institution Problem, Especially for Individuals with Psychosocial Disabilities), (İzmir Barosu Dergisi, Ocak, 2021), 30. 'Deinstitutionalization has clearly demonstrated the importance of individualized care for mentally ill persons, who constitute a diverse and heterogeneous group of people. Service planning must be tailored to the needs of specific individuals' (Lamb and Bachrach, 2001: 1043). (It should be noted here that the authors are referring to N Sartorius (1992) 'Rehabilitation and Quality of Life. Hospital and Community', *Psychiatry*, 43, 1180–81).

[76] Ibid, 47.

[77] See also the Report of the Association for Human Rights Initiative in Mental Health (Ruh Sağlığında İnsan Hakları Girişimi Derneği), entitled 'Human Rights in the Field of Mental Health Turkey 2013 Report. Problems and Solution Suggestions' (Ruh Sağlığı Alanında İnsan Hakları Türkiye 2013 Raporu. Sorunlar ve Çözüm Önerileri), https://rusihak.org.tr/wp-content/uploads/2022/03/rusihak_2013_turkiye_raporu-2.pdf (23.12.2024).

[78] TOHAD, Mevzuattan Uygulamaya Engelli Hakları İzleme Raporu 2020, Yayına Hazırlayanlar: Süleyman Akbulut Ceren Taşköprü, Toplumsal Haklar ve Araştırmalar Derneği, 1 (Baskı, Ankara, Haziran 2021), 40.

[79] Hüseyin Uğur Bakan, '2016–2020 Yılları Arasında Akdeniz Üniversitesi Adli Tıp Anabilim Dalına Medeni Hakların Kısıtlanması veya Sınırlandırılması (Vesayet ve Yasal Danışmanlık) için Yönlendirilen Olguların Değerlendirilmesi' (Evaluation of the Cases Referred to Akdeniz University Department of Forensic Medicine for Restriction or Limitation of Civil Rights (Guardianship and Legal Counselling) between 2016–2020), Expertise Thesis, Akdeniz University, Adli Tıp Ana Bilim Dalı (Forensic Medicine Department), Supervisor: Yaşar Mustafa Karagöz, 2023, 121.

and/or substance use disorder, bipolar disorder and psychotic disorder. In all age groups, dementia, psychotic disorders, bipolar disorder, substance use disorders, mental retardation, traumatic intracranial haemorrhage and stroke were found to be the most common causes of restraint. While dementia and stroke come to the forefront in the elderly population group, psychiatric disorders and traumatic intracranial haemorrhage come to the forefront in the active working age group. In the group where restraint measures by appointing a guardian or legal advisor were not sufficient and compulsory hospitalisation was decided, it was determined that psychotic disorders were at the forefront.'[80] Another research project conducted with 352 cases between 2022 and 2023 shows that for persons aged 65 and over the 'restriction rate was statistically significantly higher compared to other age groups'.[81]

The need to establish guidelines for the elaboration of such reports for each group of cases[82] and the importance of following a common path by doctors in the evaluation of legal capacity within the scope of forensic psychiatric examination[83] are emphasised. Additionally, the latest statistics[84] confirm that there has been an increase in the number of trials in the Courts of Peace, and also those dealing with guardianship.

It should be stressed that each of the above points should be reconsidered and developed further in the context of Turkey.

CONCLUSION

Our analysis highlights two interconnected issues. First, we see that the question of access to justice is being reconsidered. There is an effort under way to institute a change of direction, to introduce new means for tackling the question of disability and access to justice. In saying this, we are in no way ignoring the difficult relationship between 'legal equality' and 'access to justice'. In other words, even to have legal equality fixed as an objective, ensuring access to justice remains a complex and arduous task. Secondly, as tangible examples show us, the 'rights-based approach' is gaining pace, at least in terms of discourse. As we observe

[80] Ibid, 115.

[81] Özge Savcı Ergun, '2022 ve 2023 Yıllarında Süleyman Demirel Üniversitesi Tıp Fakültesi Adli Tıp Ana Bilim Dalınca Hukuki Ehliyet Konusunda Vesayet Raporu Düzenlenen Olguların Değerlendirilmesi' (Evaluation of Cases for Which Guardianship Reports Were Prepared on Legal Capacity by Süleyman Demirel University, Faculty of Medicine, Department of Forensic Medicine in 2022 and 2023), Expertise Thesis, Süleyman Demirel University, Adli Tıp Ana Bilim Dalı (Department of Forensic Medicine), Supervisor: Abdulkadir Yıldız, 2024, 110.

[82] Bakan, op cit, 2023, 116.

[83] Savcı Ergun, op cit, 2024, 109.

[84] Judicial Statistics 2023, Ministry of Justice General Directorate for Criminal Records and Statistic https://adlisicil.adalet.gov.tr/Resimler/SayfaDokuman/1042024101742Adalet%20%C4%B0statistikleri%202023.pdf, 27, 32 (4.3.2025).

through the implications of different actors, there is a growing conviction that 'disability should be approached from a universal human rights perspective, disabled individuals should be fully equal to other individuals in all areas of life and should be able to live independent lives, principles and practices that ensure respect for human dignity and individual autonomy should be supported, and the aid-based perspective that weakens, separates and limits the individual, and medical, charitable, patriarchal and traditional approaches that reduce disabled individuals to their disabilities and health conditions should be abandoned'.[85]

These changes are 'often described as a shift away from viewing persons with disabilities from objects to subjects',[86] which means 'a move from charity to a rights-based approach and from paternalism to empowerment'.[87] It is important to 'consider it as a shift from the withdrawal of legal capacity to the right to support for exercising legal capacity'.[88]

In CRDP, disability is conceptualised as 'a consequence of the interaction between persons with impairments and the environment. It is only when the environment fails to accommodate the needs of the individual that disability occurs[89] . . . This way of understanding disability is fundamentally different from viewing disability as a consequence of the individual's impairment. It means that it is the society's failure to create an inclusive environment that disables individuals rather than any mental or intellectual conditions attached to the person. By placing the "problem" of disability in the (inaccessible) environment, the solution is to be found there as well. The shift calls for legal, attitudinal and environmental changes.'[90]

Therefore, the 'new paradigm' which can be summarised as 'change the environment instead of fixing individuals'[91] leads us in the first instance to look more attentively to Article 12 of the CRPD on 'Equal Recognition Before the Law'.[92] This 'signals a deeper understanding of equality'.[93] As it is stated, 'the model of personhood and legal capacity embedded in Article 12 of CRPD is much more inclusive than the idea of the "rational person". It recognises the reality behind

[85] İzmir Barosu, op cit, 21.

[86] Who Gets to Decide? Right to Legal Capacity for Persons with Intellectual and Psychosocial Disabilities, Issue Paper, prepared by Anna Nilsson, Council of Europe Commissioner for Human Rights Council of Europe, April 2012, https://rm.coe.int/who-gets-to-decide-right-to-legal-capacity-for-persons-with-intellectu/16807bb0f9, 17 (2.3.2025).

[87] Ibid.

[88] Ibid.

[89] Here a reference to Article 1 and preamble (e) of the Convention is made. 'For example, if a citizen with Down's syndrome who considers applying for a certain service is provided information in easy-to-read format and adequate support and time to consider her options, she may be able to understand what the service is about and to choose whether or not to use it. In such a situation no disability arises. However, if information is only provided in standard (and to the individual inaccessible) language and no one offers to explain it to the individual in a manner that he or she understands, disability becomes a fact' (ibid).

[90] Ibid.

[91] Ibid, 21.

[92] See https://www.un.org/disabilities/documents/convention/convoptprot-e.pdf (27.2.2025).

[93] Council of Europe Commissioner for Human Rights, op cit, 5.

all persons' decision-making and emphasises support instead of stripping persons of their legal capacity to make choices. As pointed out by Michael Bach, the question is no longer: does a person have the mental capacity to exercise his/her legal capacity? The question is instead: what types of support are required for the person to exercise his or her legal capacity? This is a profound shift in the law of legal capacity.'[94]

In light of these elements, we see that the approach of the CRPD 'to personhood and legal capacity is therefore inherently different from the guardianship practices . . . where persons with intellectual and/or psychosocial disabilities, instead of being empowered to formulate their choices, are deprived of their capacity and given a guardian to take decisions on their behalf . . .'[95]

Moreover, we notice that 'the supports that Article 12 calls for can take a variety of forms including support to enable someone who communicates in alternative ways to convey his/her message to third persons; support to assist someone in their contacts with the authorities; and life planning supports to assist a person in thinking about options for living and other arrangements. Common to all these measures is that the choices rest with the individual. Third parties, ie public officials, doctors, social workers, bank employees and others must in turn take measures to enable the individual to enter into agreements and make other decisions with legal consequences (reasonable accommodation).'[96]

All this reminds us of the importance of the 'tailor-made responses',[97] since just because you do not understand something does not mean you cannot understand something else.[98] Above all 'having an intellectual and/or psychosocial disability cannot be a reason for not benefiting from the presumption of capacity'.[99]

In the second instance, it seems crucial to focus on the sense of 'inclusiveness' by thinking again of the 'ableism' that we mention in the introduction. As Parent states with reference to Dan Goodley (2014), 'ableism provides an environment in which the temperature and quantity of nutrients allow disablism to grow'.[100] As the author explains, this is a metaphor for illustrating the way in which 'ableism' and 'disablism' are co-constructed.[101] 'Disablism' defined 'as oppressive practices of society that aim to exclude, eradicate and neutralise individuals, bodies and minds that do not fit into the capitalist performance

[94] Ibid, 31.
[95] Ibid, 22.
[96] Ibid
[97] Ibid, 23.
[98] In this respect, as expressed by Valentine, 'a person's incompetence in one area (eg managing assets) should not result in his or her incompetence in other areas (certain life choices)' (2018: 133). For example, 'just because you have dementia, you should not have less right to divorce' (Valentine, 2018: 130).
[99] Council of Europe Commissioner for Human Rights, op cit, 31.
[100] Parent, op cit, 2017, 189.
[101] Ibid.

mould'.[102] Another perspective, focusing more on attitudes, defines it as 'discriminatory, oppressive or abusive behaviour, stemming from the belief that disabled people are inferior to others'.[103]

Thus, '. . . disability was not caused by loss of ability but by the pressure of an entrenched society and its institutions'.[104]

> In my bioethics course, my teacher said that people are at the heart of decisions. For example, a patient has to have one leg amputated to avoid dying. If having both legs is a very important value to him/her, even more important than living, we have to listen to him/her, accept his/her refusal to have them amputated and let him/her die. I raised my hand and asked her if the author who was making this point had given any thought to the ways in which these values are shaped by society. I explained that we live in a world that devalues disability and difference. She disagreed. In her view, values are personal and if having all members was important to a person, that should be respected. She added that it was tragic to have cancer, that it is tragic to be disabled (pointing at me). I felt a bit like crying.[105]

When we consider all these views together, the idea of 'respecting human diversity means recognising that there are many different ways to develop and flourish as human beings'[106] becomes even more obvious. And, 'focus on human rights rather than care or charity', as well as 'focus on social barriers and negative attitudes rather than individualised personal tragedies'[107] appear among the major challenges to reconsider, alongside the place of persons designated as 'legally incapable', as well as legal and judicial organisations.

To conclude, we would like to describe how an interview which we read just after the last Paralympic games stays with us. It can be found in Lucky Love, where the artist declares that 'Normality is having a disability, everyone has one, or even several'.[108] We know that we are quite far from making our world capable of developing such a capacity for seeing. However, in conjunction with existing efforts at various levels to promote another perspective on disability, it is now not impossible to imagine it. And at least, *to hope to imagine it* and to embark on new paths.

[102] Goodley, 2014 quoted by Parent, op cit, 2017, 188.

[103] Paul Miller, Sophia Parker et Sarah Gillinson, 2004, quoted by Parent, ibid.

[104] Balam Kenter, 'Radikal İhtiyaçlar Olarak Özel İhtiyaçlar: Engelliliği ve Bağımlılığı Merkeze Alan Devrimci Bir İhtiyaç Kuramına Doğru', in Eşit Haklar İçin İzleme Derneği (ed), Uluslararası Engelli Hakları Konferansı Engellilerin Adalete Erişimi, 2018, 31.

[105] This testimony of Marie-Eve Veilleux, student in bioethics is shared by Laurence Parent, op cit, 2017, 201.

[106] Khader, 2008, 6 quoted by Kenter, op cit, 2018: 35.

[107] Engelli Bireylerin Bağımsız Yaşaması İçin El Kitabı (Handbook for Independent Living of Persons with Disabilities), 2015, 50.

[108] See https://madame.lefigaro.fr/celebrites/culture/lucky-love-la-normalite-c-est-d-avoir-un-handicap-toutes-les-personnes-en-ont-un-voire-plusieurs-20241116 (12.1.2025).

REFERENCES

Açıkgöz, Aslı (2016) 'Dar Anlamda Vesayeti Gerektiren Hâller ve Vesayet Altına Almanın İşlem Ehliyeti Bakımından Sonuçları' (Cases for Legal Guardianship in the Narrow Sense and the Consequences of Legal Guardianship on the Capacity to Make Transactions), PhD Thesis, Istanbul University, Özel Hukuk Ana Bilim Dalı (Department of Private Law), Supervisor: Bilgehan Çetiner.

Aldemir, Songül (2020) 'Medeni Hukuk Çerçevesinde Vesayet İlişkisi ve Vesayeti Gerektiren Hâller' (Wardship Relationship Within the Framework of Civil Law and Situations Requiring Wardship), MA Thesis, Atatürk University, Hukuk Ana Bilim Dalı (Department of Law), Supervisor: Hatice Kübra Ercoşkun Şenol.

Bakan, Hüseyin Uğur (2023) '2016–2020 Yılları Arasında Akdeniz Üniversitesi Adli Tıp Anabilim Dalına Medeni Hakların Kısıtlanması veya Sınırlandırılması (Vesayet ve Yasal Danışmanlık) için Yönlendirilen Olguların Değerlendirilmesi' (Evaluation of the Cases Referred to Akdeniz University Department of Forensic Medicine for Restriction or Limitation of Civil Rights (Guardianship and Legal Counselling) between 2016–2020), Expertise Thesis, Akdeniz University, Adli Tıp Ana Bilim Dalı (Forensic Medicine Department), Supervisor: Yaşar Mustafa Karagöz.

Cumalıoğlu, Emre (2021) *'Koruma Amacıyla Özgürlüğün Kısıtlanması: Özellikle Psikosoyal Engelli Bireyler Bakımından 'Elverişli Kurum' Sorunu'* (Deprivation of Liberty for the Purpose of Protection: A Focus on Suitable Institution Problem, Especially for Individuals with Psychosocial Disabilities) (İzmir Barosu Dergisi, Ocak), 15–21.

Çınar, Ceyda (2024) 'Türk Medeni Hukuku Kapsamında Vesayet İlişkisi ve Vesayet Makamının İzni ile Yapılabilen İşlemler' (Under Turkish Civil Law Guardian Relationship and With the Permission of the Guardian Authority Transactions that can be Taken), MA Thesis, Istanbul Aydin University, Özel Hukuk Ana Bilim Dalı (Department of Private Law), Supervisor: Ebru Ceylan.

Erkan, Vehbi Umut, Yücer İpek (2011) 'Ayırt Etme Gücü', *AUHFD*, 60(3), 485–522.

Eyraud, Benoît (2023) 'Adopter une approche du handicap par les droits humains? La domestication en spirale de la Convention internationale sur les droits des personnes handicapées en France', *Droit et Société,* 113, 55–71.

Kenter, Balam (2018) 'Radikal İhtiyaçlar Olarak Özel İhtiyaçlar: Engelliliği ve Bağımlılığı Merkeze Alan Devrimci Bir İhtiyaç Kuramına Doğru', in Eşit Haklar İçin İzleme Derneği (ed), Uluslararası Engelli Hakları Konferansı Engellilerin Adalete Erişimi, 29–38.

Lamb, H Richard, Leona L Bachrach (2001) 'Some Perspectives on Deinstitutionalization', *Psychiatric Services*, August, 52(8), 1039–45.

Parent, Laurence (2017) 'Ableism/disablism, on dit ça comment en français?', *Canadian Journal of Disability Studies*, 6(2), 182–212. DOI: https://doi.org/10.15353/cjds.v6i2.355.

Savcı Ergün, Özge (2024) '2022 ve 2023 Yıllarında Süleyman Demirel Üniversitesi Tıp Fakültesi Adli Tıp Ana Bilim Dalınca Hukuki Ehliyet Konusunda Vesayet Raporu Düzenlenen Olguların Değerlendirilmesi' (Evaluation of Cases for Which Guardianship Reports Were Prepared on Legal Capacity by Süleyman Demirel University, Faculty of Medicine, Department of Forensic Medicine in 2022 and 2023), Expertise Thesis, Süleyman Demirel University, Adli Tıp Ana Bilim Dalı (Department of Forensic Medicine), Supervisor: Abdulkadir Yıldız.

Şimşek, A Aslı, Songur Damla (2018) 'Engellilik Çalışmalarında Adalete Erişim: Hak Temelli Farkındalık Üzerine Bir Değerlendirme', in Eşit Haklar İçin İzleme Derneği (ed), Uluslararası Engelli Haklarıte Erişimi, 97–110.

Şimşek Öner, A Aslı (2024) 'Engelli Kadınlar İçin Engelsiz Bir Adalet Mümkün mü?: Adalete Erişim Hakkı Çerçevesinde Bir İnceleme' (Is Barrier-free Justice Possible for Women with Disabilities: A Review Within the Framework of the Right to Access to Justice), *Akdeniz Üniversitesi Hukuk Fakültesi Dergisi*, Haziran Cilt: 14 – Sayı: 1, 85–115. https://doi.org/10.54704/akdhfd.1463542.

Şirin, Tolga, Ömer E Egeliği (2024) 'Aradığınız Adalete Erişilemiyor', Türkiye'de Dezavantajlı Grupların Adalete Erişim Sorunu, EŞHİD Yayınları.

Taştan, Nejat (2018) Önsöz, in Eşit Haklar İçin İzleme Derneği (ed), Uluslararası Engelli Hakları Konferansı Engellilerin Adalete Erişimi, 11–13.

TOHAD (2021) Mevzuattan Uygulamaya Engelli Hakları İzleme Raporu 2020, Yayına Hazırlayanlar: Süleyman Akbulut Ceren Taşköprü, Toplumsal Haklar ve Araştırmalar Derneği, 1. Baskı, Ankara, Haziran 2021.

Valentine, Suzanne (2018) 'Ölüm Bizi Ayırana Dek: Demans ve Boşanma İkilemi Hak Ehliyeti Sahibi Olan ve Olmayan Başvurucular Arasındaki Dengesizliğe Dair Bir Değerlendirme' in Eşit Haklar İçin İzleme Derneği (ed), Uluslararası Engelli Hakları Konferansı Engellilerin Adalete Erişimi, 129–35.

11

The Impossible Job of the Guardian and the Client Whose Assets are Placed under Guardianship

B DIJKSTERHUIS, J LANDMAN,
AND A VAANDERING-HOEKSTRA

INTRODUCTION

GUARDIANSHIP – ALSO called protective trust – is a legal measure in which a court, namely the cantonal judge, appoints a guardian to look after the financial interests of someone who is not (or no longer) able to do so him/herself (hereafter: himself): a person is temporarily or permanently unable to protect and manage his financial interests and/or assets properly. It is the assets of a person (hereafter 'the client') which are placed under guardianship when a guardian is appointed, it is not the client himself who is placed under guardianship. Once appointed, the guardian protects the client from bad financial decisions or harmful financial situations. The client retains legal capacity, but cannot independently acquire assets or dispose of his assets placed under guardianship. The legal ground for placing the assets of the client under guardianship is that someone is no longer able to make financial decisions due to physical or mental illness or because of (problematic) debts or squandering. Many people in this situation need protection from financial exploitation: these are vulnerable individuals at risk of financial abuse by others. A total of about 859,000 cantonal cases were filed in 2023. The total number of family law cases (which consist almost entirely of guardianship cases) in 2023 was 525,000.[1] Thus, more than half of the cantonal cases consisted of guardianship cases.

The guardianship measure was introduced in the Netherlands on 1 September 1982 with the introduction of title 19 in Book 1 of the Dutch Civil Code (hereafter

[1] Jaarverslag de Rechtspraak (Annual report Judiciary) 2023: 54.

the 'DCC'), meant to protect vulnerable (often elderly) persons from financial abuse.[2] In 2014, problematic debts or profligacy also became grounds for guardianship. We live in a complex society and it is therefore very difficult for many people to understand society and cope financially. Frequently, clients in guardianship are dealing with low incomes, often alongside low educational levels and other socio-economic problems which result in high levels of debt.[3] The legal framework surrounding guardianship is as follows. Guardianship is regulated in the DCC, specifically in Book 1, Title 19, articles 431 to 449. The purpose of the legislation is to protect and support people who cannot manage their financial affairs themselves. A guardian is appointed by the cantonal judge, usually at the request of the person concerned, family members or caregivers. Often taken into account in this context is Article 12 of the United Nations Convention on the Rights of Persons with Disabilities (hereafter: UNCRPD). This is a crucial human rights framework when it comes to the rights of the autonomy of clients with physical or mental health issues. Article 12 states that we need to make sure that 'safeguards shall be proportional to the degree to which such measures affect the person's rights and interests'. In other words, the state needs to interfere as little as possible with the right to autonomy of a client, whether disabled and/or under guardianship.[4] But on what grounds is it justified to interfere with the client's autonomy in the first place? To answer that question, it is important to understand what happens to the autonomy of a client when the guardian is appointed and interferes in day-to-day decisions. This will be explored in this chapter in 'Theoretical Framework – Autonomy and Paternalism' below.

There are two types of guardians: a guardian appointed from the direct circle of the person under guardianship and a professional guardian who conducts a practice as a commercial enterprise. This distinction can be traced back to article 1:435 BCC. Professional guardians are subject to stricter requirements than so-called family guardians. Both are entitled to compensation. This fee is paid from the income or assets of the person under guardianship or, if this is not possible, compensation can be requested from the municipality. In principle, a client must ensure that he has sufficient income. In many cases, this will be income from employment. But it is often the case that the income consists

[2] Act of 15 May 1981, Stb. 1981, 283, which entered into force on 1 September 1982, concerning guardianship for the protection of adults.

[3] This is a worldwide problem. See, for example, S Mullainathan and E Shafir, 'Scarcity: Why Having Too Little Means so Much', 2013; M Jacoby, 'Unjust Debts: How our Bankruptcy System Makes America More Unequal', 2024. See also (for the Dutch equivalent) T'S Jongers, Armoede uitgelegd aan mensen met geld (poverty explained to people with money), 2024.

[4] See also Hoge Raad (Dutch Supreme Court) 1 July 1983, ECLI:NL:HR:1983:AG4626: Subsidiarity and proportionality are crucial when deciding which legal measure (full guardianship or guardianship or a lighter measure) should be applied. See also more on the application of the Convention in P Vlaardingerbroek ea., Het hedendaagse personen- en familierecht, 2023: 629, 655-656; H Stelma-Roorda ea, 'A Changing Paradigm of Protection of Vulnerable Adults and its Implications for the Netherlands', *Family and Law*, February 2019; K Blankman, meerderjarigenbescherming, in W Schrama ea, *Familierecht. Een introductie*, 2023: 95–133.

of a government social or sickness benefit and a number of income support measures and allowances. It is necessary to apply for these benefits. The application process is often complex and it is easy to make a mistake when filling in the relevant forms. It is the task of the guardian to ensure that the appropriate social benefits and allowances are applied for in time. The person, in this case the guardian, who fills in the application forms is fully liable for mistakes and the financial consequences that follow.[5] For the guardian it is particularly important to be very alert not only to fill in the paperwork correctly but even more important, not to forget to apply for these benefits, as article 1:444 BCC states that the guardian will be liable to the beneficiary if he fails to exercise the care of a good guardian, unless the failure cannot be attributed to him. Good care by the guardian involves making sure the beneficiary receives the state benefits to which he is entitled.

The duties of the guardian are management of goods and finances of the client, reporting annually to the court and submitting important decisions to the court. The guardian is – in short – responsible for the client's asset management. The guardian must ensure that the budget is at least balanced. This concerns both the expenditure side and the revenue side. The cantonal judge supervises the guardian. Occasionally, where there has been inadequate guardianship another guardian will be appointed. However, the main reason for the termination of guardianship by the court is the fact that the grounds for guardianship no longer exist. Professional guardians must meet quality requirements and are supervised by a National Quality Office. There is a complaints procedure where there is dissatisfaction with a guardian.

In this chapter, we report on the role and position of the guardian in practice, and how the guardian is facilitated. We will answer the question as to what extend the legal framework and external context contribute, positively or negatively, to the task of the guardian in financial matters. We start by discussing how this relates to the autonomy of the client in question in the following section. The legislator partly restricts, and at the same time tries to protect, the autonomy of the client as much as possible in the light of Article 12 of the UNCRPD. After that, we go into the task of the guardian in theory and practice. In 'The (Family) Legal Framework' below, the legal task of the guardian according to Dutch law will be discussed. In 'The Guardian Within the Chain – The Judge and Other Chain Partners' below, the role of the judge and the other chain partners will be taken into account. The guardian in action will be described in 'The Challenges of the Guardian in Practice' below.

For our study, we conducted exploratory empirical legal research. We held interviews with guardians and also a person who got a guardian appointed. We conducted interviews with 10 people. We came into contact with five guardians

[5] A further legal consequence of such mistakes might be that all benefits should be paid back with interest and sometimes accompanied by fines. This led to the so-called Dutch 'toeslagenaffaire' (childcare benefits scandal).

through our network and a snowball method. Three were very experienced guardians, of which one had a special role within the network; and two were new ones. Moreover, we conducted an interview with two judges and two legal assistants at the court, who had been involved in many cases on guardianship. One of the authors, Jelle Landman, as a former guardian, has gained a great deal of experience with the practical problems of the profession. On 1 December 2016 Bregje Dijksterhuis attended, on request, an expert meeting on guardianship and the role of the judge. One of the key questions was whether the judge was a chain partner or the director of the whole process and moreover whether this should be considered as a judicial task at all.[6] Bregje Dijksterhuis also attended court hearings during two days at two different courts to form an impression of the work of the judges.

THEORETICAL FRAMEWORK – AUTONOMY AND PATERNALISM

Guardianship impacts on a client's autonomy. The client is no longer autonomous in relation to every decision with legal consequences through a legal act. If a decision by the client is harmful to his financial situation, the guardian can reverse certain legal actions taken by the client. In that case the legal consequences will also be reversed. However, only those legal actions which entail bad financial consequences and are harmful to the client's assets need to be reversed (ie 'reversing': a legal act by the guardian which ensures the legal act of the client has no legal effect. The initial agreement between the client and the third party in question will subsequently become void.) The law does not oblige the guardian to undo every legal action taken by the client, as long as it is attributed to so called 'good guardianship'. When the guardian acts adequately considering the situation at hand, there may be minimal interference with the client's autonomy. In that light, the law answers with respect for the autonomy of the client. The judiciary also asks guardians to stimulate the client's self-reliance. This can also be seen as a way the law respects the autonomy of the client in the sense that a guardianship goes only as far as it is needed, something the legislator is obliged to do in the light of Article 12 of the UNCRPD.[7] A guardian is held accountable by the court and is liable towards the client if he fails to be a careful guardian (art 1:444 BCC). This also applies when the autonomy of the client is harmed by the guardian. When a client feels his autonomy is not well respected or when the guardian feels the autonomy of the client is at risk, a judge can intervene.

According to Mill, the autonomy of a person is a great good. People should be autonomous to think and act, even if the consequence is that they harm themselves and/or exhibit immoral behaviour/thoughts. In other words, a person

[6] More on this meeting: Y van der Vlugt, Perspectieven op particuliere bewindvoering, 2018: 2.

[7] See also H Stelma-Roorda ea, 'A Changing Paradigm of Protection of Vulnerable Adults and its Implications for the Netherlands', *Family and Law*, February 2019; K Blankman, meerderjarigenbescherming, in W Schrama ea, *Familierecht. Een introductie*, 2021: 97–134.

should live his life independently, not controlled by external standards, but by following his own values, beliefs, wishes and considerations. Only then is a person autonomous to choose for himself.[8] This means there needs to be a certain (external) environment wherein someone can be truly autonomous. In contrast, in situations of oppression by the government, an individual does not have this capacity. This is reflected in Article 3 of the International Universal Declaration of Human Rights (hereafter: UDHR), where the right to life, freedom, and security are enshrined. To answer the question where one's autonomy ends, Article 1 of the UDHR, that states that all humans should act towards one another in a spirit of brotherhood, gives some clues. It ends where another person's freedom starts. As a famous old quote, often attributed to Oliver Wendell Holmes Jr, states 'your right to swing your arms ends just where the other man's nose begins'. According to John Stuart Mill, it is crucial whether you harm other people. Only in that case can the law step in, and it is no longer about morals.[9] For example, alcoholism (and the trade in alcohol) falls within the scope of autonomy.[10]

But what if laws are complex and therefore you are unable to navigate through the dimensions of our existing world; can you still be truly autonomous in that situation? The issue with guardianship is that a person's autonomy is (partially) taken away, at least in a financial sense, if it turns out that this person is unable to cope independently with this autonomy himself. It takes skills to be financially autonomous in our complex society. It is a sliding scale. We could look at illness or problematic debts as external factors that influence one's reasons. One is no longer in a state of being able to be autonomous. At some point it can be concluded on reasonably objective grounds that it is no longer responsible to leave this autonomy to the person himself. There is apparently sufficient interest to stop (further) financial mismanagement and to prevent or resolve debts. Otherwise, all the consequences of your decisions will keep following you and could limit your autonomy in the future. For example, if you lose your house when you cannot pay your debts, to what extent can you then still be (financially) autonomous? If a person does not know how our society and economy function due to the limitations of his mental/physical health condition or misses certain cognitive functions, one can wonder whether this person should keep his full autonomy or whether some (professional) help is needed.

The justification for protecting the client against the consequences of irresponsible financial decisions and restricting his autonomy, can be found in Dworkin's theory of paternalism.[11] 'Paternalism is the interference of a state

[8] J Mill, *On Liberty*, 1859 [2002, Publisher Boom, translation: WE Krul and FL van Holthoon]: 45–51, ch 3.

[9] J Mill, *On Liberty*, 1859 [2002, Publisher Boom, translation: WE Krul and FL van Holthoon], ch 4. The only exception Mill makes is the case of voluntary slavery. Ibid: 161. See also R Dworkin, 'Harm and the Volenti Principle' (2012) *Social Philosophy and Policy*, 29: 315–16.

[10] J Mill, *On Liberty*, 1859 [2002, Publisher Boom, translation: WE Krul and FL van Holthoon], ch 4: 143–44.

[11] G Dworkin, 'Paternalism', *The Monist*: 56: 64–84.

or an individual with another person, against their will, and defended or motivated by a claim that the person interfered with will be better off or protected from harm.'[12] In cases where guardianship is requested voluntarily by the client himself, this is a free choice. But if guardianship is requested by family or the government against one's will, one is forced into a situation where autonomy is interfered with in order to be better off or protected from harm and/or immoral behaviour. Dworkin introduces the useful concept of moralistic legal paternalism, compared to legal paternalism and legal moralism, which means that 'our justification for certain kinds of interference . . . would not be justified by concern for the person's welfare, but, out of respect for them as persons. Forcing a drug addict to get over his addiction may not be better for him, on the assumption that he prefers his addicted life to his new one, but our justification would be that his new life is a better one nevertheless.'[13] This could be applied to people with (heavy) debts and/or in harmful financial situations; therefore it is irrelevant whether the client considers his life as improved by the guardianship; the new life without debts or without the risk of financial exploitation is simply better.

One could even argue that guardianship increases the autonomy of the client. The guardian translates our complex society into a simplified version, wherein a client can understand certain decisions and their (legal) consequences. For each client, a different translation is needed because each person has more or less capacity to understand to what extent certain decisions have an impact on their life. The client can be enabled to stay autonomous to the extent that he understands the simplified version that is presented by the guardian. When it is still difficult for the client to decide, the guardian is there for the client to guide him to the right decision. When the client makes a decision on his own that has a negative impact on his assets, the guardian can protect the client from the consequences by reversing those decisions. A justification for paternalism can also be found in the fact that sometimes the individual's autonomy is advanced in the long-run by restricting his autonomy in the short-run.[14]

THE (FAMILY) LEGAL FRAMEWORK

Before describing the duties of the guardian under the law, we will give a brief overview of the genesis of guardianship. The main reasons for its introduction in 1982 were to protect vulnerable (often elderly) persons from financial abuse

[12] 'Paternalism', *The Stanford Encyclopedia of Philosophy* (Fall 2020 Edition), Edward N Zalta (ed), first sentence of the article, https://plato.stanford.edu/archives/fall2020/entries/paternalism/.

[13] G Dworkin, 'Moral Paternalism', *Law and Philosophy*, 24(3): 319. See p 313 for the distinction between legal paternalism and legal moralism: in the first case the good in question is not moral; in the second case a person sees his case as degrading but cannot change it on their own. See also G Dworkin, Harm and the Volenti principle, *Social Philosophy and Policy*, 29: 312.

[14] 'Paternalism', *The Stanford Encyclopedia of Philosophy* (Fall 2020 Edition), Edward N Zalta (ed), p 5, https://plato.stanford.edu/archives/fall2020/entries/paternalism.

and to provide a less intrusive alternative to full guardianship (guardianship that includes physical and psychological care in addition to financial protection). The intention was to respond to the increasingly ageing population and related issues. Moreover, there was a need for a more flexible asset management instrument in cases of incapacity to pay. Guardianship is a dynamic area of law that is constantly evolving to reflect changing societal needs and perceptions. Over time, the scope of guardianship has expanded, and stricter requirements are imposed upon the person of the guardian and the manner in which he or she practices his or her profession. Here we mention the key developments in this legal field: in 1995 the grounds for guardianship where expanded to include a physical or mental condition. In 2014 the 'Guardianship, Full Guardianship and Mentorship Amendment Act was introduced. This meant, firstly, the introduction of problematic debts as grounds for guardianship, and secondly the tightening of quality requirements for guardians. In 2016 the National Quality Bureau CBM for supervision of guardians was established. Finally in 2023, recommendations on guardianship were given by the National Consultation on Supervisory Expertise, 31 January 2023. Guardianship and its importance, especially in terms of the role of the guardian and the future of the protection regime, are also in the political spotlight. This is evident from a position paper by the Council for the Judiciary. In this paper, the Council for the Judiciary responds to an introductory note by a member of the House of Representatives. The initiative note is entitled 'More time, attention and protection in guardianship' (36.464).[15] The essence of the position paper is that people under guardianship are in a vulnerable position and that this position needs protection, with the judiciary playing an important role. The paper discusses issues such as supervision of (professional) guardians, promoting self-reliance, proper supervision through consultation with chain partners and further digitalisation. The idea underlying the initiative note was to adjust the guardian's tasks, so that the person under guardianship has a more central role and to reduce the number of clients per guardian. It was also proposed that from 2028 onwards, there should no longer be any profit-making guardian (or guardian organisations). The Council for the Judiciary said that the thrust of the latter proposal was not clear. Possibly, the initiative note arose from the desire to shift guardianship to the municipalities. The authors of this chapter question whether this would be a desirable development. Municipalities are often already overburdened with regard to the target group. It is questionable whether this would improve the quality of guardianship in a general sense.

[15] Position paper Council for the Judiciary and other experts for the roundtable by the Commission of Social affairs and employment on 21 March 2024. https://www.tweedekamer.nl/debat_en_vergadering/commissievergaderingen/details?id=2024A01038; Initiative Note of second chamber member Kat 'Meer tijd, aandacht en bescherming bij beschermingsbewind More time, attention and protection in guardianship' (*Kamerstukken II* 2023/24, 36.464, nr. 2).

The two grounds for guardianship are set out in article 1:431 Sub 1 of the DCC: 'The cantonal judge may institute a regime of administration over one or more of the assets that belong or will belong to an adult as entitled person; (a) for a fixed or indefinite period of time if the adult is temporarily or permanently incapable of fully looking after his property interests as a result of his physical or mental condition, or (b) for a fixed period of time if the adult is temporarily unable to fully and properly look after his property interests due to dissipation or problematic debts.' In other words, the client of the guardian is someone whose physical or mental health condition prevents him from making the right decisions when it comes to his assets, but also a person who has created problematic debts. It is important to note that guardianship is only instituted when it is truly necessary and other less intrusive measures are not sufficient to protect and support the person in managing their finances, according to the legal framework and jurisprudence.[16] Hereafter, we describe some of the situations in which the court may institute guardianship according to article 1:431, sub 1, a DCC: physical or mental condition, which mean people with mental disabilities: (1) individuals with dementia (thus elderly people who struggle with financial management due to declining cognitive skills); (2) people with other cognitive disorders and individuals with serious physical or psychiatric problems (this includes individuals with mental health conditions that affect their financial decision-making); (3) people who are temporarily unable to manage their finances due to illness or an accident; (4) individuals with complex financial issues that they cannot oversee themselves; (5) people with addiction problems who cannot manage their finances. Hereafter, we describe some of the situations in which the court may institute guardianship according to article 1:431 sub 1, b DCC: (1) problematic debt, which means struggling with serious debt problems and individuals unable to manage their finances independently due to debt; (2) profligacy, which relates to people who waste their assets due to excessive spending and people who face financial difficulties due to gambling or other addictions.

The law describes the task, legal responsibility and competence of the guardian in the DCC in article 1:435, 1:438, 1:439 1:441 and 1:444. We discuss these legal provisions below, not necessarily in that order. Article 1:438 DCC states that during the guardianship, the assets that are placed under guardianship are no longer available to the client. He cannot dispose of his assets without the permission of the guardian or the judge. If the client disposes of his assets without permission, article 1:439 DCC states that this can only be held against a third party if he or she knew or could have known about the guardianship. The guardian can reverse the legal action and thus dissolve the contract. This also applies in cases where an asset has been obtained, alienated, or burdened. To know of the existence of a guardianship, there is a register where the name and

[16] P Vlaardingerbroek ea, Het hedendaagse personen- en familierecht, 2023: 655–656.

birthdate of the client are registered. Both article 1:438 and 1:439 BCC enable the guardian to reverse certain legal actions if they have a negative effect on the financial situation of the client. This means the guardian can protect the client's assets against negative effects.

The legal task of the guardian is described in the paramount article 1:441 DCC. The guardian represents the client in and out of court. The guardian is responsible for the efficient investment of the assets of the client, insofar as these are subject to guardianship and should not be spent on the care of the client. The guardian may also perform all acts for the client that contribute to good guardianship, which is an open, legal, norm. The law describes in article 1:441 sub 2 DCC cases in which the guardian must have the permission of the client or a judge for certain legal actions. For example, the guardian needs permission to enter into an agreement for the disposal of an asset subject to the guardianship or for the acceptance of a gift for the client, which entails a financial burden or taking out a loan on behalf of the client. The guardian does not need approval for acts of ordinary management (eg for car maintenance to keep a car safe to drive), provided the expenses do not exceed €2,000.[17]

THE GUARDIAN WITHIN THE CHAIN – THE JUDGE AND OTHER CHAIN PARTNERS

The Judge – Appointment and Accountability

Before guardianship can be instituted, a request must be submitted to the cantonal judge, upon which (according to article 1:435 DCC) a judge appoints the guardian. The request indicates on what grounds the guardianship should be instituted: on the grounds of a physical or mental disability or on the grounds of problematic debts or profligacy. The request is usually submitted by the intended guardian. The latter will submit a standardised form indicating the ground on which the guardianship should be imposed and the client's mental and financial situation. Furthermore, an overview of income and expenses is given. If there are debts, the guardian will send an overview of the debts known at that time. If there are any relatives (parents, brothers, sisters, children), they must usually indicate in writing that they agree to the institution of the protection regime.

Based on this information and after the client has paid the court fee, the guardian and the client will be invited to discuss the request with the judge. If all the conditions of the guardianship are met, the judge will institute the guardianship and make a court ruling of it. This ruling will also state the remuneration the guardian will receive for his work. Depending on the client's financial situation, the guardian can apply for special assistance from the municipality for the

[17] De rechtspraak, Aanbevelingen meerderjarigbewind, Vastgesteld door het LOVT op 31 January 2023, sub B.20.

payment of the remuneration. After the court ruling is issued, the actual work of the guardian begins. Once the judge has pronounced the guardianship, the guardian and the client will receive a court order. This states that the client is under guardianship as from a certain date and what property the order covers – all or a part of the client's assets. The guardianship is entered in a central register for persons whose assets are placed under guardianship due to waste or problematic debts. Registration is also mandatory for persons for whom there is guardianship due to physical or mental conditions, where the court has decided that publication is necessary (art 1:391 DCC).

During the guardianship, the guardian is held accountable by the court according to article 1:445 DCC. the guardian needs to report on his work to the court (art 1:445 sub 1 DCC). The court controls the guardian, and the guardian needs to be aware of his legal responsibilities and liabilities. Any mistake the guardian makes may risk liability (art 1:444 DCC). In the event that serious mistakes are made by the guardian, the court can decide to terminate the guardian's position and even prevent them from being appointed again, according to article 1:448 DCC. The liability of a guardian towards his client is recorded in article 1:444 DCC. The guardian is liable if he falls short of being a careful guardian, unless this cannot be attributed to him. This is an open standard. The judiciary describes in more detail how the guardian should fulfil his duty. The 'Recommendations on adult guardianship' from the Dutch judiciary (hereafter: 'Recommendations'), provides detailed recommendations on, among other things, the establishment of guardianship, the duties of the guardian, remuneration for the guardian, complaint handling and the specific requirements for an administrator. According to the 'Recommendations', it is expected that the guardian motivates the person who is placed under the guardianship to be self-reliant.[18] This means that it is expected that the guardian will be more than just a budget manager whose role is only to manage the assets of the client. Rather, the guardian is supposed to teach the client to manage his assets on his own again – like a budget coach. This is not an easy task and can take up a lot of the guardian's time. The 'Recommendations' have a practical approach towards the legal responsibilities of the guardian according to the law. For example, they specify for which legal actions the client needs permission from the guardian, such as buying a caravan or changing homes. They also specify the legal actions for which the client does not require permission, such as buying groceries.[19] The 'Recommendations' also specify when the guardian needs authorisation from a judge for certain management acts, such as incidental expenditure above €2,000 or for investments according to more high-risk profiles.[20] The authorisation limit

[18] De rechtspraak, Aanbevelingen meerderjarigbewind, Vastgesteld door het LOVT op 31 January 2023, sub B.23.

[19] De rechtspraak, Aanbevelingen meerderjarigbewind, Vastgesteld door het LOVT op 31 January 2023, sub B.18.

[20] De rechtspraak, Aanbevelingen meerderjarigbewind, Vastgesteld door het LOVT op 31 January 2023, sub B.20.

of €2,000 is cumulative per year; so, for example for driving lessons, several holidays in one year or furnishing a house, the guardian must request prior authorisation if the costs of such expenses foreseeably exceed the authorisation limit. The guardian does not need permission for a management acts such as saving money or the normal exploitation and efficient investment or reinvestment of assets. For example, the guardian is allowed to exchange shares and bonds, limited to a defensive investment profile.[21]

The guardian takes over the entire financial management and will first try to stabilise the financial situation and draw up a balanced budget plan. If there are any debts, an inventory of these will be drawn up and a plan will be made on how to pay these debts or an appeal will be made to the municipal debt assistance or debt restructuring scheme. Usually the guardian has sophisticated software to perform his duties. If there is insufficient income, the guardian takes care of applying for benefits or other income support. The guardian regularly informs the court. For example, after a period of time has elapsed following commencement of the guardianship, an estate inventory is submitted to the court. In addition, a guardian must submit an annual account to the court. The court can ask the guardian to also make an interim report. This allows the court to check how the guardian is doing and also assess whether a less intrusive measure is now sufficient.

Other Chain Partners

The guardian may act on behalf of the client based on the court order. From the moment the court order has been made, the guardian has to deal with several chain partners in order to look after the financial interests of the client. Acting on behalf of the client with regard to financial matters also implies that the guardian must contact everyone who has any financial relationship with the client. The guardian will therefore start approaching all financially concerned parties and inform them that he is the guardian appointed by court and thus the contact person for the client and responsible for all financial matters. All parties involved, such as employers, local government, creditors and the bank, are obliged to cooperate. To carry out his work effectively, the guardian depends on a number of chain partners.

The first such partner to be approached after receiving the court order is the bank. The guardian opens two bank accounts: the management account – one to which the client has no access – and secondly, a living allowance account for the client's personal use. The client's income is paid into the management account and all necessary expenses are incurred from this account, including financial obligations such as rent. The client receives a weekly amount on the living

[21] De rechtspraak, Aanbevelingen meerderjarigbewind, Vastgesteld door het LOVT op 31 January 2023, sub B.17.

allowance account to cover his daily expenses.[22] In this account, the guardian usually deposits a limited sum per week, which the client can use for groceries and other personal expenses. The guardian closes the bank accounts owned by the client before the guardianship took effect and the balance is transferred onto the management account. The second chain partner, the city administration has an important role during the appointment process and during the guardianship itself. In cases where a guardianship has been appointed due to problematic debts, the city administration can advise (since 2021) if this is the right solution for the client (art 1:432a CC).[23] The guardian will then be ordered by a judge to inform the city administration about his action plan and the assets of the client to enable the city administration to write an advisory report. During the guardianship, it may happen that the client does not have enough income to pay for his essential needs or for the costs of the guardianship itself. In that case, the city administration can provide special welfare.[24] The third chain partners are social workers and/or health providers who are involved with the client; they also need to be informed.

One would expect that the guardian also needs to involve the family of the client, but this is not the case. When the family does get involved with the client or the guardian, it can only be done on a voluntary basis and with the client's permission. This happens regularly, as we will see in the results from the interviews.

THE CHALLENGES OF THE GUARDIAN IN PRACTICE

During our exploratory research, we held some interviews with guardians and also with a client whose assets had been placed under guardianship. We found that the day-to-day work of a guardian is very challenging. We identified several issues. Sometimes these issues had a negative effect on the liability risk for guardians and, more importantly, a negative effect on the service level for the client.

The Client

Firstly the interviewees spoke about the client's behaviour. From our interview with a client whose assets were placed under guardianship, it was clear that the guardian was a great support in his life. He states that, 'I can do everything myself, but together with my guardian (thus not independently)'.[25] His guardian

[22] De rechtspraak, Aanbevelingen meerderjarigbewind, Vastgesteld door het LOVT op 31 January 2023, sub B.5.

[23] See https://vng.nl/sites/default/files/2021-06/handreiking-adviesrecht-voor-schuldenbewind.pdf.; A Nuytinck, personen- en familierecht, relatievermogensrecht en erfrecht, 2024, nr. 250a.

[24] See https://www.rijksoverheid.nl/onderwerpen/bijstand/vraag-en-antwoord/wanneer-heb-ik-recht-op-bijzondere-bijstand.

[25] Interview 'client R'.

works together with his client. During the interview, the client asked his guardian about getting a new terrace for his balcony. The guardian asked if the client had looked at the price and the amount of money he still had in his bank account. It was clear that the guardian asked certain questions to guide the client through the decision. The guardian tried to simplify the situation at hand, so the client could make his own decision. It was a perfect first-hand example of how the guardian was able to respect the autonomy of the client. The guardian explained afterwards that the reason she can spend more time with a client is because she works with an assistant. Not every office works this way.[26] However, the legislator does not provide solutions in terms of providing the guardian with enough time to spend on respecting the autonomy of the client or helping the client to be self-reliant. In most cases, the guardian must quickly decide whether to reverse a particular legal action, often without having a complete understanding of why the client acted in the way that he did.[27]

Furthermore, the guardian needs to be able to deal with aggressive clients or clients who do not cooperate. For example, when a client has no money to buy cigarettes because the weekly amount for groceries has been spent and there are no savings left. The client may be aggressive over the phone or via e-mail and may make demands.[28] Or it happens that the client has behavioural issues (in public) and keeps being fined, which also has a negative effect on his financial situation. As a guardian, you cannot do much about a fine, but you have to manage to pay it.[29] Another example is when clients make online orders under false names. The order will be delivered and needs to be paid, because the guardian cannot reverse an online order under a false name. The online shop could not know this person's assets were placed under guardianship.[30] In one of the interviews, it was clear that sometimes the guardian held on to a contract between the client and a third party to raise awareness of a bad financial decision made by the client himself.[31] The client needs to set aside money to pay back this third party and might mean that the client does not have extra funds for a couple of months. This is only done when the financial situation allows it. If not, the client's legal action can be undone, as long as no false name was used or the third party is not a private person and could know about the guardianship through the register, as explained in 'The (Family) Legal Framework' above. The guardian is not obligated to reverse every financial decision made by the client.

Lastly, although family members do not have an official role, they often play an important and not always easy role in the whole process. The client often has family members who interfere in the decision-making process of the client.

[26] Interview M&S.
[27] Interview P.
[28] Interview M&S; Interview P.
[29] Interview P.
[30] Interview M&S; Interview M.
[31] Interview P.; Interview M&S.

One example from the interviews can illustrate this.[32] The client wanted a new couch and saw one that cost the exact amount of money that was in the savings account. The guardian advised the client not to buy this couch, but to look for a cheaper one. After a few weeks, the guardian came for a house visit and saw the new couch in the living area. The father of the client sat at the table and told the guardian that he needed to be repaid for the couch. The father had made the payment in advance for the client. In this case, the couch was bought from a private person, and the father paid for it. The guardian could not reverse the purchase of the couch. In this instance, it was lucky that the money was there to pay for the couch, but no savings were left.[33] In these types of situations where other people in the social circle think they are helping the client, it is very difficult for the guardian to control the financial situation. In another situation, the girlfriend of a client was very negative about the guardian and expressed this to the city administration. The city administration assumed this information to be true and refused to cooperate with the guardian. This frustrated the work of the guardian, and the guardian needed to work harder to prove he had acted legally and in the best interests of the client.[34]

The Chain Partners

Another important topic in the interviews was the chain partners, as noted above. The interviewees affirmed that the chain partners are mainly the court, city administration, banks and care providers. It is expected that the guardian follows their guidelines.[35] The issue is that every partner has their own (complex) working process. The guardian is expected to apprise himself of all these working processes, what role these chain partners have, and how they influence the (financial) position of the client. Often, the position of the guardian is not well understood by these chain partners. Sometimes, in the process of communicating with these chain partners, the guardian has to prove that he acts legally on behalf of his client; in comparison for example a lawyer does not have such problems. Every so often, it is expected that the guardian sits with a client when a call is made for a certain request by the client.[36] This can make the role of the guardian more complex, and the guardian cannot always act adequately in the interests of the client. Some examples from the interviews can illustrate this.

The judges came with a few remarks on autonomy and increasing self-reliance. According to one judge, for the vast majority of people under guardianship, there is not much to change with regard to financial self-reliance.

[32] Interview M&S.
[33] Interview M&S.
[34] Interview M.
[35] Interview P.
[36] Interview M&S.

There are many people with disabilities, limited intellectual abilities, or people who will never succeed. However, he did see opportunities for people who had fallen into debt due to external circumstances such as divorce or business failure. According to the judge, these people are perfectly capable of getting their lives back in order if their debts are paid off. These are the first people who ask for the debt to be cancelled. This group, who make up about 10 per cent of the total number of people under guardianship, are people for whom guardianship is not really intended.[37] The other judge came up with an anecdote where a social worker came with a request for guardianship. The intended client was assisted by a lawyer who went all the way for her, but mounted a strong defence against everything that had been requested. The social worker argued that they were acting for the intended client's own good. She had a state pension and there were two big dogs in the household that she could not afford. The judge told the lawyer he did not like what the lawyer was advocating, namely self-reliance, because in her case it would mean that eviction would start on Monday, and then there would be no guardian. The judged adjourned the hearing and said it would be wise if the social worker would rethink this. They came back and said: on second thoughts, it was a very good idea not to appoint a guardian. The judge asked himself every time: is it really necessary, especially when the debts are not that big.[38] And the same judge said: 'You often notice in this discussion that what our western society, our democracy holds in high esteem is personal autonomy and the right to get into debt is at odds with what should happen when things go completely wrong. Then there will be an imbalance.' This judge also mentioned the problem with regard to the complexity of state allowances: 'If you look at it socially, there are quite a few people who cannot see the wood for the trees. There are 27 income-dependent allowances.'[39]

On the task of the job of appointing the guardian, making them accountable (supervision), and whether this is a task of the judge at all: 'The question that keeps coming up is: is this really judicial work, supervising. The decision you take to put someone's assets under guardianship is one that interferes with someone's rights and obligations. I think that is a judicial task. Then there is a supervisory phase, just like bankruptcy. That supervision the legislature puts on the court. The actual implementation lies with the guardian, who is accountable to his client.'[40] According to this judge, looking at the workload of the canton's apparatus, two-thirds of the administration is involved in guardianship debt settlements. Since debt settlements have come into law, they have been a growth area, but a bottleneck for the judiciary that it is not valued financially. 'That explains those five-minute sessions – we get a few tens per session. If you want to make supervision a serious task, you will also have to change something in the

[37] Interview D.
[38] Interview E.
[39] Interview E.
[40] Interview E.

financing.'[41] And the other judge wondered how you can create an account in such a way that you have all the checks in it, but can still go through it efficiently. 'If the state lottery came in on the bank account in July and was also immediately removed from the account, the judges do not see this. We are supposed to supervise but resources are very limited.' [42] This judge stressed that there are judges who say supervision is not a judicial function, because judges are decision makers; that you should outsource the whole supervision and not put that in the courts. On the task of monitoring the quality of (inadequate) guardians, the other judge mentioned a firm of guardians that went bankrupt, because a lot had gone wrong. According to him, 'Just like in the legal profession, you have some rotten apples that need to be thrown out, and that is done by the judiciary. This guardian has been fired. I also know of an office in Den Helder from whom we collectively took away all the clients, he was fired everywhere.'[43]

Concerning prevention, one of the judges mentioned that it could probably be done differently and better, for example, by proper selection by means of careful upfront screening. 'The companies you deal with the most, such as housing associations and energy companies, can play a signalling role. If you identify at an early stage that people are at risk of getting into financial trouble and make sure they are helped by debt assistance rather than being sent from pillar to post, you create an alternative route to guardianship.'[44] He also mentioned an intermediate form, which would allow the client his dignity by, for example, a monthly allowance instead of weekly payment, or paying part of his own fixed expenses so that he still feels in control. This judge also made some observations about guardians and their incentive to help their clients and make them more self-reliant: 'you have guardians who really became administrators out of conviction, but those cases then come up for hearing before those five years to be lifted. You have guardians who really want to help the clients, who often come from social care. They put in a huge number of hours with clients, also to make them financially self-reliant. These are the ones who are often the first to knock on the door to ask for ending guardianship. Those go down to their own success. Because they are good, that caseload only increases; they get burnt out or the quality of their work deteriorates. It is very cynical but as a guardian you have little to gain from guiding your client towards financial self-sufficiency. When the guardianship is installed it is easy money-making. It is income management what they do; paying clients' fixed expenses and trying to prevent them from getting into more debt.'[45]

With regard to the other chain partners the interviewees made some helpful observations. Firstly, the bank needs to process the requests of the guardian. Some banks have a special desk for guardians to make sure the requests are taken

[41] Interview E.
[42] Interview D.
[43] Interview E.
[44] Interview D.
[45] Interview D.

care of within 24 hours. Unfortunately, most banks do not have such a special desk and the processing time of a request can run up to 10 working days.[46] When an existing bank account of the client is placed under guardianship, the bank is held responsible for making sure, that from the moment the request has been received from the guardian, no money flows out of the existing bank account of the client according to article 4:24a Financial Supervision Act. For the bank, a person whose assets are placed under guardianship means extra administration and liability costs. The guardian and the client are seen as burdens. In the case of a guardianship, some banks therefore charge extra administration costs, which the guardian needs to pay.[47] Secondly, the process of requesting special welfare at the city administration is not always well organised. This could mean that during the process, certain essential expenses cannot be covered, and the client must wait until the city administration approves the request for special welfare.[48] Often, there is no policy for dealing with guardians. This means that when a guardian wants to take care of something on behalf of the client, the city administration does not always cooperate well. Although the guardian can legally act on behalf of the client, the city administration demands that the client appear in person or make a call in person.[49] Thirdly, the guardian must communicate with healthcare providers or social workers. They do not always understand the role of the guardian, which sometimes leads to misunderstanding and frustration.[50] For example, the guardian is expected to save money for emergency cases. If a washing machine breaks down, it needs to be replaced. But if a client has behavioural issues and keeps being fined, for example for not buying a train ticket or for yelling at a police officer, it is difficult to save money. Then, a social worker who works with the client does not always understand that there is no money for a new washing machine, bike, or coat. For a guardian, it is frustrating that sometimes there appears to be no understanding of the fact that there is a limited amount of money and no awareness of what financial position the client is in.[51] One of the guardians we spoke with, told us that they inform social workers themselves by giving a presentation about the role and task of a guardian.[52] The social workers were very surprised, and were helped to understand the guardian's position. Not all guardians are in a position to invest time and money in these activities.[53] To conclude, an important remark on cooperation by the chain partners by one of the judges was that: 'I strongly feel that everyone is doing

[46] Interview M&S.
[47] Interview J.
[48] Interview M&S.
[49] Interview M&S.
[50] Interview P.
[51] Interview P.
[52] Interview M&S.
[53] Interview P.

their thing; we are doing our thing, the guardian, social workers; I do not feel that the overall picture is being looked at. There should be a holistic approach.'[54]

The Conditions under which a Guardian Needs to Perform its Tasks

The work of the guardian involves all kinds of day-to-day practicalities. As mentioned earlier, the professional guardian has a business to run. He is an entrepreneur, appointed by court. This gives the guardian a special position with great responsibilities and challenges. Imagine your own day-to-day business and the administrative work that comes with it. Then imagine the guardian, with 100 clients who each have their own day-to-day business and administrative questions. The work of a guardian is very diverse, from paying rent, the mortgage, or the electricity bill each month, to helping with the holiday budget or giving advice on buying new furniture.[55] We can also think of dealing with debts, (criminal) lawsuits, seizures, fines, or losing a debit card.[56] Additionally, each client has their own wishes, and they need help in a different ways. The client should not know about his savings, because otherwise they might be totally wasted.[57] The guardian needs to be concerned with every client on a different level.

The framework of the autonomy of the client, as discussed in 'The Chain Partners' above, is not something a guardian is aware of when doing his job. For example, there cannot be a discussion about rent that must be paid or other monthly costs. Because the guardian is held accountable for the asset management of the client and due to limited time, the guardian is busy ensuring that all financial obligations are fulfilled by the client.[58] The guardian has a practical approach to the day-to-day workload and has no time to explain to the client why certain things are done in a certain way or to discuss the effects on his autonomy.[59] The guardian can only deliberate with the client about the amount of money that is available to spend.[60]

If we speak about conditions, resources are the paramount concern for most guardians. Guardians are paid a low statutory amount per client per month, which does not reflect the cost and responsibilities a guardian faces. As a result, guardians need to accept more clients than they can easily handle to cover their costs and earn a decent income. Guardians take on 100 clients per employee, while research has found that an employee can take on a maximum of 70

[54] Interview E.
[55] Interview M&S.
[56] Interview P; Interview M&S.
[57] Interview M&S.
[58] Interview P.
[59] Interview J.
[60] Interview P.

clients.[61] Therefore, some guardians make a choice and only accept easy clients who have no (serious) illnesses and preferably no debts. Other guardians solve this problem by working with assistants who can take on administrative work, while the guardian leads.[62] On the whole, the workload is very high and it is estimated that guardians work pro bono one-third of the time. This became apparent from an interview with the chairman of one of the trade associations for administrators.[63] The interviewee added that if there was more time, the guardian could work with the client to raise awareness about why the guardian took certain actions. According to him, this might contribute to making the client more self-reliant, something the guardian is obligated to do according to the judiciary's recommendations, and reflects Article 12 of the UNCRPD. This could also prevent clients from falling back into old patterns after the guardianship ends.

Furthermore there is the importance of being educated. A guardian needs to be educated very broadly because, for example, it could be that a person's large real estate portfolio with rented properties is placed under guardianship. The guardian suddenly needs to know about tenancy law. Or, in the case of an old lady whose large art collection is placed under guardianship, the guardian needs to know about the conservation of valuable art.[64] These two examples are not very common, but when they do occur, it has a big impact on the day-to-day workload and the liability risk of a guardian. A guardian is allowed to hire expertise, but often it will take more time to provide a good service, and the guardian cannot charge for these extra hours. Moreover, think of the fact that the guardian is there for clients with problematic debts, but also for clients with mental/physical health issues. These two types of groups require different approaches. Guardians are not always adequately trained for this.

The guardian needs to know about specific laws and legal procedures that apply to the client's situation.[65] The Netherlands has a complex social security system, which makes the work of guardians even more complex. Not only does the guardian need a broad education, but he must also be empathic and be able to guard against becoming emotionally involved with clients.[66] In other words, guardians should have a strong personality, be well educated, show understanding, and also be protective of themselves. Currently, there is no special training for guardians. Because all clients are different, needing help in different ways, and because the day-to-day workload is very broad, it is important to have guardians 'who can switch fast from task to task and are able to work on different task at

[61] W Vermeulen ea, Bekostiging en beloning van beschermingsbewind bij schulden, *rapport i.o.v. ministerie van sociale zaken en werkgelegenheid*, 2022: 38.

[62] Interview P.

[63] Interview G.

[64] Interview J.

[65] Interview J.

[66] Interview J; Interview P.

the same time'.[67] This interviewee explained that, actually, a guardian almost needs to have a form of ADHD to do the work properly.

The public image of the guardian is also a concern. In the past, there have been scandals involving guardians who have committed fraud. In one case, for example, the client's money was used by a guardian to make payments to prevent the bankruptcy of his own office.[68] Cases of fraud still occur and the court is not fully equipped to prevent this at an early stage because the legal case needs to be founded on evidence.[69] In the meantime, the damage has already been done. From one of the interviews, it was clear that it is difficult to communicate with institutions because of this image problem.[70] There is a lot of resistance to cooperating with guardians.[71] This has a negative effect on the client. Administrative processes take more time, while the client cannot take care of things personally. That is why the guardian is there in the first place. It also does not help that guardians are not well organised as a profession, as lawyers or doctors are. There are several associations for guardians, but they each work in their own way and do not work well together. For example, there is no knowledge database or best practice available. Due to this lack of unity among guardians and their associations, the interests of the guardians cannot be well presented to the legislator.[72]

The complex work environment of guardians, their questionable public image, and the limited resources that are available to them increase the chances of making mistakes. Most guardians receive many complaints, since clients file complaints more readily nowadays. Also, more guardians are being held liable by clients. As noted earlier, the law states that the guardian has a liability towards the client (art 1:444 DCC). The guardian must answer to the court. This takes (unpaid) time. Often the cause of the complaint is not the conduct of the guardian himself, but the fact that the chain partners do not cooperate well.[73] Chain partners do not have a direct liability to the client, so it is the guardian who has to defend his position and has to explain his actions. From one of the interviews, it was clear that if more complaints followed in the future, the guardian would quit the job.[74]

Lastly there is the legislator, who according to the interviewees, does not make the job of a guardian much easier. The legislator has created a complex social security system, and at the same time, the guardian can be held accountable and liable for any mistakes he makes.[75] The legislator determines the

[67] Interview P; Interview M&S.
[68] Interview C&A.
[69] Interview C&A.
[70] Interview M.
[71] Ibid; Interview P; Interview M&S.
[72] Interview J; Interview P.
[73] Interview M&S.
[74] Interview M&S.
[75] Interview P; Interview J; Interview M.

compensation of the guardian, education requirements, and the way guardians need to report to the court. But the legislator does not provide solutions to make sure chain partners cooperate, the right resources are available, or guardians get a seat at the table when thinking of new legislation for guardianship.[76] For example, it would be easier if all clients were obliged to be registered. Now there needs to be a good reason to register the client before a judge decides to do so. If there is no registration, then the guardian cannot reverse the legal action of the client. This is because of article 1:439 DCC which states that a legal act cannot be held against a third party when he could have known about the guardianship. What happens in practice is that the guardian sends the decision of the court to the third party who is involved. Often, this is enough to reverse the legal action taken by the client, but the third party is not obliged to cooperate.[77]

CONCLUSION AND POSSIBLE SOLUTIONS

The issue in this chapter is the extent to which the legal framework and external context contribute, positively or negatively, to the task of the guardian in financial matters. The law is formulated with open standards, and the guardian may perform all acts that contribute to good guardianship. A guardian has the legal capacity to reverse certain legal actions that are harmful to the financial situation of the client, so he is provided with the legal capacity to fulfil his duty. A client also needs permission for certain actions that could have a great effect on their financial situation or entail a great risk. In this way, a guardian can prevent certain legal actions with negative financial consequences if necessary. However, in practice, this is not always possible if, for example, a client uses a false name when making online orders or receives fines that cannot be reversed, or family members try to help and buy things with the client's money.

We found that the job of guardians is challenging due to both internal and external factors that frustrate their work. What the law asks of guardians is not well reflected in their financial compensation. It is expected that guardians are (fully) informed about our complex society, as well as the law, and they must be broadly educated. The judiciary also asks the guardian to encourage the client's self-reliance. The approach to do so might differ in cases where clients have health issues or problematic debts. Either way it is expected of the guardian to serve both target groups. The guardian cannot perform his task comprehensively, due to limited time and money. None the less, he is held accountable by the court and faces the risk of liability with regard to the client. Furthermore, the guardian needs to deal with several parties, who each have their own procedures and conditions. For example banks see a person whose assets are placed under guardianship as extra administration and liability costs and therefore

[76] Interview J.
[77] Interview M&S.

the guardian and the client are seen as burdens. Some banks therefore charge extra administration costs. In some cases, a guardian cannot adequately meet the needs of his clients because of complicated administration processes at the bank or city administration that take too long. The law does not yet provide a solution for this matter.

The legislator states that we need to interfere as little as possible with the autonomy of the client, in the context of Article 12 UNCRPD. We found that the guardian cannot always do the job according to their own view of how it should be carried out. One of the solutions could and should perhaps, especially in the light of the challenges of this profession be higher compensation per client, so the guardian does not have to take on more clients than he can handle. The legislator could oblige partners in the chain to facilitate guardians. There could be specified training that includes finances, law, social aspects, communication skills, and awareness regarding the influence the guardian has on the life of a client. A solution could also be an association for guardians to raise awareness of the role and task of the guardian, so that, for example, chain partners know what the job of the guardian entails. An example is the presentation some guardians have given about their work to social workers. This could be the task of a professional organisation for guardians. They could also make the interests of guardians known to policymakers and legislators. They could work on a knowledge database with best practices, so the guardians are able to learn from one another.

The question remains: how can the guardian equipped to carry out his role? It now seems that the guardian has to surrender to external factors that he cannot influence, but that do affect his day-to-day work negatively and hinder the performance of this role. There is a high chance of making mistakes, and at the same time, he is held accountable and bears a great risk of liability. Simultaneously the client's autonomy could be violated. It is also unhelpful that there is no distinction between a guardian who is there for a client with mental of physical health issues and a client who has problematic debts, because each requires a different approach. We need more research to find solutions, and the legislator needs to step in urgently to assist guardians more fully in carrying out their responsibilities.

12

Unaccompanied Ukrainian Children and Separated Ukrainian Children in Poland

MAŁGORZATA FUSZARA AND JACEK KURCZEWSKI

As a result of Russia's aggression against Ukraine, a massive number of Ukrainians fled abroad – primarily to Poland. According to the estimates of the Polish Border Guard, in the period of six months between 24 February and September 2022, 6,366,000 Ukrainians entered the country. These numbers do not account for all arrivals, because many people did not travel directly from Ukraine, but rather crossed the Ukrainian border with other countries and then made their way into Poland. Those cases are not recorded in the statistics (Fuszara 2022).

The attack was unexpected, and the refugee wave it triggered was enormous. Poland had no prior experience with rising to a challenge of this nature. There were no action plans and no procedures. Furthermore, there was no infrastructure: no reception points, no shelters, no food distribution facilities, no pre-trained staff. To be able to imagine the sheer number of people needed to offer help it is first essential to understand the scale of the influx of Ukrainians, including children who arrived without their parents. It is very difficult to determine how many such children came. Particularly in the initial period, they were difficult even to pinpoint geographically to a specific location. Some of them, for example, were travelling to reunite with their parents working in Poland or in other European countries. Their legal status was also difficult to categorise; some had, for instance, left Ukraine with a grandparent. Legal differences between Poland and Ukraine complicated the issue even further. Nonetheless, according to rough estimates, children made up about 35–40 per cent of all Ukrainian groups arriving in the country. Many of them travelled without their parents.

When discussing children crossing into Poland without a legal guardian, it is probably best to identify two separate categories. The first is children travelling individually (unaccompanied minors), while the second is children in institutional care, evacuated in groups.

CHILDREN TRAVELLING INDIVIDUALLY (UNACCOMPANIED MINORS)

Some children travelled with family members other than their parents; others with neighbours; others completely alone. It is very difficult to estimate the total number who crossed. Based on the numbers of applications for the appointment of a temporary guardian, the number was in the tens of thousands. Some parents put their children on buses or trains going into Poland while they themselves stayed to fight in Ukraine. Particularly, in the initial days when the territorial reach of Russia's aggression was not yet known, the prevailing impulse was to save the children first of all.

Problems began immediately at the border. In the early days of the war, the Ukrainian border guard let almost everyone cross without any checks. The Polish border guard tried to verify whether the parents had agreed for the children to leave Ukraine and whether the children were in someone's care. Due to the extraordinary circumstances, nearly any type of document sufficed as evidence. Polish notaries[1] volunteered to notarise documents allowing carers to cross the border with the children in their care. Some parents took great risks by posting on social media that their children were en route to Poland, listing the details of the train or bus the child was travelling on, attaching a photo of the child, and making a public appeal for somebody to look after the child in question.

The absence of legal regulation on the Ukrainian side ended on 12 March 2022, when the government of Ukraine passed Resolution No 264. It mandated that children younger than 16 should travel with a legal guardian, while those over the age of 16 could leave the territory of Ukraine if they wished, whether or not they had the consent of their parents or legal guardians. However, Polish law requires that children aged 16–18 must have a legal guardian. In consequence, children aged 16 were allowed to cross into Poland without the consent of their guardian(s), but they were required to either find a temporary guardian or be placed in institutional care (a children's home or a similar facility). NGOs working with Ukrainian youths in the 16–18 age group believe that a large proportion of them neither enter the temporary guardianship procedure nor report to any institution (Krawczak 2022). Some of them believe themselves fully capable, in line with Ukrainian law, to make independent decisions to leave the country, to take up a job, etc. Others simply prefer to steer clear of all and any Polish institutions, including the courts that appoint temporary guardians. They tend to seek out informal groups of Ukrainians to lease a house together as housemates. In many cases they also work, though mostly unofficially. An NGO lawyer who

[1] See: https://www.adwokatura.gdansk.pl/upload/files/451_anyFile_file_lista_notariuszy_–_pomoc_dla_ukrainy.pdf – the list of Polish notaries who volunteered to assist Ukrainian refugees.

works with youths gave an example of a boy living in such a shared house. The landlord was not aware that the boy was a minor. When the matter came to light, the boy asked the landlord to become his temporary guardian. He agreed, and the courts processed the appointment accordingly (Krawczak 2022).

In Poland, a new special law was passed too: namely, the law on assistance to be provided to citizens of Ukraine in relation to the military conflict on the territory of Ukraine (12 March 2022).[2] The law introduced the new institution of a 'temporary guardian', to be appointed by a family court. Preference in appointing a temporary guardian was to be given to the child's relatives. The list of individuals and institutions who had the right to submit a temporary guardianship application (ie to ask the court to find a temporary guardian for the child specified in the application) was quite exhaustive. It included border guard officials, heads of municipalities, city mayors, heads of various local government units (starosta, marszałek województwa), public prosecutors, police officers, heads of social welfare units, representatives of international or non-governmental organisations providing assistance to foreigners, persons having actual custody of a minor at the time, persons who took custody of a minor after the minor entered the territory of the Republic of Poland and who were exercising such custody on the day of submitting the application, and finally other persons or entities as part of their general responsibilities.

As illustrated by data provided by the Polish justice ministry, temporary guardianship cases were most numerous in the first year following the Russian invasion, and tapered off later.

The distribution of the cases across courts was deeply uneven. While it might be reasonable to expect that most cases would be lodged with the courts located in the vicinity of the Polish-Ukrainian border (and while that was actually true for a brief initial period), typically the applications to appoint a temporary guardian were not filed immediately upon arrival of the minor into the country. Often, the time to deal with the matter only came after reaching cities with big communities of Ukrainians who had also fled the war. In some of the regions with the heaviest influx of refugees, the numbers of cases were relatively low. For

Table 12.1 Temporary guardianship cases regarding Ukrainian minors in family courts

Year	Number of cases (reported)	Number of cases (rulings issued)	Number of minors covered by the rulings
2022	23,955	23,777	25,486
2023	7,134	5,905	6,669
2024	6,710	5,536	6,188
2025	4,507	3,715	3,989

Source: Polish Ministry of Justice

[2] The law of 12 March 2022 on assistance to be provided to citizens of Ukraine in relation to the military conflict on the territory of Ukraine, *Polish Journal of Laws* of 2022, item 583.

instance, in the Rzeszów region that directly borders Ukraine, in 2022 the courts received only 623 temporary guardianship applications[3] (ie fewer than 3 per cent of the total), whereas the court district of Wrocław, located all the way to the west of Poland, had 3,008 cases (13 per cent), and the Gdańsk district all the way on the coast to the north had 2,979 cases (12 per cent). The majority of cases were recorded in the courts in Warsaw, which received numerous refugees (3,179 cases, 13 per cent). The disparity is even clearer when looking at the data broken down further into courts in Warsaw's specific boroughs. One court in a single borough of Warsaw heard nearly twice as many temporary guardianship cases as the entire border-adjacent Rzeszów district: the court in Warsaw borough of Praga heard 1,163 cases in 2022 compared to the Rzeszów district's 623. Since temporary guardianship applications tended to be filed with the courts in the biggest cities, the courts there struggled under the burden, in particular because the time limit for issuing a ruling in these cases is only three days. However, over subsequent years the distribution of the cases reflects the fact that refugees were finding long-term homes in regions and cities other than Warsaw. In the first three quarters of 2024, the courts in the Warsaw district heard 485 cases, while the highest number recorded was in the Wrocław district (775) followed by the Katowice district in the south of the country (867).

According to NGOs, these official numbers are not an accurate reflection of the number of children who arrived in Poland without legal guardians. Some carers of refugee children were not even aware that they should request the

Table 12.2 Temporary guardianship cases regarding Ukrainian minors in family courts split by court districts

Court district (*apelacja*)	**2022**	**2023**	**2024**	**2025**
Warsaw	3,179 (13%)	707 (10%)	650 (10%)	460 (10%)
Białystok	749 (3%)	200 (3%)	163 (2%)	94 (2%)
Gdańsk	2,979 (12%)	768 (11%)	629 (9%)	412 (9%)
Katowice	2,718 (11%)	1,047 (16%)	1045 (17%)	614 (14%)
Kraków	3,129 (13%)	963 (13%)	888 (13%)	640 (15%)
Lublin	1,833 (8%)	548 (7%)	546 (8%)	485 (11%)
Łódź	2,257 (9%)	870 (12%)	811 (12%)	508 (11%)
Poznań	1,850 (8%)	567 (8%)	471 (7%)	280 (6%)
Rzeszów	623 (3%)	160 (2%)	190 (3%)	180 (4%)
Szczecin	1,630 (7%)	390 (5%)	351 (5%)	236 (5%)
Wrocław	3,008 (13%)	914 (13%)	966 (14%)	598 (13%)

Source: Polish Ministry of Justice. Calculations: authors' own

[3] *Source*: Polish Ministry of Justice. Calculations: authors' own.

legal status of a temporary guardian. Some minors, in particular those aged 16–18, already see themselves as adults, since they can leave Ukraine without the consent of their guardians. Some refugees avoid contact with any institutions on principle, because they are afraid of institutional interference (eg in the way care is provided).

Temporary guardianship is a completely new institution in the Polish legal system. It was created to ensure that Ukrainian minors are in someone's care, but also to create a pathway for these minors to function in society: to access school enrolment, medical care, social services, etc. Consequently, it was crucial for the procedure to be fast. The courts were given a three-day timeline for handling applications to appoint temporary guardians. This proved difficult to comply with, especially in the most overwhelming early months when the family courts in major cities were flooded with applications.

The legal provisions governing the matter were worded fairly generally, leaving room for a variety of approaches as to how the cases were handled in the courtroom. Interviews with family court judges[4] suggest that two main approaches had emerged, both solidly rooted in the wording of the new provisions. The first was to hold a hearing with all parties present, and hear both of the parties in every case. This is based on the wording of article 25(12), which reads: 'In matters concerning the appointment of a temporary guardian, the court issues its ruling following the non-trial procedure, after holding a hearing. The court considers testimony from the temporary guardian candidate, from the person in whose custody the minor remains at the moment, and from the minor, as long as the minor's mental development, health status and maturity permit it, taking the minor's reasonable wishes into account if possible.'[5] One of the judges we interviewed, who took the approach of always hearing both the temporary guardian candidate and the minor, said that she 'could not imagine appointing a guardian for a minor without having spoken to the minor in question'. This approach was both time and labour intensive. It often required interviewing young children, usually with the assistance of an interpreter, given that most of the children spoke no Polish.

The second approach was based on the wording of article 25(13), whereby the judge is allowed to waive the requirement of testimony: 'When there is compelling reason, if the temporary guardian candidate is the person in whose custody the minor is at the time, the circumstances of the case leave no doubt that the custody is being exercised in an appropriate manner, and if doing so is conducive to safeguarding the welfare of the minor, the court may carry out the proceedings to take evidence solely on the basis of documentation, and hear the case in closed session.'[6] This approach dominated in the big cities where the volume of

[4] For the purposes of this study we interviewed four judges who had experience handling temporary guardianship applications, in various regions of Poland.

[5] The law of 12 March 2022 on assistance to be provided to citizens of Ukraine in relation to the military conflict on the territory of Ukraine, *Polish Journal of Laws* of 2022, item 583.

[6] The law of 12 March 2022 on assistance to be provided to citizens of Ukraine in relation to the military conflict on the territory of Ukraine, *Polish Journal of Laws* of 2022, item 583.

applications was very high. Clear-cut cases were heard in camera, with hearings held only in cases with complicating factors, where the judge believed it was necessary to hear the testimony of the candidate and the minor.[7]

We learned from the interviews with judges that they initially feared being overwhelmed with cases and the challenges of having to manage their staggering new workload. The applications added an extra caseload on top of an already challenging regular caseload, and it required fast, efficient handling. Some courts were accepting up to 30 new temporary guardianship applications daily, and so initially each judge had to hear 12–15 cases per day, which translated into extremely long working hours. The courts, which generally had to handle the extra caseload without any extra funding, adapted in various ways. Some hired dual Polish-Ukrainian speakers to help the applicants fill in forms, which also helped mitigate problems stemming from the applicants' unfamiliarity with the language and the procedures. This also weeded out incomplete applications (eg those missing key attachments) and was a way of 'troubleshooting' formal and technical issues.[8] Where small courts were inundated with applications due to children being relocated to the area en masse, as part of foster care institutions or orphanages, judges from larger cities were assigned to come and stay in the town for a specific time (eg a week), to help process the applications. This tended to be voluntary, with judges themselves offering to take up the assignments.

When the influx of these applications started impacting the courts, the Association of Family Judges ran several webinars. The key decision was what to prioritise. As one judge expressed the issue: Was it more important to focus on formalities, dotting the I's and crossing the T's, or was it better to focus on efficiency, making sure that all children had temporary guardians assigned as quickly as possible? It was collectively determined that speed and efficiency should be prioritised, because appointing guardians was necessary for enrolling children in school, sorting out healthcare, and drawing social welfare benefits. During the webinars, the judges also decided that it would be helpful to set out in the text of the ruling the rights of the temporary guardian, so that those reading the ruling would have immediate clarity in that respect. As a result, the rulings included a passage explaining that the temporary guardian is authorised temporarily to represent the minor in matters including healthcare (treatment, diagnosis, tests, hospital stays, medication, surgery, and rehabilitation), therapy,

[7] Based on data from 29 courts, the Helsinki Foundation estimated that the proportion of cases heard in closed session to those heard in open session was 2:1. In: Ada Tymińska, *Dzieci z pieczy zastępczej oraz małoletni bez opieki z Ukrainy: ocena ex-post regulacji i praktyki stosowania specustawy ukraińskiej,* Fundacja Helsińska Warszawa 2022.

[8] As noted by the judges, this was especially important in the initial period, when there were no application forms and the conditions that the application had to meet were only set out in the law, which presented a difficulty. In March 2022, the Ministry of Justice prepared a bilingual (Polish–Ukrainian) form, rendering the process much easier. The forms are available online: Formularze dotyczące opiekuna tymczasowego – w wersjach językowych: polskiej i ukraińskiej – Ministerstwo Sprawiedliwości – Portal Gov.pl. A similar form had also been drawn up at the time by the Association of Family Judges.

education (diagnosis, therapeutical appointments, school classes, extracurriculars) and trips undertaken for recreational purposes.

This is not required by the law, and the idea that the ruling should list this information is not generally binding; it was simply an idea circulated among the judges. In effect, two forms of rulings have come into circulation. The judges who participated in working out this idea issued rulings with this specific information added. Other judges, in contrast, believed that the role of a guardian is sufficiently well defined in the provisions of the Family and Guardianship Code, and therefore chose not to offer any more details in the rulings they issued.

Another issue in the days immediately following the invasion was whether the provisions of Polish or Ukrainian law apply to the refugees or whether, further complicating matters, the Polish law on foreigners applies instead. The latter option seemed better suited to the circumstances but would be hard to implement: for instance, the law on foreigners requires that a curator be appointed for a minor for the duration of guardianship proceedings. Given the sheer numbers of incoming minors, finding curators would be extremely difficult if not outright impossible. The issue became moot when, on 12 March 2022, parliament adopted the law on assistance to be provided to citizens of Ukraine in relation to the military conflict on the territory of Ukraine,[9] creating the new institution of temporary guardianship. As a side effect, it meant that Polish law would apply to matters of temporary guardianship. However, in other types of cases heard by Polish family courts (eg for determination of paternity), Ukrainian law sometimes applies.

We asked the judges whether any clear categories could be distinguished among the cases they had encountered. There was consensus that only one division made sense: namely, the clear-cut cases and all the rest. The clear-cut cases included mainly those where the applications asked for a relative of the minor to be appointed as a temporary guardian. Typically, the relatives were grandmothers or other women in the minor's family who had come to Poland with children of their own and were additionally looking after other members of their extended families. They already had de facto custody of the children and were simply looking for a confirmation of the status quo. As noted in the NGO report, in the early days of 2022 nearly 96 per cent of applications pertained to these situations (Tymińska 2022). The less clear-cut cases involved temporary guardianship candidates who were unrelated to the minor. Here, it proved considerably more difficult to determine the best decision, in particular when an adult man was applying for guardianship of an adolescent girl. Certain risks had to be taken into consideration, such as the potential for sexual abuse or trafficking, but in more practical and immediate terms there was the suspicion of potential benefits fraud (seeking the guardianship to claim the cash benefits that the guardians were eligible to draw). The judges who insisted on speaking to every minor took great care to explain to

[9] The law of 12 March 2022 on assistance to be provided to citizens of Ukraine in relation to the military conflict on the territory of Ukraine, *Polish Journal of Laws* of 2022, item 583. The law was made retroactive and applicable to all persons who had left Ukraine due to the Russian invasion.

the minors that they were encouraged to report any problems, fears or dangers to the court or to another authority, because the guardianship arrangement was temporary and modifiable as needed. One of the judges, when asked about cases that she remembered as being out of the ordinary, spoke about a young woman aged 17 and her 18-year old boyfriend, who was requesting the appointment as her temporary guardian. The judge believed the case to be difficult because the resulting situation would put the young woman legally and factually into a position of dependence on her boyfriend. However, denying the application would mean that the young woman would be placed in institutional care, due to the absence of other temporary guardian candidates. Ultimately, the judge granted the application, but made sure to instruct the young woman in the presence of her partner that she was always free to apply for modification of the ruling should the circumstances between her and her partner change.

Another unusual case was a minor who played a sport competitively. A Polish sports coach brought him into the country. The plan was originally for the boy to stay with the coach and his wife for only a brief period, and then to travel onward to a different pre-arranged location. However, a few days after the boy's arrival the coach applied for temporary guardianship. The boy had acclimatised well and there were good opportunities for him to continue training, and so the coach and his wife had decided that they would take him in and care for him, rather than sending him to another place where he would have to try once again to become settled. The judge heard the testimony of the boy, who said he would very much prefer to stay where he was, because the coach was very knowledgeable about his needs and they had good rapport. The case was unusual in that the temporary guardianship candidate had no prior relationship with the boy and their acquaintance was very brief. However, the judge found that their short time living together provided a sufficiently good basis for the decision. Another situation that a judge recalled as unusual was quite difficult as well. In the early days of the invasion, an adolescent girl got into a car with several Ukrainian women she did not know, claiming that she was fleeing the war. The women had no relationship with her. They allowed her to travel with them into Poland but declined guardianship once they were all safely across the border. The judge therefore approached a lawyer from a list of volunteers who had made herself available to serve as a temporary guardian in cases where there was a specific need.[10] The lawyer was appointed to the role, while at the same time a search was launched for the parents of the adolescent girl in Ukraine. When her mother was found, she expressed a preference for her daughter to remain in Poland. It soon turned out that the adolescent girl was displaying enormously challenging behaviours and was engaging into criminal conduct. She was ultimately placed in an institutional care facility for troubled youth in Poland, with consent of the mother, who remained in Ukraine.

[10] From the very beginning of the refugee crisis, lawyers had been offering pro bono assistance to refugees. There were also coordinators of this assistance in each court district. See https://www.prawo.pl/prawnicy-sady/adwokaci-i-radcy-dla-ukrainy-listy,513758.html.

The judges, who preferred to issue rulings in closed session, tended nonetheless to hold a hearing when the case was not clear-cut, and also when the minor in question was an older teenager, capable of speaking about their relationship with the temporary guardianship candidate. As a result, the judge was able to learn, for example, that the candidate was not the minor's relative but was a member of a family with whom the minor's family had a relationship, or that the two had known each other for a long time.

As for hearing the perspectives of younger children who had fled Ukraine, this proved a very difficult task. Normally when there is a need for a child to testify, it takes place in a purpose-designed, tranquil, non-threatening space. However, this was very rarely possible in temporary guardianship cases, where the court's caseload was low. Typically, with dozens of cases to be examined every day, it was not practicable. In effect, judges had to hear the children's testimony in the regular courtrooms. They took pains to try to develop a measure of rapport with the children and make sure that conversations felt as natural as possible. While the focus was usually not on the traumatic events of the war, the stories of the children were nonetheless emotionally difficult for the judges to hear and process, since they often involved discussing the reasons why the children's parents had stayed behind in Ukraine, choosing to send their children abroad, sometimes with people who were not even family members. Most typically, parents stayed in Ukraine due to family obligations (to look after other family members, persons with disabilities, elderly parents, grandparents), professional obligations (judges medical personnel, public prosecutors, etc) or to defend their country. The judges – all of them women, as is typical for family courts in Poland – said in the interviews that they had found it difficult not to compare the children's stories with their own situations and imagine the decisions they would have to make under similar circumstances.

Another layer of difficulty was that taking testimony from the children nearly always required the assistance of an interpreter. Approaches to this issue varied across courts. Some relied on persons hired ad hoc, but most quickly identified the interpreters who were tackling the situation particularly skilfully, and tried to ensure these interpreters were present at all hearings. Usually, their skillset included not only speaking the language but also serving as a guide to cultural (and other) differences. One of the judges who emphasised the importance of the interpreters said she relied mostly on one female interpreter, who was Ukrainian-born and raised but had been living in Poland for many years. According to the provisions of the law, the judge explained, that taking testimony consists in a conversation between the judge and the child. In reality, the pathway is: judge – interpreter – child – interpreter – judge; from the child's perspective, the conversation is with the interpreter, not with the judge. It is the interpreter who asks questions and listens to the answers. In effect, the interpreter's skills and abilities are crucial, and must extend far beyond their linguistic qualifications.

As long as there was a candidate to serve as the temporary guardian, applications were granted very quickly. The judges we interviewed mentioned many times that the very tight statutory time limit of three days effectively made it impossible to verify whether the temporary guardianship candidate was actually going to provide good care to the minor. NGOs encountered situations in which temporary guardians had to be stripped of the role, for instance due to violence and abuse (Tymińska 2022). The judges we interviewed said they were not aware of any such instances involving temporary guardians, but they did know of relatively numerous interventions that had to be made due to domestic violence and alcohol abuse on the part of Ukrainian women, usually the children's mothers. Attempts to collect the child from the kindergarten while drunk; being many hours late for kindergarten or school pick-up because 'the child will be okay to wait'; marks on children's bodies suggesting domestic violence – all of these caused numerous interventions by staff from the childcare and healthcare facilities, including relevant reports being filed with courts. None of the persons at fault were temporary guardians. However, the three-day time limit resulted in unequal treatment of Polish and Ukrainian children. To be awarded custody of a Polish child, it is necessary to meet numerous strict requirements: pass an interview with a court-appointed curator, complete training, etc. No such requirements have to be met with regard to Ukrainian children. Consequently, while the relevant NGOs accepted that due to the extraordinary circumstances the procedure had to be swift and simple, they are now proposing that the relevant training should be completed after appointment, and that the timeline for the procedure should be extended to 14 days now that the inflow of cases has eased, to allow for proper verification of the candidates.

The situation was more complicated in the cases where no candidate came forward to serve as the temporary guardian. The courts approached lawyers, family assistance centres (which are part of the social welfare system) and NGOs to find volunteers to step into the role in those cases. However, it was quite rare for this need to arise, and most typically cases could be heard and resolved promptly, ensuring that all children had a temporary guardian if needed.

CHILDREN FROM EVACUATED INSTITUTIONAL CARE FACILITIES

The number of children evacuated from institutional care facilities (children's home, orphanages, etc) is difficult to estimate with any degree of accuracy. Ukrainian authorities officially note that 1,868 children from 100 care facilities were evacuated from areas directly affected by Russian attacks in 2022 alone.[11] Using data obtained from the Polish interior ministry, Give Children Strength, an NGO that works with children, calculated that in April 2022 the number of Ukrainian children in institutional care evacuated to Poland was 2,048. Accommodation for them was found in buildings that normally housed

[11] Inspection report. Monitoring of the Observance of Rights of Ukrainian Children Evacuated to the Republic of Poland (unpublished). The inspection ('monitoring visit') took place in May 2024. The report was drafted without consultation with the relevant Polish authorities.

healthcare facilities, in holiday homes, in hotels, etc. They continued to live with the same group and with the same carers as they did back home (A Krawczak, 2022). The exact figure is difficult to estimate because as soon as the war began, a number of NGOs, both Polish and those based in other countries, immediately started facilitating the evacuation of orphanages, children's homes and similar institutions. The border was wide open, and the exact numbers of the people who crossed it are difficult, if not impossible, to calculate. Orphanages and children's homes in Ukraine are significantly different from similar institutions in Western Europe and in Poland in terms of size and of the reasons why children are placed there. Data provided by UNICEF and UNHCR[12] and international NGOs (Save the Children 2022) suggest that at the time of Russia's invasion, there may have been up to 100,000 children in the Ukrainian system of full-time institutional care. According to international NGOs, only 10–20 per cent of them had no parents, and approximately 82 per cent of them had been placed in the care facility at the request of the parents or guardians (Hope and Homes for Children, 2015).[13] The facilities tended to be large, housing up to 100 children. In contrast, the total number of children in institutional care in Poland is approximately 17,000, and children's homes have been largely phased out in favour of small, family-sized foster homes. The legal status of children placed in institutional care is also different. In Ukraine, parents who request such placement for their children retain the full scope of parental rights. This has naturally caused numerous difficulties after the children's arrival in Poland, since it is difficult to establish who has the relevant rights and responsibilities, and to what extent. The evacuees often arrived with no documents, and this further complicated matters.

The evacuation of entire children's homes was often accomplished with the initiative and assistance of NGOs (such as SOS Wioski Dziecięce, Happy Kids, Klub Inteligencji Katolickiej) in cooperation with local authorities that helped find suitable accommodation. The adults in charge of the children at the time of arrival were usually appointed to serve as their temporary guardians. This once again caused a differentiation of the situation between Polish and Ukrainian children, since in effect Ukrainian carers became guardians to dozens of children each, which was not an option in Poland beforehand.

[12] 'Nearly 100,000 children, half of them with disabilities, live in institutional care and boarding schools in Ukraine. Many of these children have living relatives or legal guardians. We have received reports of institutions seeking to move children to safety in neighbouring countries or beyond. While recognizing that, under specific circumstances, humanitarian evacuations can be lifesaving and welcoming efforts to bring children to safety, it is critical that special measures be taken in the best interest of the children.' *Unaccompanied and separated children fleeing escalating conflict in Ukraine must be protected*, joint statement by UNICEF Executive Director Catherine Russell and United Nations High Commissioner for Refugees Filippo Grandi, 7 March 2022.
See https://www.unicef.org/press-releases/unaccompanied-and-separated-children-fleeing-escalating-conflict-ukraine-must-be#:~:text=%22UNICEF%20and%.

[13] The Illusion of Protection. An Analytical Report Based on the Findings a Comprehensive Study of the Child Protection System in Ukraine, https://www.hopeandhomes.org/content/uploads/2024/11/ English-v.pdf.

The legal status of these children is currently quite complicated. Under official agreements between Poland and Ukraine, carers and guardians are assigned by the relevant Ukrainian authorities, while Poland is only responsible for securing accommodation, welfare assistance, and additional assistance (medical, psychological, etc) as needed. On 30 June 2022, the Ukrainian ministry of social policy and the Polish ministry of labour and social policy signed a declaration 'on social welfare provision to children affected by war and armed conflict', which outlines the framework for cooperation in providing care to evacuees in institutional care. Under the declaration, Poland is obliged: to facilitate the return of minors to Ukraine after the cessation of hostilities; to ensure that ongoing adoption processes are not accelerated and new ones are not initiated; to register minors in the relevant IT systems; and to facilitate maintaining close contact between children evacuated from the same institution (in practice, this means that Ukraine refuses to allow large care institutions to be split into new smaller ones). This hinders proper social welfare provision. Disputes between Ukrainian and Polish authorities concerning the care of children also occur in other contexts and, according to the judges, are likely to continue generating problems in the future. The judges noted, for instance, that cases of Ukrainian mothers leaving their newborn children in hospital are on the rise. According to the judges we interviewed, these children could easily be placed in families, yet Ukrainian authorities disallow the placement of Ukrainian children in Polish families. In the absence of Ukrainian families to step into the role, these children stay in institutional care, which creates worse outcomes in terms of their development.

According to data made available by the ministry of labour and social policy, there were 800 children in institutional care in Poland in December 2024. They live in 33 homes, with the largest one housing 188 children and the smallest ones having just a few children each. The children are cared for by 81 carers. Only one institution has more than 100 residents (specifically, it is the one with 188 children). Two have more than 70, a further three have more than 20 children each (varying from 24 to 53), 18 homes have between 10 and 18 children each, and the rest have fewer than 10 children each.

The reasons for the decreasing number of children in institutional care emerge from the report of the Ukrainian inspectors following their visits to these institutions.[14] One institution, for example, had 113 children in its care at the time of its evacuation in 2022. In May 2024, 97 children remained, aged 3 to 17. As outlined in the report, three of the children were orphans, the parents of 58 had lost their parental rights, and 18 children had been placed in the facility due to 'difficult life circumstances'. Since evacuation from Ukraine, 34 children had left: 12 of them returned to boarding schools; six reached the age of

[14] Inspection report. Monitoring of the Observance of Rights of Ukrainian Children Evacuated to the Republic of Poland (unpublished). The inspection ('monitoring visit') took place in May 2024. The report was drafted without consultation with the relevant Polish authorities.

majority and left the facility; four were moved into individual care; 12 returned to their Ukrainian parents. The situation in other, smaller facilities is similar. In one of them, there were 40 children at the time of evacuation, but only 35 (including three children with disabilities) in May 2024. Three of them were orphans, 12 had parents who had lost their parental rights, and another 12 had been placed in care due to 'difficult life circumstances'. Out of the five children who had left the facility, one reunited with the parents, one was adopted by a Ukrainian family, one reached the age of majority, and two were moved to another facility. In general, the number of children and youths evacuated from Ukraine and remaining in institutional care in Poland has been steadily decreasing due to these general reasons: some of the children reach the age of majority and leave the facilities; some return to Ukraine to stay with their parents; some choose to study at boarding schools. Some have also been transferred outside of Poland with the consent of the Ukrainian authorities, usually in larger groups. The evacuation further abroad (ie beyond Poland) of a children's home from Mariupol was at the heart of a situation that was, in the authors' opinion, most fraught in terms of possible violations of human rights and children's rights. A group of 60 children evacuated from a care institution in Mariupol arrived in Kazimierz Dolny, where they were housed in a hotel operated by the Association of Journalists. Inspections by Polish state institutions normally focus on living conditions, accommodation, food, etc. However, on this occasion the inspectors discovered that the children were being cared for not only by their previous Ukrainian carers, but also by new carers affiliated with Loving Families and Homes for Orphans, an American organisation led by pastor Matt Shea, a man charged with domestic terrorism in the USA, with a reputation for inciting violence and promoting the idea of religious war. The pastor claimed to be preparing children for adoption in the United States, and to be doing so in cooperation with the Ukrainian consulate. The case generated a large public and media response. The Polish family welfare authority stepped in, taking the case to court. The court appointed Ukrainian carers to serve as temporary guardians for the children, alongside one Polish carer, and ruled to disallow the removal of the children beyond the municipality of Kazimierz Dolny. Yet despite the court's order the children were moved to Switzerland, with full consent and support of the Ukrainian consul. According to the report by Giving Children Strength, 'the children were allowed to leave Poland in contravention of the ruling of the Polish court, meaning that the ruling was effectively irrelevant, symbolic, and merely designed to reassure the public. The children were allowed to leave Poland based on the decision of the persons with authority under Ukrainian law, namely the headmistress of the orphanage and the consul general of Ukraine, because they were subject to Ukrainian law. The children had never entered the Polish foster care system at all, so the Polish authorities had no right to enforce any decisions related to the location or the further fate of children' (Krawczak 2022, 366).

Problems also emerged on a more individual scale. The case of two children, aged 10 and 7, garnered a lot of attention in Poland. The children arrived with their foster mother, who then died while already in Poland. The children were placed with a female police officer specialising in juvenile cases. Two years later, the woman was formally named as their foster mother. The children's mental health had suffered enormously over the course of these events, to the point that the 10-year-old boy was diagnosed with post-traumatic stress disorder. However, more than two years after their arrival in Poland, Ukrainian authorities demanded that the children be returned to Ukraine. Hostilities are ongoing in the area from which the children originally arrived, and they would be placed in an orphanage on their return there.[15] The matter is currently subject to negotiations between the Polish ministry and the Ukrainian consulate.

These two examples demonstrate the difficulties that arise in the context of providing care to children evacuated from Ukraine. Problems also stem from attempts to delineate the powers and competences of the relevant Polish and Ukrainian authorities. Often, they are also rooted in the differing approaches to what constitutes the best interest of the child. Furthermore, as the case of the children's home relocated from Kazimierz Dolny demonstrates, human trafficking is a risk. Given that the numbers of refugees passing through Poland are in the millions, it is impossible to ensure that every single person receives the necessary standard of protection. To mitigate the risks, it is compulsory to keep up-to-date records on children without legal guardians in Poland. However, since many adults and minors alike try to stay out of sight of the authorities, such record-keeping is extremely difficult in practice.

FINAL COMMENTS

Special circumstances call for special measures. In the face of the tragic Russian invasion of Ukraine and the refugee crisis it triggered, an enormous effort was needed to rise to the challenge, both by the Polish state and by its individual citizens (Fuszara 2022, Fuszara 2024, Kurczewski 2022). New comprehensive legal regulations were also needed, to lay the groundwork for new solutions in the area of healthcare, accommodation, social welfare services, access to education, jurisdiction, applicability of the new laws, etc. With regard to children, in particular those who arrived in Poland without parents and legal guardians, education and healthcare were areas of utmost concern.

In terms of education, it was decided (Krajewska 2022) that Ukrainian children would be given the choice between enrolling in the Polish school system, attending Ukrainian schools in Poland, enrolling in online Ukrainian schools, as these forms of education. According to data published in October 2024 by

[15] Dariusz Faron i Paweł Figurski, Dała dzieciom dom. Dała dzieciom dom, teraz dostała pismo z Ukrainy. 'Nie chcę nawet myśleć o szoku, który przeżyją'.Accessed on 15 December 2024. Similar information was obtained during an interview with a high-ranking employee of the Polish ministry of labour and social welfare.

the deputy minister Joanna Mucha, there were 248,000 students from Ukraine enrolled in Polish schools at the time. Out of that number, 179,700 were children who had arrived following the attack of 24 February 2022. Despite the implementation of numerous incentives (eg the payment of the child benefit is now contingent on the child being enrolled in school), the number of Ukrainian children in the Polish school system is holding steady, rather than increasing.[16] Legally, the situation of Ukrainian refugee children is different compared to Polish children, in that the former are welcome to enrol in Polish schools but have no such obligation, in contrast to the latter, for whom school attendance is compulsory. Ukrainian children who are not enrolled in schools are technically obliged to enrol with Ukrainian schools online. However, compliance is difficult to ensure or even monitor, and in practice the matter ultimately rests with the parents and guardians.

In terms of custody of children who have come to Poland without parents or legal guardians, the new institution of temporary guardianship is pivotal. The relevant laws were drafted with great haste, with virtually no time for consultation with the judges who were tasked with implementing them. Various difficulties emerged in practice. Some of them were technical in nature, consisting for instance in the inadequate number of interpreters (only sworn interpreters are allowed to appear in court, and the profession is highly regulated), in the failures of applicants to rectify formal problems with the applications (undermining the courts' ability to process the applications smoothly), and in the sheer number of applications flooding the family courts within a very short time frame. The courts coped as best they could, finding the assistance of dual Ukrainian-Polish speakers to help with the paperwork, temporarily waiving the sworn interpreter requirement to allow non-sworn interpreters to step in and help out, hiring extra staff to assist in filling in the applications, assigning judges to temporary short-term placements where the caseload was particularly overwhelming, etc.

However, it was difficulties of a different nature that proved most challenging. The notion of temporary guardianship was outlined in the new laws only in most general terms, and so had to be developed organically in practice. Some judges issued rulings that specified the scope of authority of the temporary guardians while others did not, granting custody but not listing specifics. There is no case law to offer guidance on potential conflict of rights (if, for instance, a parent arrives from Ukraine while a temporary guardian has been appointed for the child). The judges we interviewed believed that the rights of the parent should prevail in that scenario. However, the matter is currently legally unresolved. Some judges also assumed that temporary guardianship ceases when the child and temporary guardian return to Ukraine, and must be re-established on their next arrival into Poland – however, the law is far from clear on the matter,

[16] Information from deputy minister Joanna Mucha presented at the session of the Sejm Committee on Education and Science regarding Ukrainian students in the Polish school system. Ukraińskie dzieci w szkołach i 800+. 'Prawie dokładnie w tych samych liczbach' – Bankier.pl.

even though such situations are actually quite common. Judges' professional associations organised numerous training courses and webinars to address the issues as they arose, and to foster the development of a shared approach to these legal challenges.

The number of temporary guardianship cases has now significantly decreased, but the courts are presently facing new challenges resulting from the influx of Ukrainian refugees. Some of these issues are largely procedural: for instance, Ukrainian law applies to matters such as the denial of the paternity of the mother's husband. Other are more practical. Even if the paternity of the mother's husband is evidently impossible – if, for instance, the pregnant woman and her husband have not seen each other for two years, because the husband has been in Ukraine and the wife has been in Poland throughout this time – it is legally necessary to notify the mother's husband of the pending case to deny his paternity. One of the judges we interviewed asked, rather rhetorically: how is a notice of a hearing in Poland supposed to reach a man in Ukraine's war zone or on the frontline? Family courts do try to find ways of contact (such as e-mail), but in reality it is often completely impossible to ensure that the notice finds its intended recipient. The subject matter is too delicate and has too much potential impact not to make at least an attempt to notify the person concerned. Yet the best interest of the child remains the overriding principle, and there is no doubt that it is better for the child to be recognised by the biological father.

Another point of contention (emphasised by the judges we interviewed) is the refusal on the part of the Ukrainian authorities to uphold rulings issued by Polish courts in what Polish judges consider in the children's best interest: dividing large facilities into smaller ones, for instance, or placing newborns left in hospitals by Ukrainian mothers in the care of Polish families. In the absence of consent from the Ukrainian authorities, the children must be placed in institutional rather than family care.

Cultural differences are also an issue. While there are many similarities between the culture in Poland and Ukraine, certain differences persist. One of them, as mentioned above, is alcohol consumption while caring for a child. While the problem is not entirely absent in Poland, it is much less prevalent (according to the unanimous opinion of the judges we interviewed) – and, crucially, there is a difference in attitudes. Ukrainian mothers do not view it as a problem, nor do they view certain behaviours that are treated in Poland as domestic violence as problematic. In general, all the judges we interviewed noted that attitudes of adults towards children differ between Ukraine and Poland. According to judges who have served in family courts for many years, it is like 'going back to the 1990s in Poland'. Children are regarded as deserving of lesser respect, and violence is used as a 'child-raising method'. These observations are confirmed by the monitoring report drafted by Ukrainian inspectors following their visits to children's homes evacuated to Poland. The homes are staffed by Ukrainian carers and Polish law is not applicable, except in situations where the police or the prosecutor's office are notified of a crime. The Ukrainian report documents the occurrence of various forms of abuse (eg physical violence, withdrawal of food as punishment, sleep disruption), all of which are classified as 'child-raising methods'.

It is likely that the approach to children in the Ukrainian community will evolve to converge with the standards now prevalent in Western Europe and in Poland. However, it is difficult to predict when this might happen. Mobility is an issue: many individuals, families and groups leave Poland for other countries or return to Ukraine. The absence of strong roots in any one place makes predictions for the future rather tricky. Continued research on developments in the Ukrainian community in Poland and the legal solutions that were formulated during the refugee crisis would certainly offer valuable insight.

Is there any general lesson to be learned from the handling of the refugee crisis? In studying the Polish response to the situation, Nassim Taleb's *The Black Swan. The Impact of the Highly Improbable* (2007) is often cited. Taleb claims that we are used to existing in a 'Mediocristan' condition created by our past experiences, and we plan for the future, both our own and of our entire societies, on the basis of these 'mediocre' expectations. Yet this renders us vulnerable to unpredictable, extraordinary events. He argues that we should always be ready to encounter 'Extremistan', the condition of random, thoroughly unexpected phenomena that are bound to occur sooner or later. The swiftness with which new legal mechanisms were developed and implemented to assist the millions of arriving refugees demonstrates that the legal system is capable of adjusting much more flexibly than we tend to assume. With that new appreciation of its strengths and weaknesses, we must now work on improving it even further. The perfect time to do so is right now. The present moment, when the situation in Poland and in the other countries that have welcomed the influx of refugees is relatively stable, creates a perfect opportunity to do this work.

REFERENCES

Faron, Dariusz and Figurski, Paweł (2024) 'Dała dzieciom dom', Dała dzieciom dom, teraz dostała pismo z Ukrainy. 'Nie chcę nawet myśleć o szoku, który przeżyją', Accessed on 15 December 2024.

Fuszara, Małgorzata (2022): 'Wojna, ucieczki i pomaganie', in M Fuszara (ed), *Masowa pomoc w masowej ucieczce. Społeczeństwo polskie wobec migracji wojennej z Ukrainy* (ISNS UW, Warszawa), 7–18, https://isns.uw.edu.pl/pliki/wydawnictwa/Ukraina_WWW.pdf.

Fuszara, Małgorzata (2024), Polish Relief Effort for Ukrainian Refugees, in Societas/Communitas nr 1(37) 2024, ISNS UW Warszawa, 149–82, https://societas-communitas.isns.uw.edu.pl/issue/16527.

Inspection report. Monitoring of the Observance of Rights of Ukrainian Children Evacuated to the Republic of Poland (unpublished).

Krajewska, Anna (2022), 'Dzieci-uchodźcy z Ukrainy w polskim systemie edukacji', in *Masowa pomoc w masowej ucieczce. Społeczeństwo polskie wobec migracji wojennej z Ukrainy* (ISNS UW, Warszawa), 77–96, https://isns.uw.edu.pl/pliki/wydawnictwa/Ukraina_WWW.pdf.

Krawczak, Anna (2022), Sytuacja dzieci ukraińskich w Polsce, report published by Giving Children Strength (Dajemy dzieciom siłę), Warszawa 2022, 355, https://fdds.pl/_Resources/Persistent/5/e/8/9/5e8940d252b5fdcadd95e8a2d5a2daea07b11e29/Dzieci%20si%C4%99%20licz%C4%85%20 2022%20-%20Ukraina.pdf.

Kurczewski, Jacek (2022), 'Ius insitum – obowiązek pomocy i prawo do pomocy', in M Fuszara (ed), *Masowa pomoc w masowej ucieczce. Społeczeństwo polskie wobec migracji wojennej z Ukrainy* (ISNS UW, Warszawa), 135–46, https://isns.uw.edu.pl/pliki/wydawnictwa/Ukraina_WWW.pdf.

Taleb, Nassim Nicholas (2007), *The Black Swan: The Impact of the Highly Improbable.* Random House (US), Allen Lane (UK).

The Illusion of Protection. An Analytical Report Based on the Findings a Comprehensive Study of the Child Protection System in Ukraine, https://www.hopeandhomes.org/content/uploads/2024/11/English-v.pdf.

Tashkinova Oksana, 'The Family Situation of Ukrainian Female Forced Migrants in Poland', *Societas/Communitas*,1(37) 45–52.

Tymińska, Ada (2022), *Dzieci z pieczy zastępczej oraz małoletni bez opieki z Ukrainy: ocena ex-post regulacji i praktyki stosowania specustawy ukraińskiej,* Fundacja Helsińska.

Ukraine: Children without Caregivers Risk Being Forgotten. Save the Children 2022, https://www.savethechildren.net/news/ukraine-children-without-caregivers-risk-being-forgotten.

The law of 12 March 2022 on assistance to be provided to citizens of Ukraine in relation to the military conflict on the territory of Ukraine, *Polish Journal of Laws* of 2022, item 583.

13

Concluding Observations

MAVIS MACLEAN

SOCIOLOGISTS OF LAW are accustomed to thinking carefully about how their approach to legal studies may be of benefit not only to fellow scholars, but also to legal practitioners and those who seek their help, whether to support a claim to their home or their income, or for the enjoyment of family life with partners, parents and children.

The current regulation of family life has its origins in the values associated with longstanding moral and religious codes, but these are now often subject to question and variation as the development of family life becomes more complex, more international, more heterogeneous and open to different ways of organising the family to the benefit of as many family members as possible. But any particular form of family group organisation may be threatened when a member differs from the more generally held norms of family behaviour, as a result of extreme age (whether old or young), or physical or mental capacity which affects physical and mental health or ability. Colour blindness may not be noticed, but a complete lack of vision may make it difficult for a family as a group to function without support, while a person without sight may need help as an individual to take up or maintain a position in a family group especially as a breadwinner or parent.

Problems may arise concerning the need for social or welfare care, for financial arrangements about ownership of a home or inheritance, or for access where there has been parental separation. There may be existing legal rules which have developed to deal with such problems. But these laws may be too complex for the layman to understand, and it may be too costly for family members to seek legal help in achieving a solution to their problems. In the UK, we were pleased to be approached by Sarah Castle, the Official Solicitor for England and Wales, who took the initiative in alerting this group of socio legal family lawyers to the importance of family law in the many cases coming to her notice regarding legal competence. Many aspects of family life can be affected by arguments about a vulnerable individual's legal capacity to make decisions affecting others, arising from health or disability issues which may create problems in every area of life. These may include conflicting views on the validity of a marriage or a will, legitimacy, rights of residence in a country, parental rights, inheritance rights, and lifestyle and possible compensation for example in cases of deprivation of liberty due to physical incapacity, and many more. We begin in chapter two with the Official Solicitor's account of supporting those with legal problems, but who lack capacity.

Growing awareness of these kinds of current concerns about how a legal framework might meet such needs includes ideas about how to protect those who may be affected by the behaviour of a vulnerable individual, or on the other hand how to protect the rights of such an individual, and this dichotomy has been leading to complex debates in many countries. We were fortunate in having as the authors of our third chapter members of the FL-EUR Project team founded in Amsterdam in 2919. Their first project looked at the empowerment and protection of vulnerable adults, triggered by the rapidly ageing populations in developed countries, and the coming into force of the United Nations Convention of Rights of Persons with Disabilities. This chapter shows how the work of the UN has moved on from the traditional paternalistic approach, to protection through restriction of an adult's legal capacity towards a new focus on promoting, protecting and ensuring the full and equal enjoyment of all human rights and fundamental freedoms by persons with disabilities, and how to promote respect for their inherent dignity. The definition of these persons includes those who have long-term physical mental or sensory impairments, which – in interaction with other issues – may hinder full and effective participation in society on an equal basis with others. The FL-EUR report includes an up-to-date description of the range of recent statutory requirements that now affect these issues across the EU.

The chapters that then follow bring together local accounts of the current ways of responding to legal incapacity in the UK, Germany, Australia, Spain, Argentina, France, Turkey, the Netherlands, Bulgaria and Poland.

In our workshop, we learned of some surprising developments. From the UK, we heard about the OS 'standing in the shoes' of those who lack capacity, including the story of an elderly gentleman who received compensation for separation from his pet cat. He lived alone and had been taken into care against his will when worried neighbours, anxious about his ability to look after himself, reported his case to the local authority and requested help. But after further investigation and protest from his friends, the case came to the Court of Protection where DJ Mort found in his favour in January 2015. The man was sent home and awarded compensation from the local authority for wrongful deprivation of liberty and separation from his cat, Fluffy. This example shows how difficult it may be to identify the specific needs of a vulnerable person living alone, and perhaps indicates the need for caution in enforcing deprivation of liberty. But at the same time, this local authority might be regarded as having acted very responsibly in avoiding the risk of harm to this elderly and infirm man.

In chapter four, we hear of difficulties arising at the other end of the age range, where the welfare of a child may be at risk as a result of the mental or physical disability of a parent, but the disabled person has the right not to be discriminated against as a result of their disability. Under Article 23 of the UN Convention on the Rights of Persons with Disabilities, the state has a duty to take effective measures to ensure that the disabled person does not suffer discrimination, but it will result in the state being required to supplement the resources of the parent to ensure this. In addition, a child has the right to be protected against all forms of neglect and negligent behaviours, or physical or mental violence, while in the care of parents (Article 19 UN Convention on the Rights of the Child). Furthermore, decision making about the upholding of these rights by professionals will require a parent to prove that their parenting is good enough to avoid the risk of harm. This raises the question of how far the state should be focusing on its responsibility to offer support and how far on making parents prove their capacity. Again we see questions arising about the role of law and of social policy. Do the key questions lie in the area of social policy about concern for providing support for families with these difficulties, or do they fall in the area of family law in requiring parents to prove their capacity? What comes first, welfare or justice?

There is an emerging debate about the roles of welfare and justice, where a family member suffers an incapacity. This underlies the questions addressed in chapter five, which looks at the Australian approach to guardianship and support or control for people with disabilities, asking whose interests are being protected following the operation of the recent Guardianship and Administration Act 2019 in the state of Victoria. The law concerning legal incapacity in Australia is the responsibility of State Governments, rather than the Federal Government. This includes the power to make laws to support people with disabilities affecting their decision-making capacity. But so far in this comparison, in Victoria the move towards a more rights-based approach seems not to have affected the kinds of cases coming before the courts. The legislation appears to be supporting developed current practice, rather than promoting reform.

We continued to look further afield at the impact of the growing move towards more legislation to defend the rights of disabled people, stressing their access to dignity, autonomy and freedom in a number of jurisdictions. In chapter six, we were able to examine the situation in Spain following Spanish State Law 8/2021, based on equal rights for disabled people to dignity, autonomy and freedom to make decisions. But each autonomous community in Spain has its own jurisdiction over laws relating to social assistance, and there is considerable regional diversity. In the Autonomous Community of Aragon, the new federal law 8/2021 was only partially applied because of the existence of their own regional law, Aragon Law 3/2024. There is still concern about the impact of giving legal effect to the decision for the disabled or impaired person, and allowing respect for the will and preferences of the disabled person to underpin the law. So instead of having a legal guardian who will make decisions, the State Law now requires that the disabled person should have support from a person, known as a de facto guardian, who will work with them in making plans and will follow their wishes and preferences. The most inspiring impact of the new state principle, according to Professor Novales, is that it will no longer be possible for courts in Aragon to deprive anyone of their legal capacity. There will be different forms of guardianship (eg de facto, notarised de facto . . .), according to the specific needs of the disabled persons. Meanwhile discussion regarding the success of this ambitious development continues.

Overall, the recent approaches to responding to the difficulties arising from disability have been leading to the development of decisions based on the rights of the individual with recourse to court if required, in contrast to the earlier traditional needs-based approach which relied on state support – and professional decision making remains current. The latter may include discussion of the needs to be met by the state, and there may be a variety of ways of managing a situation which continue to include access to state support. The key question that arises is whether it is possible in practice both to retain flexibility and to value the differing elements of both approaches.

In Bulgaria, the new rights-based ideas were at first welcomed, and legislation to that effect was prepared in 2016, with an emphasis on supported decision making to replace substitute decision making, and also to provide some protection for the disabled person. In some instances, this could be seen as empowerment, such as home-based services and personal assistance. But the Bill on Physical Persons and Supported Decision Making did not reach the statute book. The lengthy and delicate discussion of supported decision making lost out in the political context in Bulgaria at the time, which was weakened by COVID-19, when liberal and democratic ideas were threatened, and the conservative attitude of academics and decision makers impeded progress, so that the wishes and preferences but not the will of the impaired person remain the dominant reference point.

Following these two chapters on the different approaches to legislating for the disabled to provide the necessary support for them and their families, chapter eight describes a very different development in Argentina, where a study was carried out of how those whose lives are affected by various pieces of legislation view the experience as also including an element of control. The research looked at how adolescents in care homes understood access to justice. The study used an inductive approach, which intersects child welfare, legal frameworks and child development. Following abuse or abandonment, adolescents in care homes were encouraged to express their relationship with the justice system though participation in artwork, plays and workshops. The results showed how the young people perceived access to support or control.

In the final part of this volume we explore the ideologies and frameworks underlying the development of policy concerning capacity. For example, in France we see the strength of the judicial model, as compared with the focus on community responsibility in the Netherlands. And we close with an account of the impact of an emergency situation in Poland, where large numbers of young

Ukrainian children – often unaccompanied – had to be cared for within a legal framework based on requiring the presence of guardians for young people.

The contrasts between the aims and outcomes of the approaches discussed in this volume are clear, and, as so often in our experience of comparative work, bring the stimulation of awareness of alternative approaches to long-standing issues and hopefully greater willingness to think carefully about what direction to take. Legal rights and sympathetic understanding are both essential. The question that is emerging relates to how we might enable justice and welfare to work together. We hope to address this in future international discussion at the IISL Onati, to whom we are indebted for the ideas presented in this volume.

Index

www.ingramcontent.com/pod-product-compliance
Ingram Content Group UK Ltd.
Pitfield, Milton Keynes, MK11 3LW, UK
UKHW020810290926
15470UKWH00003B/1074